A Writer's Britain

A Writer's Britain

Margaret Drabble

 **Thames & Hudson**

An earlier version of this book was published in 1979 as
A Writer's Britain: Landscape in Literature

This edition first published in 2009 in hardcover in the United States
of America by Thames & Hudson Inc., 500 Fifth Avenue, New York,
New York 10110

thamesandhudsonusa.com

Library of Congress Catalog Card Number 2009900140

ISBN 978-0-500-51493-1

Printed and bound in Germany by Bercker

CONTENTS

FOREWORD

The British have long been known for their love of landscape, and English literature, like English painting, is rich in evocations of what Shakespeare patriotically proclaimed as 'this other Eden, Demi-Paradise'. Indeed, at the beginning of the nineteenth century love of nature seemed almost to replace love of mankind as a subject for literature. Despite an uncertain climate and a large-scale industrial revolution, English writers have persisted in seeing and praising the distinctive beauties of their own country, some of them finding beauty in the most unexpected corners, in slag heaps and urban wildernesses, in suburban streets and railway stations, in docks and cobbled alleys. Again and again, we find a passionate attachment to the places of childhood, and an almost mystic devotion to the land itself. Generations of exiles have longed for the green fields of home, and expressed their longing in their own words, or the words of others. 'Oh, to be in England now that April's there', sighed Browning (though he really preferred Italy), and every April his words must echo through innumerable minds. Even the cynical Byron could not suppress a surge of enthusiasm at the sight of the white cliffs of Dover and the green fields of Kent. Most travellers returning from grander, wilder, more picturesque scenery feel the same delight.

The desire to turn landscape into art seems a natural one, though it is hard to say precisely why painters and writers should labour to reproduce in paint or words what each of us can see with our own eyes. But we all see differently, and every writer's work is a record both of himself and of the age in which he lives, as well as of the particular places he describes. The appreciation of landscape has evolved over the years, and fashions in viewing scenery have changed; in recent years much has been written about the painter's attitude to landscape, but less about the writer's, though writers have been affected by and have helped to create the same fashions, the same new awarenesses. The word 'landscape' itself is relatively new, dating from the end of the sixteenth century: the word 'scenery' is even more recent, dating from the late eighteenth century. Both are so familiar that it is hard to imagine how writers managed without them. Perhaps, as some believe, the ability to enjoy scenery for its own sake is as recent as the language we use to describe it. If this is a new faculty, how did it arise, and why did the English develop it to such a marked degree?

These are unanswerable questions, but they are intriguing, and this book prove a lifetime to pursue them all.

Nathaniel Hawthorne, visiting the Lake District in 1855, comments,

> On the rudest surface of English earth, there is seen the effect of centuries of civilization, so that you do not quite get at naked Nature anywhere. And then every point of beauty is so well known, and has been described so much, that one must needs look through other people's eyes, and feel as if he were seeing a picture rather than a reality . . .

Young men, he says, 'might sometimes yearn for a fresher draught. But an American likes it.' And so, I think, do most of us; those who enjoy reading gain great pleasure from associating places with lines of poetry, with scenes from novels. One pleasure reinforces the other. Even those who do not read cannot choose but see certain landscapes through the eyes of the writers that discovered them. The vision of countless visitors who have never read a word of Walter Scott has been formed by Scott's poems and novels. Knowingly or unknowingly, we have all been influenced by the writers who went before us, and the popularity of the great literary shrines of Britain shows how irresistibly many are drawn to retrace, in the most literal sense, their footsteps.

Another of the attractions of landscape seems to lie in the fact that it represents at once the changing and the unchanging. Places on the whole change more slowly than people, and nothing evokes the past more powerfully than a visit to the remembered places of childhood. Most writers return again and again to childhood, seeing in a pond, a field, a tree, a church some reminder of what they once were. Sometimes the journey to the past ends in tragedy: George Orwell's hero tries to find the pond where he once saw huge carp swimming, and finds nothing but a new housing estate. How can one ever find the farm near Knutsford which Elizabeth Gaskell describes with such intensity of feeling? To most of us today, Knutsford is a service station on a motorway, and Cranford is a town of the mind. Yet there are places that remain unchanged: the moors behind Haworth are the same as when Emily Brontë walked them, and although Tintern Abbey has suffered successive waves of restoration and dilapidation, the valley of the Wye itself is much as it was when Wordsworth first saw it, as it was when the Cistercians first built there.

This book, then, combines journeys both in place and in time. There are many ways of reading landscape, as historians, archaeologists, geologists and painters have demonstrated. Writers have contributed their own perceptions, and through their words we can see the past that has vanished, and the present that remains. I hope that this book will convey the pleasure and excitement with which the subject inspired me.

Margaret Drabble
1979

SACRED PLACES

'There has never been an age, however rude and uncultivated, in which the love of landscape has not been in some way manifested.' So said the painter John Constable, and one's instinct is to agree with him. Yet it is at the same time clear that, however the people of the Dark and Middle Ages saw Britain, their vision and their landscapes must have been very different from ours, and their love must have been manifested in different ways. Is it possible to imagine their world, and how they perceived it? There are clues, in art, in architecture, in Anglo-Saxon, Celtic and medieval poetry, in the Latin lives of the saints, in the names of places and the English language itself. They are no more than clues, but they offer an irresistible appeal. There are places in Britain – Stonehenge, Glastonbury, Silbury Hill, Offa's Dyke, Badbury Rings, Hadrian's Wall, the Pilgrim's Way – as well as a host of minor sites – barrows, ancient little woods, solitary standing stones, even milestones – that give to the least historically minded visitor a shiver of contact, an apprehension of lingering barbarity or sanctity, an intimation of the distant past. The dullest documents can come to life, transporting us back to a world not so very different from our own. Here is King Edmund's charter to Bishop Aelfric, granting him land in Berkshire in AD 944:

> First to the east side of the estate at Amwell, then south straight to the ditch of the waterslade, then along the ditch to the south end to the true estate boundary, then up to the great tumulus beneath the wild garlic wood, then from the tumulus up along stone way to the tall crucifix at Hawk Thorn, then from Hawk Thorn to the tall thorn tree at Icknield Way, then to the third thorn tree at bog-myrtle hanger . . . then up to Hill of Trouble, then west to rough lynchet, along the rough lynchet to the heathen burial places . . .

As Ronald Blythe, the historian of modern English village life, wrote in *The Listener* on 20 April 1978 (reviewing *Signposts to the Past: Place Names and the History of England* by Margaret Gelling), 'The vividness of the route becomes so natural and overwhelming that we feel we have been trudging along near Didcot in the tenth century.' Our vision may be distorted, human nature may have changed almost out of recognition, but we can still feel a sense of closeness, a living link: we know the hawthorns and the wild garlic, although the wayside crucifixes have largely vanished.

Most modern historians, however, have stressed differences in attitude, for we no longer believe in universal human nature and eternal aesthetic standards. Kenneth Clark in *Landscape into Art* makes the point that the medieval mind saw nature as hostile, dwelt on its horrors rather than its beauties, sought safety rather than the wilderness. The great forests were inimical to human life, dangerous and wolf-infested, an obstacle to be hacked and cleared and burned down before man could survive. The population of Britain in the Middle Ages was tiny, the waste expanses vast, and each little settlement was a precarious endeavour. Walled cities shut out marauders, both animal and human: nature could be perceived as beautiful only when men had the leisure and skill to build walled gardens. The lofty prospect had no appeal; no man before Petrarch, the first Renaissance man, is known to have climbed a mountain for the sake of the view. In *The Making of the English Landscape*, W. G. Hoskins says that the Old English 'had no eye for scenery, any more than other hard-working farmers of later centuries'; they were too busy fighting against roots and brambles.

A contemporary account of the building of Fountains Abbey illustrates the difficulties that early settlers encountered on inhospitable terrain. In 1132 Archbishop Thurston of York allocated to a group of dissenting monks from St Mary's Abbey, York, 'a place remote and uninhabited, set with thorns, amongst the hollows of the mountains and rocks, more fit, it seemed, for the lair of wild beasts than for human use'. So it was described by Serlo, one of the first band of monks to leave York for the new foundation, in a dictation made about 1207 to Hugh of Kirkstall. Matthew Paris, writing not many years later in his *Historia Anglorum*, agreed – he called the site 'a place of horror and of vast solitude, in a deep and gloomy valley about three miles from Ripon, where they began in extreme poverty to build a church'. Not a word of the beauties of Skeldale.

Serlo tells us that when the monks first moved to their new land, their only shelter was a thatched hut which they built round the stem of a great elm. The winter was so harsh that they were reduced to stewing the leaves of this elm for food next summer. No wonder the medicinal springs after which the abbey was named did not at this stage move them to poetry. We look upon Fountains and Rievaulx, Tintern and Valle Crucis as buildings of exceptional beauty in exceptionally beautiful natural surroundings; even Furness, overtaken by railways and industry, still demonstrates what we consider the Cistercian eye for landscape – for we are accustomed to seeing these abbeys as tourist attractions. But the monks had no such interests or intentions: they built by rivers for practical reasons, but beyond that, they were moved less by a sense of beauty than by a desire to avoid the corruptions and ease of town life. The monks left St Mary's for Fountains because St Mary's had become corrupt and indulgent, not because they had any positive feeling for the countryside.

They left, in short, to avoid the distractions of beauty, rather than to seek them, following the advice of that great reformer of monastic life, Bernard of Clairvaux, who condemned costly church ornaments and the gratification of the senses. All things 'beautiful to the eye, soft to the ear, agreeable to the smell, sweet to the taste and pleasant to the touch' must be accounted as 'dross and dung', he declared. Decoration was a distraction; what, he wrote in *Apologia ad Willelmum* (*c.* 1130), did the brethren engaged in reading in the cloisters need with the fantasies of medieval sculpture, with

> those unclean monkeys? those fierce lions? those monstrous centaurs? those semi-human beings? those spotted tigers? those fighting warriors? those huntsmen blowing their horns? Here you behold several bodies beneath one head; there again several heads beneath one body. Here you see a quadruped with the tail of a serpent; there a fish with the head of a quadruped ... In fine, on all sides there appears so rich and amazing a variety of forms that it is more delightful to read the marbles than the manuscripts ...

This austere attitude towards ornament included natural beauty, as well as man-made. Not only did the early Christians not admire the same kind of scenery as we do; many thought it wrong to enjoy this world's beauty at all. St Anselm, Archbishop of Canterbury in the early twelfth century, considered that 'the delight of the senses is rarely good, mostly bad'. The admiration of red roses involves the senses of sight and smell in evil, and the sense of hearing is also infected 'when someone sits in a garden to look at the herbs, listen to stories and breathe the scent of the flowers'. Such pleasures were better avoided, the devout were warned. For this reason, the Early Fathers chose to build their monasteries and cells on the remote islands that surround Britain's coasts, where they could avoid both persecution and temptation. They established themselves in desolate spots such as Iona, Lindisfarne, Papa Westray (named after its hermits), Ramsey, St Michael's Mount, and Bardsey, where the bones of 20,000 saints are said to be buried. St Guthlac even managed to find an inland island, at Crowland, in the Lincolnshire Fens, where he lived in solitude.

We have plenty of descriptions of the austere lives of the Early Fathers: Adamnan, in his *Life* of Columba, describes the bitter storms that lashed Iona, and the holy life of the saint, whose bed was a rock, whose pillow was a stone, whose broth was nettle soup. Bede tells us of St Cuthbert's retreat to Farne Island, even more desolate than Lindisfarne, where his cell was surrounded by a wall higher than a man, 'but within, by excavating the rock, he made it much deeper, to prevent the eyes and thoughts from wandering, that the mind might be wholly bent on heavenly things, and the inhabitant might behold nothing from his residence but the heavens above him . . .' Aelred of Rievaulx spent his time not in appreciating the glory of Ryedale, but in the infirmary, suffering from rheumatism, gallstones, dysentery, and bronchial complaints exacerbated, we presume, by the bitter cold.

This is, no doubt, half the picture, but perhaps it is only half. Asceticism did not destroy all natural feeling, though it expressed itself in ways mysterious to us, acceptable to the Church. Cuthbert loved the wild life of the Northumbrian coast: Bede reports in his *Life* that a monk saw him once standing all night in the sea, praying, and 'at daybreak he came out, knelt down on the sand, and prayed. Two seals came out of the water, dried his feet with their fur, and warmed his limbs with their breath . . .' He kept the crows from his barley simply by speaking to them, and they apologized to him when he reproached them for stealing thatch for their nests from his hut. He was particularly fond of the eider ducks, which came to be known as St Cuthbert's ducks: Reginald of Durham gives a lively account of these friendly creatures, which were so tame that they would allow themselves to be stroked and petted, would come running when he called, and would build their nests in people's houses. 'They even come to your table and build under your bed', says Reginald, and goes on to describe Cuthbert's protective attitude towards his feathered flock, and the way they would rush to him for shelter in storms and troubles.

When Cuthbert's tomb was opened in 1927, one of the treasures found was a silk robe colourfully embroidered with seals or porpoises, fishes, and eider ducks. In 1381 a Newcastle craftsman was paid twelve pence for providing a design for a duck to ornament the Neville screen in Durham Cathedral.

These simple and miraculous tales of saints and animals are deeply rooted in place, in a feeling for a way of life which, austere though it was, maintained a close and affectionate contact with nature. The medieval mind interpreted nature in allegorical terms: the winter-flowering hawthorns at Glastonbury are from the Holy Thorn, sprung from the staff of Joseph of Arimathea which took root as he rested on his travels from the Holy Land with the Blood of the Cross; the poet of the *Lyfe of Joseph*, written *c.* 1502 (probably a Glastonbury monk), says they

Do burge and bere grene leaves at Christmas
As fresshe as other yn May, when the nightingale
Wrestes out her notes musycall as pure as glas . . .

The red moss on the stones at Holywell in Wales (*Jungermannia asplenoides* and *Byssus jolythus*) is the blood-stained hair of the martyred St Winefride – but it is also beautiful, as the Welsh poet Tudur Aled acknowledges when he writes,

And the breeze that comes from it
Is as the honey-bees first swarming
A sweet odour over the turf
Of musk or balm in the midst of the world . . .
The drops of her blood are as the red shower
Of the berries of the wild rose,
The tears of Christ from the height of the Cross . . .

Even the early Celtic poets and hermits had a profound and developed love of place: they may not have produced landscapes, in the organized, mountaintop Renaissance sense, but they certainly loved their seclusions. An Irish author of the tenth century writes:

I have a hut in the wood, none knows it but my Lord; an ash tree this side, a hazel on the other, a great tree on a mound encloses it.

Two heathery doorposts for support, and a lintel of honey-suckle; around its close the wood sheds its nuts upon fat swine.

The size of my hut, small yet not small, a place of familiar paths; the she-bird in its dress of blackbird colour sings a melodious strain from its gable.

The stags of Druim Rolach leap out of its stream of trim meadows; from them red Roighne can be seen . . .

Peaceful, in crowds, a grave host of the countryside, an assembly at my house; foxes come to the woods before it – it is delightful . . .

Fruits of rowan, black sloes of the dark blackthorn; foods of whorts, spare berries . . .

A clutch of eggs, honey, produce of heath-peas, God has sent it; sweet apples, red bog-berries, whortleberries . . .

There is no hostility to natural beauty here. Nor can one believe that even the earliest of pilgrims failed to be impressed by the drama of a site like St Michael's Mount, as were later poets like Spenser, Drayton and Milton. Why else, after all, should the 'great vision of the guarded mount', the legend of the apparition of the Archangel, have been allocated to this strange semi-island, if not through some sense that it was an appropriate place for angelic visitation?

In Anglo-Saxon literature, I think we can trace a positive liking for the bleak and desolate, a melancholy and nostalgia that provide a powerful strain in our national feeling for landscape, though they were partially suppressed during the bright Renaissance, and rose again with the Gothic revival and the Romantic movement. Kenneth Clark tells us that the poet of *Beowulf* describes Grendel's mere only for its terrors, which may be true, but at the same time it is clear that the poet and his audience enjoyed those terrors. He tells us of Grendel and his mother:

> . . . These two live
> In a little-known country, wolf-slopes, windswept headlands,
> Perilous paths across the boggy moors, where a mountain stream
> Plunges under the mist-covered cliffs,
> Rushes through a fissure. It is not far from here,
> If measured in miles, that the lake stands
> Shadowed by trees stiff with hoar frost.
> A wood, firmly-rooted, frowns over the water . . .

This is the kind of landscape that Tolkien, centuries later, was to bring to millions. Even in the early Middle Ages, we find a strong sense of the beauty of decay and dereliction, more commonly associated with the Gothic revival; in *The Ruin* a poet sings of transience, of a deserted and ruined city (thought by some to be Bath, abandoned by the Romans):

> Wonderful is this wall of stone, wrecked by fate.
> The city buildings crumble, the bold works of giants decay.
> Roofs have caved in, towers collapsed,
> Barred gates are gone, gateways have gaping mouths, hoar frost
>   clings to mortar.
> Ceilings save nothing from the fury of storms, worn away,
>   tottering,
> Undermined by age. The earth's embrace,
> Its clumsy grip, has claimed the mighty craftsmen;

They are perished, gone. A hundred generations of men
Have passed away since then. This wall, grey with lichen
And red of hue, outlived kingdom after kingdom,
Weathers wild storms . . .

If this were by a late eighteenth-century writer, instead of by one of the ninth century, we would certainly describe it as admiring rather than horror-struck. Similarly the Anglo-Saxon riddles that tell of icebergs and anchors, ships and storms, and the longer poem *The Seafarer*, show love as well as hardship: the seafarer, like Tennyson's Ulysses, cannot rest from travel, he despises the comfortable wine-flushed city dwellers, he sings of the icy sea, the hail, 'coldest of grain'; he declares,

The cry of the gannet was all my gladness,
The call of the curlew, not the laughter of men,
The mewing gull, not the sweetness of mead,
There, storms echoed off the rocky cliffs; the ice-feathered tern
Answered them . . .

Our language itself preserves some of the attributes of our early land-scapes, and our ways of looking at them: it is no accident that Tennyson is so fond of words such as glimmer, wan, dim, ghastly, misty, dusk, chill, dreary, drooping, sodden, drenched and dewy – most of them words that have no counterparts in the brighter languages of the South – for they describe the half-tones, the melancholy, the dim wetness of a Northern world.

But medieval life was not all rain and hailstorms. The warfare and stoicism of the Anglo-Saxons gradually gave way to a literature of spring, of joy, of hawthorn blossoms and nightingales, of cherries and roses, of the greenwood. Forests were not merely places of darkness, haunted by wolves and demons: they provided shelter for lovers like the woman in 'The Nut Brown Maid', who was prepared to cut her hair and her skirt and endure the wind and the weather for her outlawed love. They were the abode of Robin Hood, who haunts our literature from the fourteenth century, some say earlier. The Robin Hood ballads, such as 'The Birth of Robin Hood', portray the greenwood as a bright and summery place:

And mony ane sings o'grass, o'grass,
And mony ane sings o'corn,
And mony ane sings o' Robin Hood,
Kens little whare he was born.
It wasna in the ha', the ha'
Nor in the painted bower,
But it was in the gude green-wood,
Among the lily-flower.

Legend has surrounded the great oaks of Sherwood Forest, some of which still survive, until they have become symbols of protection, keeping watch over the poor and the simple, hiding the peasant and the outlaw from the taxman, sheltering egalitarian subversives like Mildar and Malder in the folk song of the Cutty Wren:

O where are you going, said Mildar to Malder,
O we may not tell you, said Fessel to Fose,
We're off to the green wood, said John the Red Nose,
We're off to the green wood, said John the Red Nose.
And what will you do there, said Mildar to Malder,
O we may not tell you, said Fessel to Fose,
We will shoot the Cutty Wren, said John the Red Nose,
We will shoot the Cutty Wren, said John the Red Nose.
And who'll get the spare ribs, said Mildar to Malder,
O we may not tell you, said Fessel to Fose,
We will give them all to the poor, said John the Red Nose,
We will give them all to the poor, said John the Red Nose.

From the late Middle Ages at least, the forest became a place of freedom, in legend if not in reality, where all men were equal, where the landscape belonged to all. Nature sided with the oppressed, against the artificial boundaries of ownership. This significance endures; in the nineteenth century the Lancashire radical Samuel Bamford wrote in his autobiography, *Early Days* (1849), that he loved the ballads of Robin Hood – 'And I was quite delighted with the idea of a free life in the merrie green-wood'. More recently, E. M. Forster's Maurice escapes from the sexual hypocrisy and inhibition of Edwardian England to the forests with his lover, and Arnold Wesker quotes the Cutty Wren in his attack on the rigidity of the class structure in *Chips with Everything*.

Nature's greenery even at its most untamed was not merely something to be hacked and burned: it represented fertility and renewal, green knights rode out of its 'wondrously wild woods', green children were born from it. It sprang back, abundant and indestructible; its green men adorn public-house signposts to this day, and leap up again in a novel by Kingsley Amis, and in a poem by Molly Holden, 'The Green Man':

> A divinity dominates my garden in August.
> He stands at the head of the patch I reserve
> for wild flowers – or weeds, as you choose.
> He is cloaked in green from head to foot,
> in layer upon layer of shifting spade-shaped leaves,
> faceless, armless, mysterious,
> eight feet high, silent and unmoving.
> Now, who is this? whence came this shrouded majesty?

He is, it appears, a disused clothes-line post covered with convolvulus, but to the poet he is the garden's master, with two tendrils twirling on his head 'like the fillet of some Gaulish god, / and pure white flowers, in turn, without / incongruity, lie on his shoulders, his hair'.

Chaucer's pilgrims set off to Canterbury in no mood of penitence or self-punishment, but in holiday high spirits, engendered by the sweet showers of April and the budding shoots; many of their tales are more pagan than Christian in tone, and in Chaucer even the conventional medieval imagery of rose gardens and nightingales has a bright and spring-time freshness. The statue of Venus in 'The Knight's Tale', rising from the green and glittering waves, and crowned with a garland of fresh roses, is a premonition of Botticelli. The poor nymphs and hamadryads that run forlornly disinherited from their homes in the same story are very much alive in Chaucer's imagination, and the trees felled for Arcite's funeral pyre (in lines 2061–66) are the trees of old England, not of classical Greece:

But how the fyr was maked up on highte,
And eek the names how the treës highte,
As ook, fivre, birch, asp, alder, holm, popler,
Wilow, elm, plane, ash, box, chasteyn, lind, laurer,
Mapul, thorn, beech, hasel, ew, whippel-tree
How they weren feld, shal not be told for me.

Even William Langland, a more austere and devout poet, also writing in the late fourteenth century, has his vision of Piers Plowman 'in a summer season, when soft was the sun', as he is walking, apparently for pleasure, on the Malvern Hills. The *Oxford Book of Medieval English Verse* may disappoint the landscape-hunter with its tedious disputes between owls and nightingales, holly bushes and ivy plants, but it also has that magical lyric, 'Now springes the spray', the first line of which is springtime in action, springtime unfolding into words. The Welsh poet Dafydd ap Gwilym sang a little earlier in the same century,

Welcome, with your lovely greenwood choir, summery month of May for which I long! Like a potent knight, an amorous boon, the green-tangled lord of the wildwood, comrade of love and of the birds, whom lovers remember... the faultless month of May is coming, with its heart set on conquering every green glen... A thick shade, clothing the highways, has draped every place with its green web...

Clearly pagan joy was strong enough to reassert itself, and to drive its green shoot through the blood, despite the warnings of Christianity; the Christian stories themselves put on a brighter colouring. In the Cherry-Tree Carol, Joseph and Mary walk in an orchard green

Where was berries and cherries
As thick as might be seen.
O then bespoke Mary,
So meek and so mild,
'Pluck me one cherry, Joseph,
For I am with child.'

O then bespoke Joseph
With words so unkind,
'Let him pluck thee a cherry
That brought thee with child.'
O then bespoke the babe
Within his mother's womb,
'Bow down then the tallest tree
For my mother to have some.'

This is no Biblical landscape, but an English orchard. Similarly the shepherd Jolly Wat, who goes to Bethlehem at Christ's nativity, is a thoroughly English shepherd, as he kneels by the baby and says:

'Jesu, I offer to thee here my pipe,
My skirt, my tar-box, and my scrip;
Home to my felowes now will I skip,
And also look unto my shepe.'
Ut hoy!
For in his pipe he made so much joy.

Ut hoy! is a cheerful cry, and Christianity softened, and became lighter of heart, as the centuries passed. It also grew prosperous and worldly: in the eighth century, Bede was able to describe Britain as a fertile land, 'rich in grain and timber; it has good pasturage for cattle and draught animals, and vines are cultivated in various localities . . . it is well known for its plentiful springs and rivers abounding in fish.' (Figs and grapes were known to the Romans in Britain, though they may not have grown as far north as Bede's Northumberland.) The abbeys and monasteries flourished, eventually losing all traces of their self-denying origins. The Cistercians in particular were responsible for teaching the arts of agriculture, for draining marsh and fen, for the growing wool trade. Huge flocks of monastic sheep grazed on the chalk and limestone uplands of Yorkshire and Lincolnshire, in Wales and the Cotswolds: early in the twelfth century, according to Hoskins, the nuns of Holy Trinity Abbey at Caen had a flock of 1,700 sheep grazing on Minchinhampton Common in the Cotswolds. Rival abbeys in Yorkshire built miles of drystone walls to settle boundary disputes, and despite centuries of change these walls still stand, an essential feature of the landscape. The new wealth built not only walls, but churches. From the early thirteenth century, spires began to spring up in the Fens of Lincolnshire and Norfolk, followed by the towers of Somerset and Suffolk. Southwell Minster, in Nottinghamshire, is a glorious example of craftsmanship which did not ignore nature or nature's images: the chapter-house (1295–1300) is decorated with the most realistic and lovingly observed carvings of maple, oak, hawthorn, vine, ivy and hop, the first of its kind in Britain, evidence of a new spirit, which Nikolaus Pevsner also detects in the philosophy of St Thomas Aquinas, in St Francis's sense of oneness with the universe, in the botanic descriptions of Albertus Magnus. Of this new way of seeing, this new art, Pevsner writes:

> And is not the balance of Southwell something deeper too than a balance of nature and style or of the imitative and the decorative? Is it not perhaps also a balance of God and the World, the invisible and the visible? Could these leaves of the English countryside, with all their freshness, move us so deeply if they were not carved in that spirit which filled the saints and poets and thinkers of the thirteenth century, the spirit of religious respect for the loveliness of created nature?

Love of this world, as St Bernard warned, can go too far, and although it is hard to see anything profane in the leaves of Southwell, descriptions of the wealthy shrine of Thomas à Becket at Canterbury make it sound rather shockingly opulent. In *Gesta Pontificum* William of Malmesbury, writing of the cathedral in 1125, said, 'Nothing like it could be seen in England either for the light of its glass windows, the gleaming of its marble pavements, or the many coloured paintings which led the wandering eyes to the panelled ceiling above.' Later pilgrims commented on the riches that had accumulated at the shrine. Hard though it is for us to imagine the cathedrals and abbeys in their brightly coloured pre-Reformation glory, it is easy to see why such wealth attracted Henry VIII's attention: equally easy to suppose that Bernard of the Cistercians would have disliked such ostentation. The Dissolution changed the face of Britain, destroying some of our finest buildings, creating some of our finest ruins, and subtly altering our attitude to beauty and ornament – or perhaps restoring it to an earlier ideal? Ivy-clad ruins by sylvan rivers are more in keeping with the British notion of beauty than shrines blazing with gold and jewels. The uninitiated British visitor tends to recoil with alarm from the gilded glories of Italian and Austrian Baroque and Rococo, with a feeling that such manifestations are somehow irreligious, profane: our eyes have been trained by the grey northern light, by our grey Gothic cathedrals, and we forget that these cathedrals were also once brilliant with colour. We prefer them as they are. The Dissolution, despite its wanton destruction, gave England images and scenes of ruin incomparable for their atmosphere, invaluable subject matter for a later generation of Picturesque and Romantic writers: the ruins themselves helped to develop our sensibility.

One of the earliest poets to strike the Gothic note was John Milton. *Il Penseroso* (1645) is a celebrated expression of the 'dim religious' feeling that later poets were to feel when they encountered high lonely towers, peaceful hermitages and mossy cells:

> But let my due feet never fail,
> To walk the studious Cloysters pale,
> And love the high embowed Roof,
> With antick Pillars massy proof,
> And storied Windows richly dight,
> Casting a dim religious light.
> There let the pealing Organ blow,
> To the full voic'd Quire below,
> In Service high, and Anthems cleer,
> As may with sweetnes, through mine ear
> Dissolve me into extasies,
> And bring all Heav'n before mine eyes.

This is 'poetic' feeling in Milton, not moral or religious; when he wrote elsewhere of the inhabitants of pale cloisters, he anathematized them as 'swan-eating, canary-sucking prelates'. He had no praises for the rich, self-indulgent monastic life, with its sixteen-course meals; nor did he even approve of the 'fugitive and cloistered virtue' he praises in *Il Penseroso*. The addition of splendid ruins to the landscape undoubtedly fortified a certain strain of British feeling, already expressed by the Anglo-Saxon poet quoted earlier. Rose Macaulay in her splendid account, *Pleasure of Ruins*, has pointed out that 'the authors' of *Titus Andronicus* (as she cautiously describes them) 'find it natural, even for troops, to turn aside to gaze at these wasted buildings that stood in decayed or shattered beauty about their own countryside' – for in Act 5 a Gothic soldier, supposedly fighting in Rome in the third century, reports that

> ... from our troops I strayed
> To gaze upon a ruinous monastery,
> And as I earnestly did fix mine eye
> Upon the wasted building ...

Macaulay goes on to quote John Webster, in whose *Duchess of Malfi* Antonio declares:

> I do love these ancient ruins:
> We never tread upon them, but we set
> Our foot upon some reverend history ...

and says that by 1628 antiquarian lovers of 'rust and old monuments' and ruined abbeys had become common enough to furnish a subject for satire in John Earle's *Microcosmographie*. Walls are quickly dilapidated: grass grows over stone in a generation. Sometimes the sentiment inspired by these pre-Reformation ruins was of religious outrage: the destruction of the holy shrine of Walsingham moved an anonymous poet to a sorrowful lament:

> Bitter, bitter, oh to behould the grasse to growe,
> Where the walls of Walsingham so stately did show
> Levell, levell with the ground the towres do lye

Which with their golden glittering tops pearsed once to the skye.
Where were gates, no gates are nowe; the waies are unknown . . .

This is not pleasurable melancholy: it is a lament for desecration. But on the whole the ruins provided an occasion for moral reflection or poetic sadness. Here is Laurence Sterne, contemplating the remains of Byland Abbey, near Rievaulx, in characteristically sentimental mood. He wrote to Eliza, his last love:

> When I am at Coxwold in the summer, what a sweet companion will thy idea be unto me; and what new pleasures will it afford me when I go to visit my nuns! – I give this title to an afternoon pilgrimage I frequently make to the ruins of a Benedictine Monastery, about a mile and a half from my cottage.
>
> These remains are situated on the banks of a clear gliding stream; on the opposite side whereof rises a bold ridge of hills, thick with wood – and finely varied by jutting rocks and broken precipices; and these are so very abrupt, that they now not only by their magnitude, but by the shade they cast, increase the solemnity of the place. – Many parts of the ruin are still entire; the refectory is almost perfect, and a great part of the chapel has hitherto defied the power of time. – A few bunches of elders grow fantastically among the broken columns and contrast, with their verdure, the dark green ivy which clings to the walls. – But it is not all solitude and silence! – A few cottages are scattered here and there in the suburbs of this venerable pile, which has, I suppose, furnished the materials for erecting them.
>
> To this place, after my coffee, unless prevented by inclement skies, I guide my daily steps. The pathway leads, by a gentle descent, thro' many beautiful and embowering thickets, – which gradually prepare the mind for the deep impressions which this solemn place never fails to make on mine. – There I rest against a pillar till some affecting sentiment brings tears upon my cheek: – sometimes I sit me down upon a stone, and pluck up the weeds that grow about it, – then, perhaps, I lean over a neighbouring gate, and watch the

gliding brook before me, and listen to its gentle murmurs; they are oftentimes in unison with my feelings. Here it is I catch those sombre tints of sentiment which I sometimes give to the world – to humanize and rob it of its spleen.

It is a short step from this to Sterne's contemporary, Thomas Gray, in his country churchyard at Stoke Poges, reflecting on transience, obscurity, and fame.

Monastic ruins sometimes stirred sentiments other than outrage or solemn thought: for some, Catholicism equalled superstition, and monks were bloated villains, for whom no crime was too horrid. The Gothic novel exploited this vein: 'Monk' Lewis, in his notorious novel *The Monk* (1796), made abbeys and cloisters the setting for terrible deeds of darkness. Gray was told that Netley Abbey was haunted. More surprisingly, Walter Scott in *Marmion* revels in the story of a woman entombed alive in the 'solemn, huge and dark red pile' of Lindisfarne, by captors whom she defiantly addresses as 'vassal slaves of bloody Rome'. In the footnotes he makes much fun of the posthumous travels of the bones of St Cuthbert, which were carried from Lindisfarne to Scotland:

> The saint was, however, a most capricious fellow-traveller; which was the more intolerable, as, like Sinbad's Old Man of the Sea, he journeyed upon the shoulders of his companions. They paraded him through Scotland for several years, and came as far West as Withern, in Galloway, whence they attempted to sail for Ireland, but were driven back by tempests. He at length made a halt at Norham; from thence he went to Melrose, where he remained stationary for a short time, and then caused himself to be launched upon the Tweed in a stone coffin . . .

An equally irreverent attitude to the miraculous and the Romantic is shown by Jane Austen in *Northanger Abbey* (begun in 1798), a book which might, one feels, have ended abbey-sentiment for all time. But it still lingers on; and we find a fine expression of it in Henry James, who, with his susceptibility to English history, proved a perfect victim. One of the high points of his tour of England recorded in *English Hours* was a visit to a friend at Wenlock Abbey in Shropshire, an abbey converted to a private dwelling house, which had for James the added charm of being private property not open to the public:

> I returned to the habitation of my friend . . . through an old Norman portal, massively arched and quaintly sculptured, across whose hollow threshold the eye of fancy might see the ghosts of monks and the shadows of abbots pass noiselessly to and fro. This aperture admits you to a beautiful ambulatory of the thirteenth century – a long stone gallery or cloister, repeated in two stories, with the interstices of its traceries now glazed, but with its long, low, narrow, charming vista still perfect and picturesque, with its flags worn away by monkish sandals and with huge round-arched doorways opening from its inner side into great rooms roofed like cathedrals. These rooms are furnished with narrow windows, of almost defensive aspect, set in embrasures three feet deep and ornamented with little grotesque mediæval faces. To see one of the small monkish masks grinning at you while you dress and undress, or while you look up in the intervals of inspiration from your letter-writing, is a mere detail in the entertainment of living in a *ci-devant* priory. This entertainment is inexhaustible; for every step you take in such a house confronts you in one way or another with the remote past. You devour the documentary, you inhale the historic. Adjoining the house is a beautiful ruin, part of the walls and windows and bases of the piers of the magnificent church administered by the predecessor of your host, the mitred abbot. These relics are very desultory, but they are still abundant, and they testify to the great scale and the stately beauty of the abbey. You may lie upon the grass at the base of an ivied fragment, measure the girth of the great stumps of the central columns, half smothered in soft creepers, and think how strange it is that in this quiet hollow, in the midst of lonely hills, so exquisite and elaborate a work of art should have risen. It is but an hour's walk to another great ruin, which has held together more completely. There the central tower stands erect to half its altitude and the round

arches and massive pillars of the nave make a perfect vista on the unencumbered turf. You get an impression that when catholic England was in her prime great abbeys were as thick as milestones.

After Wenlock, Ludlow, although 'the most impressive and magnificent of ruins', was merely a ruin, and as such on view to any passing traveller.

The Church of England has produced a host of literary vicars, many of whom used their country livings as a means to pursue their interest in natural history, archaeology, topography, and poetry. Country churches and parsonages summon up an image of a quiet, peaceable way of life, deeply rooted in community and tradition, the seasons strongly accentuated by church festivals. Tolerant of eccentricities, not insisting on an excessive degree of devotion or pastoral care, the Church has harboured major and minor talents – the gallant Robert Herrick, the bizarre Sterne, the naturalist Gilbert White, the well-fed James Woodforde, the witty Sydney Smith, the eccentric R. S. Hawker of Morwenstow, the depressive and hard-drinking Thomas Parnell, the realist George Crabbe, and the austere Welsh nationalist R. S. Thomas, to name but a few. Their poems and letters and diaries provide a special kind of map of England, a map of its remote corners, its slow changes. The churches themselves are among our oldest unchanged landmarks, and many of their vicars have, in various ways, seen themselves as custodians of our heritage.

Not that all of them were happy to find themselves in such quiet corners. Herrick, whom we recall as the poet of an Arcadian world of primroses, cowslips and daffodils, was not at all pleased at being appointed to the pretty parish of Dean Prior, in idyllic Devon: he complained that the people were 'currish', rude and churlish, protested that

> More discontents I never had
> Since I was born, than here:
> Where I have been, and still am sad
> In this dull Devonshire.

His parting shot when ejected under Cromwell in 1647 was locally long remembered:

Dean Bourn Farewell; I never look to see
Dean, or thy warty incivility.

But back he went, in 1660, and died and was buried there fourteen years later. Over a century after that, Sydney Smith was equally perturbed to find that the Residence Bill of 1808 would oblige him to desert the pleasures of literary London and Holland House for his Yorkshire parish of Foston, where he feared to become a vegetable. His efforts to transform himself into a farming clergyman he turned into comedy, writing to *The Farmer's Magazine* to complain of his ploughing oxen: 'They could not bear hot weather, nor wet weather, nor go well down hill. It took 5 men to shoe an ox. They ran against my gate-posts, lay down in the cart whenever they got tired, and ran away at the sight of a stranger' (1819). But unlike Herrick, Smith was charmed by his move, ten years later, to the West Country; his home at Combe Florey was 'a most parsonic parsonage, like the parsonages described in novels', and the milder climate in his new 'valley of flowers' delighted him (letter to Lady Gray, 13 July 1829).

Others loved the countryside for its own sake. Gilbert White's Selborne has become a place of pilgrimage not because he was a saintly vicar but because he described it with such affection.

Robert Francis Kilvert, writing, significantly, after the Romantic movement had aroused a passion for scenery in most educated people, fills his diary with enthusiastic descriptions of sunsets, views, ruined churches, flowers, animals, birds. Some passages are dramatic and grandiose: an evening sky on 14 March 1871 in the Welsh borders he found

> tremendous, electrifying . . . I never saw anything to equal it I think, even among the high Alps. One's first involuntary thought in the presence of these magnificent sights is to lift up the heart to God and humbly thank him for having made the earth so beautiful. An intense glare of primrose light streamed from the west deepening into rose and crimson. There was not a flake of snow anywhere but on the mountains . . .

But he is at his best when describing the daily round, the common task: baptizing babies, chasing birds out of the church, planting lettuces. His surroundings were idyllic. Here is a characteristic entry:

> March 24, 1871. After luncheon I spent a happy half hour in the lovely warm afternoon wandering about Clyro churchyard among the graves. I sat awhile in the old Catholic tomb of the 'Relict of Thomas Bridgwater' . . . This is my favourite tomb . . . A small and irreverent spider came running swiftly towards me across the flat tombstone and scuttling over the sacred words and memories with most indecent haste and levity. Here it was very quiet and peaceful, nothing to disturb the stillness but the subdued village voices and the cawing of the rooks nesting and brooding in the tops of the high trees in the Castle clump . . .

There were also those whose vision and sanctity consecrated the places where they lived, and made their names symbols of Christian endeavour. Such a place is Little Gidding, which T. S. Eliot celebrated in *The Four Quartets* as a place 'where prayer has been valid'. Little Gidding, with its small church and manor house, was the home of Nicholas Ferrar's Anglican community in the seventeenth century, a community which led a life of simplicity, prayer and service, in a unique quiet blend of mysticism and practical, well-managed common sense.

> . . . If you came this way,
> Taking the route you would be likely to take
> From the place you would be likely to come from,
> If you came this way in may time, you would find the hedges
> White again in May, with voluptuary sweetness.
> It would be the same at the end of the journey,
> If you came at night like a broken king,
> If you came by day not knowing what you came for,
> It would be the same, when you leave the rough road
> And turn behind the pig-sty to the dull façade
> And the tombstone. And what you thought you came for

Is only a shell, a husk of meaning
From which the purpose breaks only when it is fulfilled
If at all. Either you had no purpose
Or the purpose is beyond the end you figured
And is altered in fulfilment. There are other places
Which also are the world's end, some at the sea jaws,
Or over a dark lake, in a desert or a city –
But this is the nearest, in place and time.
Now and in England.

The pig-sty and the tombstone – Eliot stresses the ordinary nature of the revelation (Ferrar's grave has no name). The landscape is of the same kind: simple, English, undramatic. When Ferrar and his family first arrived at Little Gidding, the church was full of straw, disguised as 'hay-barn and Hog-sty': they restored it themselves. Even now, the place is well off the usual tourist track, although its name, to readers of poetry, is famous.

But perhaps the model and archetype of clergymen was the poet George Herbert, of the same age as Nicholas Ferrar, and a close friend: he made Ferrar his literary executor on his early death in 1633 at the age of thirty-nine. Herbert's poetry is the essence of all that many consider best in Anglicanism. It is straightforward, pure, homely in its imagery, practical, at times melancholy, yet tinged with the joy and light of genius. Herbert was the perfect country minister, careful of his flock, generous, humble, kindly, a Good Samaritan. Izaak Walton, in his *Life*, tells the story of Herbert's arriving 'soiled and discomposed' at a musical gathering at Salisbury because he had stopped to help a carrier's overburdened horse. Like Ferrar, he was practical as well as good: he restored his first church, at Leighton Bromswold near Huntingdon, from dereliction, and did the same for the parsonage and church at Bemerton, just outside Salisbury, where he ended his days. Such little country churches, such quiet livings, in such ordinary places – they could not contrast more with the great abbeys of the Middle Ages, just as Herbert's verse, with its imagery of everyday affairs, could hardly be more different from the grandiose visions of Milton. Yet both are part of the fabric of the landscape, hallowed by association, by history itself. (The literary associations of

Bemerton were enriched when Herbert's home was purchased in the late twentieth century by the Indian-born poet and novelist Vikram Seth.)

The seventeenth century also produced two of our finest Christian mystical poets, who saw the natural world as an expression of God's glory. In the Middle Ages, as we have seen, natural beauty was often considered suspect, a temptation of the devil, rather than an embodiment of the Lord. This feeling has by now almost totally vanished from our consciousness: we are far more likely to agree with Thomas Traherne, who believed that 'this visible world is wonderfully to be delighted in'. Traherne was a shoemaker's son, born in or near Hereford in *c.* 1636. His family was poor and he remained, by choice, a poor priest, but nevertheless believed his 'entrance to the world was saluted and surrounded by innumerable joys'. His delight in nature was as intense as Wordsworth's was to be: he saw the corn as 'orient and immortal wheat, which never should be reaped, nor was ever sown', and tells us in *First Century*, 'You never enjoy the world aright, till the Sea itself floweth in your veins, till you are clothed with the Heavens and Crowned with the Stars: and perceive yourself to be the sole Heir of the whole world.' He had his moments of fear, but even in those nature comforted him. In *Third Century* he writes:

> Another time, in a lowering and sad evening, being alone in a field when all things were dead and quiet, a certain want and horror fell upon me, beyond imagination. The unprofitableness and silence of the place dissatisfied me, its wideness terrified me . . . I was a weak and little child . . . Yet something also of Hope and Expectation comforted me from every border. This taught me that I was concerned in all the world: and that in the remotest Borders the causes of peace delight me, and the Beauties of the Earth when seen were made to entertain me . . .

To Traherne, natural things were glorious, and to know them was glorious: he was so far from believing that this world was a fallen world, a poor sinful copy of heaven, that he thought the 'stars as fair now, as they were in Eden, the sun as bright, the sea as pure . . . the lands as rich as ever they were'. This would certainly have been considered a heretical view by the Early Fathers, but to us it does not seem particularly unorthodox, so conditioned have we been by the Romantic movement to seek God in nature. But Traherne preceded Romanticism by a century and a half: he saw with his own eyes.

So did Henry Vaughan, though his language is more conventionally metaphysical, more ornamented with conceits. He was a great admirer of Herbert, as his poetry shows, and although not so consistently successful, he has moments of true vision: it was he who saw in God 'a deep but dazzling darkness', and who tells us, calmly and familiarly,

> I saw Eternity the other night,
> Like a great ring of pure and endless light . . .

But his verse is also coloured by the spirit of the landscapes of his youth, and particularly by the waters of the river Usk, 'fresh as the air, and clear as Glass', which he called his Helicon; he saw the grace of God in a water-fall, and for him the very stones were full of praise for the Lord:

> So hills and valleys into singing break,
> And though poor stones have neither speech nor tongue,
> While active winds and streams both run and speak,
> Yet stones are deep in admiration.

It is surely not entirely coincidental that these two poets, Traherne and Vaughan, both of whom seemed to sense a living bond with the natural world, should both have been born in the countryside of the Welsh borders, where man might well see God in every hill and every valley; as we have seen, even the less inspired Kilvert felt the same.

The pantheism of the Romantic movement is too large a subject to embark upon in this chapter, but space must be made for Gerard Manley Hopkins, who, although in a sense a nature poet, and writing after the great Romantics, was doctrinally a Romantic in his attitude to landscape. He was a Jesuit (he had converted to Catholicism in 1866), and his poetry shows the conflicts between his sense of vocation as a poet and his vocation as a priest. There is also a conflict between his instinctive response to natural beauty, and his desire to consecrate that beauty, through his verse, to God.

He was a close observer of nature, as his notebooks and sketches show. He admired Tennyson's precision, Crabbe's realism, and commented in a letter to Richard Watson Dixon in December 1881 that Byron's school had 'a deep feeling but the most untrustworthy and barbarous eye'. He perceived with the greatest intensity. On 18 May 1870 he writes in his *Journal*:

> I do not think I have ever seen anything more beautiful than the bluebell I have been looking at. I know the beauty of our Lord by it. Its inscape is mixed of strength and grace, like an ash tree. The head is strongly drawn backwards and arched down like a cutwater drawing itself back from the line of the keel. The lines of the bell strike and overlie this, rayed but not symmetrically . . .

And so he continues, in this and many similar passages, trying to catch the essence, the form, the 'inscape', to use his own word, of each living scene and object. His poems on the destruction of nature show a more deeply felt anguish than that manifested in conventional laments for fallen avenues and chopped trees. In 'Binsey Poplars' he writes of the felling of poplars near Oxford in 1879:

> O if we but knew what we do
> When we delve or hew –
> Hack and rack the growing green!
> Since country is só tender
> To touch, her being so slender . . .

And in his *Journal* on 8 April 1873 he writes, 'The ash tree growing in the corner of the garden was felled. It was lopped first: I heard the sound and looking out and seeing it maimed there came at that moment a great pang and I wished to die and not to see the inscapes of this world destroyed any more'. Beauty was God's; we knew the Lord through it, and by destroying it, we destroyed his kingdom. His descriptions of Oxford are striking; he saw her as

Towery city and branchy between towers;
Cuckoo-echoing, bell-swarmèd, lark-charmèd, rook-racked,
    river-rounded,

though he did not shrink from describing also her 'base and brickish skirt', now so much extended by spreading housing and industrial estates and ring roads. Equally vivid are his evocations of the countryside round Stonyhurst College in Lancashire, which he captures in phrases like these: 'Parlick ridge like a pale goldfish skin without body. The plain about Clitheroe was sponged out by a tall white storm of rain' (16 August 1873). But the landscapes which moved him most were those of Wales, where he spent some of the happiest years of his life at St Beuno's College, St Asaph, between 1874 and 1877. These years produced his most joyful poetry, in which love of God and love of nature are fused in violent passion. The connection between the two is movingly and innocently revealed in one of his first impressions of the region, on 6 September 1874. Walking with a friend, he climbed a hill near the college, and gazed at the view of the valley up towards Ruthin and down to the sea:

> The heights of Snowdon were hidden by the clouds but not from distance or dimness. The nearer hills, the other side of the valley, shewed a hard and beautifully detached and glimmering brim against the light, which was lifting there. All the length of the valley the skyline of the hills was flowing written all along upon the sky. A blue bloom, a sort of meal, seemed to have spread upon the distant south, enclosed by a basin of hills. Looking all round but most in looking far up the valley I felt an instress and charm of Wales. Indeed in coming here I began to feel a desire to do something for the conversion of Wales . . .

He makes the same connection in his sonnet 'In the Valley of the Elwy':

> Lovely the woods, waters, meadows, coombes, vales,
> All the air things wear that build this world of Wales;
> Only the inmate does not correspond . . .

In other poems, his praise pours forth undimmed by his priestly concern for the Welsh Protestant soul – in 'The Windhover', 'Pied Beauty', 'Spring', 'The Starlight Night', and perhaps above all in 'Hurrahing in Harvest':

> Summer ends now; now barbarous in beauty, the stooks arise
> Around; up above, what wind-walks! What lovely behaviour
> Of silk-sack clouds! Has wilder, wilful-wavier
> Meal-drift moulded ever or melted across skies?
> I walk, I lift up, I lift up heart, eyes,
> Down all that glory in the heavens to glean our Saviour . . .

This poem, he said in a letter to Robert Bridges, 'was the outcome of half an hour of extreme enthusiasm as I walked home alone one day from fishing in the Elwy' (16 July 1878). Yet always, in Hopkins, there is the concern to give beauty back to God, 'beauty's self and beauty's giver': a visit to Holywell on 8 October 1874 seemed to offer a theme of the union of beauty and sacrifice. He and a friend bathed at the well 'and returned very joyously. The sight of the water in the well as clear as glass, greenish like beryl or aquamarine, trembling at the surface with the force of the springs, and shaping out the five foils of the well quite drew and held my eyes to it.' Here we catch some of the spirit of the early Welsh poets: it is no coincidence that Hopkins was drawn to study Welsh and was much affected by its rhythms, for he found the rhythms deeply embodied in the landscape itself, noting on 8 August 1874:

> I looked into a lovely comb that gave me the instress of *Weeping Winefride*, which all the west country seems to me to have: soft maroon or rosy cocoa-dust-coloured handkerchiefs of plough-fields, sometimes delicately combed with rows of green, their hedges bending in flowing outlines and now misted a little by the beginning of twilight ran down into it upon the shoulders of the hills; in the bottom crooked rows of rich tall elms, foreshortened by position, wound through it . . .

The 'buoyancy and abundance' of the water of St Winefride's Well flows up into his language and his rhythms, 'the spring in place leading back the thoughts by its spring in time to its spring in eternity'. Hopkins never finished his verse tragedy about St Winefride's martyrdom, and the well is no longer as it was in Hopkins's day, for mining operations have diverted the spring and it is now fed from a reservoir, but much of the landscape is unspoiled, and even that which has vanished lives on in his poetry.

For many of us today, lacking Hopkins's convictions, the perception of God in nature is as close as we get to religious experience. Thomas Gray's sentiments on visiting the Grande Chartreuse have been echoed by many a holiday-maker and tourist: he writes in a letter to Richard West on 16 November 1739:

> I own I have not, as yet, anywhere met with those grand and simple works of Art, that are to amaze one, and whose sight one is the better for: but those of Nature have astonished me beyond expression. In our little journey up to the Grande Chartreuse, I do not remember to have gone ten paces without an exclamation, that there was no restraining: Not a precipice, not a torrent, not a cliff, but is pregnant with religion and poetry. There are certain scenes that would awe an atheist into belief, without the help of other argument.

Wordsworth was to feel the same, in the Wye valley near the ruins of Tintern Abbey – where, noticeably, it was nature that moved him, not the religious associations of the ruins. Some orthodox Christians look down on this worship-in-the-open-air approach, but Michael Paffard, in his book *The Unattended Moment*, has collected an impressive array of testimony from Christians and non-Christians alike: Wordsworth and Osbert Sitwell, T. F. Powys and Arthur Quiller-Couch, Vladimir Nabokov and C. Day Lewis, Leonard Woolf and Julian Huxley – they and many others have borne witness to moments of profound and mystic insight through the natural world, to moments of joy and of terror, of the rose and the yew tree.

A religious or pantheistic reverence for nature comes particularly easily to children: I remember that years ago, when a group of us was returning from a school outing to the Yorkshire moors, we started singing hymns in the coach, and were reprimanded for our irreverence. We were highly indignant at the prohibition, because most of us felt more moved to praise the Lord after a day in the open air than in school prayers. Had not George Fox himself seen his vision on Pendle Hill? In his *Journal* he describes being moved by the Lord to climb this hill in the year 1652, which he did with difficulty: 'When I was come atop of it, I saw Lancashire sea; and there atop of the hill I was moved to sound the day of the Lord; and the Lord let me see in what places He had a great people to be gathered . . .' As he was resting that night, the bare room in which he lay was flooded with a vision 'of a great people in white raiment'– a vision which Canon Rawnsley decided was the effect of the sun on Farleton Knott and Whitbarrow Scar. Be that as it may, Fox certainly associated God's calling with the open air, and at Firbank preached on a rock on a hillside as Christ had done before, telling the gathering that 'the steeple house and the ground on which it stood were no more holy than that mountain'. John Wesley followed, almost literally, in his footsteps, preaching in Cumberland, and after a gathering at the little village of Lorton, he wrote in his *Journal* for 15 May 1759 that his congregation 'found God to be a God both of the hills and valleys, and nowhere more present than in the mountains of Cumberland'. Views from mountain tops have in the past stirred complex emotions: the agnostic Bernard Levin writing of a visit to Malvern for the Malvern Festival refers to one of our earliest Biblical associations when he writes, 'There is no more English spot in all England, and few more beautiful; the view from my bedroom window was so extensive and spectacular that I was disappointed not to find Satan at my elbow promising me everything I could see if I would only fall down and worship him.' A far cry from George Fox's vision, but nevertheless kin to it.

Other writers have been stirred not only by nature itself, but by associations of worship and sanctity: T. S. Eliot has made Little Gidding and East Coker places of literary as well as architectural or religious pilgrimage, and Dr Johnson, the most matter-of-fact of men, wrote, 'That man is little to be envied, whose patriotism would not gain force upon the plain of Marathon, or whose piety would not grow warmer among the ruins of Iona!' Even D. H. Lawrence, whose religious impulses had very little in common with orthodox Christianity, could respond passionately to the most traditional of Christian images. In chapter 7 of *The Rainbow* he describes a visit to Lincoln Cathedral in these terms:

> He had promised her, that one by one, they should visit all the cathedrals of England. They began with Lincoln, which he knew well.
>
> He began to get excited as the time drew near to set off. What was it that changed him so much? She was almost angry, coming as she did from the Skrebenskys'. But now he ran on alone. His very breast seemed to open its doors to watch for the great church brooding over the town. His soul ran ahead.
>
> When he saw the cathedral in the distance, dark blue lifted watchful in the sky, his heart leapt. It was the sign in heaven, it was the Spirit hovering like a dove, like an eagle over the earth. He turned his glowing, ecstatic face to her, his mouth opened with a strange, ecstatic grin.
>
> 'There she is,' he said.
>
> The 'she' irritated her. Why 'she'? It was 'it'. What was the cathedral, a big building, a thing of the past, obsolete, to excite him to such a pitch? She began to stir herself to readiness.
>
> They passed up the steep hill, he eager as a pilgrim arriving at the shrine. As they came near the precinct, with castle on one side and cathedral on the other, his veins seemed to break into fiery blossom, he was transported.
>
> They had passed through the gate, and the great west front was before them, with all its breadth and ornament.
>
> 'It was a false front,' he said, looking at the golden stone and the twin towers, and loving them just the same. In a little ecstasy he found himself in the porch, on the brink of the unrevealed. He looked up to the lovely unfolding of the stone. He was to pass within to the perfect womb.

Then he pushed open the door, and the great, pillared gloom was before him, in which his soul shuddered and rose from her nest. His soul leapt, soared up into the great church. His body stood still, absorbed by the height. His soul leapt up into the gloom, into possession, it reeled, it swooned with a great escape, it quivered in the womb, in the hush and the gloom of fecundity, like seed of procreation in ecstasy.

She too was overcome with wonder and awe. She followed him in his progress. Here, the twilight was the very essence of life, the coloured darkness was the embryo of all light, and the day. Here, the very first dawn was breaking, the very last sunset sinking, and the immemorial darkness, whereof life's day would blossom and fall away again, re-echoed peace and profound immemorial silence.

Away from time, always outside of time! Between east and west, between dawn and sunset, the church lay like a seed in silence, dark before germination, silenced after death. Containing birth and death, potential with all the noise and transition of life, the cathedral remained hushed, a great, involved seed, whereof the flower would be radiant life inconceivable, but whose beginning and whose end were the circle of silence. Spanned round with the rainbow, the jewelled gloom folded music upon silence, light upon darkness, fecundity upon death as a seed folds leaf upon leaf and silence upon the root and the flower, hushing up the secret of all between its parts, the death out of which it fell, the life into which it has dropped, the immortality it involves, and the death it will embrace again.

Here, in the church, 'before' and 'after' were folded together.

No two writers could be less similar than Lawrence and T. S. Eliot, no religions further apart than the dark gods of the one and the High Anglicanism of the other, yet both feel the same awe, the same sense of the present in the past, when confronted by these enduring symbols of spiritual history. Eliot, in *Murder in the Cathedral*, has the last words:

For wherever a saint has dwelt, wherever a martyr has given
    his blood for the blood of Christ,
There is holy ground, and the sanctity shall not depart from it
Though armies trample over it, though sightseers come with
    guide books looking over it;
From where the western seas gnaw at the coast of Iona,
To the death in the desert, the prayer in forgotten places by
    the broken imperial column,
From such ground springs that which forever renews the earth
Though it is forever denied. Therefore, O God, we thank Thee
Who hast given such blessing to Canterbury.

THE PASTORAL VISION

English literature is rich in descriptions of country life and country labour, though very few were written by the labourers themselves. The landlord and the ploughman have, literally, different perspectives: the first sees the lordly hilltop view, the second sees what is under his nose or under his boots, and his vision fails when he tries to look up. Most of our surviving early literature was written to please the landlords, by the climbing artists to whom they extend their patronage, but there is a certain amount of commentary from ground level; this commentary increased in volume and protest as educational and social opportunities increased, until in the nineteenth century a whole range of intermediate voices make themselves heard. Nor were the social origins of the earliest writers as rigidly determined as they appear at first sight: if we are to believe Bede, the poet Caedmon worked as a herdsman until the Muse called him. We shall never know who wrote the Anglo-Saxon riddle in the Exeter Book (No. 21) which gives a description of ploughing, and describes the ox as 'grey enemy of the forest', but whoever it was has left us one of the only accurate accounts of the Anglo-Saxon plough. Aelfric's *Colloquium*, written in Latin in the late tenth or early eleventh century to give beginners practice in speaking Latin, reveals a good deal about working life in Anglo-Saxon England. His characters are from the *ceorl* or slave classes, and he brings them to life in dialogue; ploughmen, shepherds, oxherds, fishermen and cobblers give accounts of their trades, and Aelfric had enough sympathy with the ploughman's long and weary day to make his interrogator address him with the words, 'O, how toilsome it is − ', to which the ploughman replies, 'It is great toil, sir, because I am not free.' By the time of the Peasants' Revolt of 1381, the labourers had found other spokesmen: John Ball's text,

When Adam delved and Eve span
Who was then the gentleman?

runs as a perpetual and pertinent refrain to the most courtly and ideal descriptions of pastoral bliss.

It was not until the eighteenth century that the first crop of verifiable ploughmen poets began to emerge – Stephen Duck, Robert Burns, John Clare – but earlier writers did not live wholly in a world of literary allusion. Spenser's first true English pastoral of 1579, *The Shepheardes Calendar*, shows a better understanding of the hardships of a shepherd's life than most courtiers possessed. Milton, the most scholarly of authors, may have viewed nature through the spectacles of old books, but he also saw it with his own eyes: his grandfather was a yeoman farmer, his father's home in Hammersmith was in the depths of the Middlesex countryside, and Horton in Buckinghamshire where he spent the years 1635–38 was yet more rural. The flowers that strew the hearse of Lycidas are real, not symbolic or classical flowers:

> The tufted Crow-toe, and pale Gessamine,
> The white Pink, and the Pansie freakt with jet,
> The glowing Violet,
> The Musk-rose, and the well attir'd Woodbine,
> With Cowslips wan that hang the pensive hed,
> And every flower that sad embroidery wears . . .

Bookish though he was, Milton would walk three or four hours of an afternoon for pleasure, and the hungry unfed sheep of his verse are not copied blindly from Virgil.

The classical myth of a Virgilian Golden Age was contrasted, even by Virgil, with the real labours of real farmers and real peasants: the Biblical vision of Paradise has, from the beginnings of time, been accompanied by the myth of the Fall. Man was born to labour; the fruits of the earth do not fall into the hand or offer themselves to the mouth, as some poets so prettily suggest. When Virgil in Eclogue IV tells us that goats shall walk home, their udders taut with milk, and nobody herding them; the ox will have no fear of the lion . . . Then grapes shall hang wild and reddening on thorn trees and honey sweat like dew from the hard bark of oaks . . . The soil shall need no harrowing, the vine no pruning knife, and the tough ploughman may at last unyoke his oxen

he knows he is imagining an impossible world, a golden Utopia, one that haunts mankind largely because of its impossibility, its contrast with the grim realities of toil, dispossession, famine, plague. Andrew Marvell's garden is, as his language suggests, a luxurious trap:

What wondrous life is this I lead!
Ripe apples drop about my head;
The luscious clusters of the vine
Upon my mouth do crush their wine;
The nectaren, and curious peach,
Into my hands themselves do reach;
Stumbling on melons, as I pass,
Insnar'd with Flow'rs, I fall on Grass.

In another poem, 'The Mower against Gardens' (1681), he condemns man's adulteration of nature, his search for the cultivated, the rare and the exotic:

The Tulip, white, did for complexion seek;
And learn'd to interline its cheek:
Its onion root they then so high did hold
That One was for a Meadow sold.

Behind these images lies the concept of natural nature, the Garden of Eden of unfallen man – but, as Marvell implies, there was never any such place, except in the mind. Milton is of the same opinion (Book IV, lines 131–49): Satan's vision of Paradise is fine enough, and indeed Horace Walpole claimed it was the poetic inspiration of English landscape gardens such as Hagley and Stourhead:

> So on he fares, and to the border comes
> Of Eden, where delicious Paradise,
> Now nearer, Crowns with her enclosure green,
> As with a rural mound the champain head
> Of a steep wilderness, whose hairie sides
> With thicket overgrown, grottesque and wilde,
> Access deni'd; and overhead up grew
> Insuperable highth of loftiest shade,
> Cedar, and Pine, and Firr, and branching Palm,
> A Silvan Scene . . .
> And higher then that wall a circling row
> Of goodliest Trees loaden with fairest Fruit,
> Blossoms and Fruits at once of golden hue
>   Appeerd, with gay enameld colours mixt . . .

The plants in Paradise are 'poured forth profuse' by nature, not arranged in beds and curious knots by 'nice art'. Yet even here, labour is necessary (Book V, lines 212–15): Adam and Eve set off to their daily labours –

>   . . . where any row
> Of Fruit-trees overwoodie reached too farr
> Thir pampered boughes, and needed hands to check
> Fruitless imbraces; or they led the Vine
> To wed her Elm . . .

What is Eve describing but 'nice art', when she speaks of directing the clasping ivy where to climb, or of winding woodbine round the arbour? Their Eden is fruitful enough, but it needs tending nevertheless; indeed, Eve suggests they can hardly keep pace with it (Book IX, lines 209–11):

>   . . . what we by day
> Lop overgrown, or prune, or prop, or bind,
> One night or two with wanton growth derides,
> Tending to wilde.

Unable to conceive a state in which labour was unnecessary, Milton creates an over-fruitful, over-abundant, fiercely procreative world, which man has to cull and check – a pleasanter state, certainly, than the lot of the settler hacking at tree roots, or digging turnips out of the frozen earth, but nevertheless fraught with its own dangers and problems. In *Comus* (lines 710–23), praise of nature's bounty is put into the mouth of the tempter:

> Wherefore did Nature powre her bounties forth,
> With such a full and unwithdrawing hand,
> Covering the earth with odours, fruits, and flocks,
> Thronging the Seas with spawn innumerable,
> But all to please, and sate the curious taste?
>   . . . if all the world
> Should in a pet of temperance feed on Pulse,
> Drink the clear stream, and nothing wear but Freize,
> Th'all-giver would be unthank't, would be unprais'd,
> Not half his riches known . . .

If we reject nature's gifts, she will be 'strangled with her waste fertility'. This is clearly nonsense, as the tempted Lady firmly retorts, but it is a powerful vision, and as one can see in *Paradise Lost*, Milton's ideas on temperance and bounty were highly ambiguous.

The truth is that labour itself is natural, at least in the British climate: there may be South Sea islands where it is unnecessary, or colonies where the realities of it can be ignored by the British consumer, but we all feel the sinister artificiality of the Britain Thomas Carew presents in 'To Saxham', where

> The Pheasant, Partridge and the Lark
> Flew to my house, as to the Ark.
> The willing Oxe, of himselfe came
> Home to the slaughter, with the Lamb,
> And every beast did thither bring
> Himselfe to be an offering.

> The scalie herd, more pleasure took
> Bath'd in the dish than in the brook.

One does not need to be a vegetarian to see the faults of this line of reasoning: what of the farmer, the shepherd, the fisherman? Their lives of bondage and labour are not even given credit, perhaps because the poet could not bear to contemplate them.

Poems like Carew's are characteristic of a literature that tried to avoid a confrontation with the facts of labour. He praised the country house life, where the lord was patron and host of the artist, where riches spilled from an effortlessly replenished cornucopia. This generous image persists to this day: in the twentieth century W. B. Yeats wrote with admiration of ancestral houses, and a life where all was 'accustomed, ceremonious', and in the 1920s Ottoline Morrell at Garsington clearly saw herself in the old style, the benevolent benefactress, although her guests made fun of her behind her back. In 1616 Ben Jonson was the guest of Philip Sidney's younger brother Robert at Penshurst, and wrote (in 'To Penshurst') of its broad beeches and chestnut shade, its purpled pheasants lying in the fields waiting to be slaughtered, its fat aged carps:

> The early cherry, with the later plum,
> Fig, grape and quince, each in his time doth come:
> The blushing apricot and woolly peach
> Hang on thy walls, that every child may reach.
> And though thy walls be of the countrey stone,
> They are reared with no mans ruine, no mans grone,
> There's none, that dwell about them, wish them downe;
> But all come in, the farmer and the clowne . . .

Jonson does seem aware that such riches are justifiable only if they are hospitably shared, but nevertheless, like Carew, manages to suggest that no real sweat was spent on producing them. Workers and servants, in this ideal world, remain invisible: the guest was tended by unseen hands. The country house of Uppark, where H. G. Wells's mother was housekeeper, was built with the servants' quarters landscaped out of sight, underground, because their intrusive presence would spoil the view. Wells himself in *The Time Machine* projected a future in which the labouring classes lived in tunnels and caves beneath the earth, emerging at night to prey on the pretty, helpless, useless upper classes – a savage prediction of what might happen if workers and consumers became even more sharply differentiated. In *Akenfield* (1969) Ronald Blythe records the experience of servants in a country house in Suffolk, who were taught to keep strictly out of sight:

> We must never be seen from the house; it was forbidden. And if people were sitting on the terrace or on the lawn, and you had a great barrow-load of weeds, you might have to push it as much as a mile to keep out of view . . . None of the village people was allowed into the garden. Definitely not. Trades-people came to their door and never saw the main gardens. Work in front of the house had to be done secretly. About seven in the morning we would tiptoe about the terrace, sweeping the leaves, tying things up, never making a sound, so that nobody in the bedrooms could hear the work being done. This is what luxury means – perfect consideration.

From the Renaissance on, England produced reams of pastoral verse, imitations of Virgil and Theocritus, and imitations of imitations, a tradition that died hard, lingering on until Thomas Hardy, still haunting the memory. In the pastoral convention, courtiers played at being shepherds: Spenser, who could write sympathetically of Cuddie and Thenot and their 'ragged rontes' (bullocks) shivering in the winter's rage, also commemorated his friend Philip Sidney as Astrophel, 'the pride of shepherds' praise, the rustic lasses' love', and saw nothing ridiculous in describing this worldly and sophisticated soldier and poet as one who could

> Pipe, and daunce, and caroll sweet
> Emongst the shepheards in their shearing feast

in a landscape of crystal wells and shady groves. The masque of *Comus* was performed at Ludlow, another hospitable country house, by the daughter and sons of the Earl of Bridgewater, and ends with a rustic dance of country shepherds. They are dismissed at the end in these words:

> Back Shepherds, back anough your play,
> Till next Sun-shine holiday,
> Here be without duck or nod
> Other trippings to be trod
> Of lighter toes . . .

One longs to know what the conscripted dancers made of their part in this courtly fantasy. Did they, like Bottom the Weaver and his colleagues in *A Midsummer Night's Dream*, enjoy their temporary release from work, or were they reluctant performers, indignant at this travesty intruding on their working life? What did they make of their ducking and nodding and of their peremptory dismissal to make way for lighter feet? Surely some of the spectators must have felt, as Hippolyta did,

> I love not to see wretchedness o'ercharged
> And duty in his service perishing.

Poets and critics themselves became impatient with the pastoral, as it grew increasingly fantastic. In 1772 John Aikin roundly declared, 'Pastoral poetry is a native of happier climes, where the face of nature, and the manners of the people are widely different from those of our northern regions. What is reality on the soft Arcadian and Sicilian plains, is all fiction here.' In *The Prophecy of Famine* (1763), Charles Churchill's shepherds huddle in a cave in bleak Scotland, amongst barren rocks and ragged flocks, thorns and thistles, where 'half-starved spiders preyed on half-starved flies'. Wordsworth's shepherds in the Lake District spend much of their time laboriously battling with the elements, rescuing their sheep from swollen rivers and snowdrifts and mountain ledges, instead of piping songs in sunny olive groves. Yet the country life was not universally hard; in certain places, at certain times, it had its brighter moments.

The pastoral has some reality. Even Churchill's Jockey 'with meikle art could on the bag-pipes play', and his Sawney

> ... without remorse could bawl
> Home's madrigals, and ditties from Fingal.

Robert Bloomfield, although he defiantly threw his old hat into the horse pond when he left his job as a farm boy, aged fourteen, in 1781, looked back with some nostalgia to his days in Suffolk, and the farm near Honington where he worked; his hero Giles is a boy of all trades, carting turnips, minding pigs, fetching reluctant cows from pasture, and scaring birds. The pleasures of haymaking and harvest feasts were real enough, even to those who recognized that the farmer's seasonal bounty was only a bribe, a temporary respite. The milkwoman poet Ann Yearsley, who in true eighteenth-century style was persuaded to rename herself Lactilla, knew from experience the hardship of poverty, and the misery of tending cows in winter, yet even she was charmed by the pastoral dream: although she had never read or heard of poets such as Dryden, Spenser and Thomson, she knew and admired a translation of Virgil's *Georgics*, and decked her poems (published in 1785) with classical references learned from pictures in the print-shop windows of Bristol, where she sold her milk from door to door.

Love for the land, and indignation at the exploitation of labour, go hand in hand in the poetry of the best of the rural poets, of whom Stephen Duck was one of the earliest. He was a tasker from Wiltshire, educated at a Charity school at the beginning of the eighteenth century; he worked as a hired labourer, and his poem 'The Thresher's Labour' gives a grim picture of sweat and toil. The winter's tasks are worst:

> When sooty Pease we thresh, you scarce can know
> Our native Colour, as from Work we go:
> The Sweat, the Dust, the suffocating Smoke,
> Make us so much like Ethiopians look,
> We scare our wives, when Ev'ning brings us home;
> And frighted Infants think the Bugbear come.

The summer is not much better; after hours of haymaking the labourer is too tired to profit from a break:

> Down our parch'd Throats we scarce the Bread can get;
> And, quite o'erspent with Toil, but faintly eat,
> Nor can the Bottle only answer all;
> The Bottle and the Beer are both too small.

The farmer is a despot, shouting at his workmen for their laziness or carelessness, scraping 'the stubble with his greedy hand'. Duck envies the shepherds their leisure, for they can tell a merry tale, while the thresher's voice is lost, 'drowned by the louder Flail'. Yet even Duck could appreciate the beauty of a ripe unmown field at dawn, and join in the 'loud Huzzas' that proclaim the harvest done.

Duck could describe a cornfield from the reaper's viewpoint, Bloomfield the 'fresh parallels' of a newly ploughed field. Neither of them was very good at the distant prospect, the organized pictorial scene, the hilltop view. When Bloomfield in the days of his literary success travelled to Dorking in 1803, he was astonished by the romantic scenery of Leith Hill and Box Hill, the highest eminences he had ever seen. John Clare, much the greatest poet and most complex sensibility of the three, had the same difficulties in contemplating a lofty or distant view. To him, the landscape was not a backdrop; the land was known intimately, tree by tree, field by field. Romantic scenery is not, of course, the best arable land: Duck's Wiltshire, Bloomfield's Suffolk and John Clare's Northamptonshire are either fairly flat or undulating, and offer little in the way of the Picturesque. Before looking more closely at Clare's attitude to his much loved and very ordinary village of Helpston, perhaps we ought to look at *The Seasons* of James Thomson. Thomson was one of the first poets to make landscape his central subject; he was immensely popular with both landlord and peasant, his work was highly influential, and he was master of the extended prospect. Thomson was born in the Border country of Scotland, near Kelso, and spent his childhood at Southdean where his father was minister. One of his biographers, Douglas Grant, insists that it was the landscape of these early years that trained

Thomson's eye: Grant describes the distant prospects of the Cheviots, the nearer desolate stretches of moorland with tufted marshes and spongy hillocks, and says,

> When Thomson, in obedience to his sensibility, stood upon the high places about his home, and turned his back to the hills, he would see laid out before him the long sweep of a delightful pastoral landscape. The English countryside owes its beauty to the cloistered grace of many particulars, a brook, a coppice, a beanfield, or a handful of primroses in a hedge; but in the Borders these particulars lose their identity in the panorama. The eye moves down a valley, follows it until it widens and enters another, and continues on across a plain which is bounded only by the horizon. This landscape is ordered into foreground, middle distance and distance, as deliberately as though it had been arranged by some great seventeenth century artist, a Salvator Rosa or a Gaspar Poussin . . . this landscape trained Thomson to observe and describe nature in a particular way . . .

This may or may not be so: other writers have suggested that Thomson's eye for composition was trained not by nature but by familiarity with the work of the painters Grant mentions, whose vogue in the eighteenth century was immense. And Thomson, unlike most other poets of nature, did not stay long in the regions of his youth or yearn unduly for them in absence: in 1725, aged twenty-five, he set off for London, never to return. In the south he embarked on a comfortable life, visiting many fashionable country houses, first as tutor, then as guest, and undoubtedly had the opportunity to study the works of Rosa, Poussin and Claude, with which his own poems are so often compared – though the first *Season* he composed, 'Winter', perhaps owes more to his native Borders and contains fewer luminous golden views than the later ones. However it came about, either the real or the painted landscapes of southern England increasingly charmed him, and 'Spring', 'Summer' and 'Autumn' present a new version of pastoral, in which Thomson responds enthusiastically both to the Sublime and to the everyday, agricultural aspects of nature, to its pictorial and its useful qualities – not yet forced to recognize, as were later generations, a conflict between the two.

Although his classical allusions are plentiful, Thomson rejects the unseen-hands view of the countryside; he peoples the calm eighteenth-century landscape of England with happy haymakers, with swains gathering nuts or ploughing, with shepherds and villagers dipping and shearing sheep – even with swains admiring the wonders of the rainbow. He recognizes that prosperity depends on labour, and that therefore labour ought to have its own dignity. He is one of the first poets to celebrate the substance rather than the proceeds of prosperity; he sings not of lavish feasts of carp and pheasant, but of the beauties of well-tended flocks, well-cultivated fields. This attitude developed into that of the sensible, estate-managing heroes of Jane Austen, who like rich meadows, snug and comfortable valleys, fine timber and neat farmhouses.

Thomson, in fact, though the son of a poor minister from a small parish, has the landlord's perspective, acquired by association and patronage. Gainsborough and his contemporaries pleased their subjects by painting them seated happily amidst their neat, productive pastures: his portrait of Mr and Mrs Andrews is, as John Berger in *Ways of Seeing* pointed out, not only a picture of Mr and Mrs Andrews enjoying the beauties of unperverted and uncorrupted nature, but also a celebration of their complacent ownership of a rich and glowing cornfield, a flock of sheep in the middle distance, and some woods in the far distance. Thomson pleases his patrons in much the same manner, depicting their handsome estates and gardens in words rather than paint. Some critics have complained that Thomson's landscapes are mere lists and catalogues of wealth, but most see them as careful compositions, organized according to recognizable rules, and 'mellowed through and through' as Christopher Hussey writes in *The Picturesque*, 'in a bath of Claudian light'. Nobody can deny that he favours a high viewpoint – his favourite view is from a hilltop, whence he can oversee, survey, command the prospect. The very language is the language of the landowner rather than of the earthbound peasant: peasants do not often climb hills to rejoice in the vision of what is not theirs, whereas lords have a marked predilection for viewing their property, and showing it proudly to their guests. Thomson's vision is that of the man of land and leisure, of wide horizons and cultured

responses; his landscapes are not wild and untamed, but civilized and fruitful. Here is a characteristic passage from 'Summer', describing the view from
the hilltop at Sheen :

>   . . . Say, shall we wind
> Along the streams? Or walk the smiling mead?
> Or court the forest glades? Or wander wild
> Among the waving harvests? Or ascend,
> While radiant Summer opens all its pride,
> Thy hill, delightful Shene? Here let us sweep
> The boundless landscape; now the raptured eye,
> Exulting, swift to huge Augusta send,
> Now to the sister-hills that skirt her plain,
> To lofty Harrow now, and now to where
> Majestic Windsor lifts his princely brow.
> In lovely contrast to this glorious view,
> Calmly magnificent, then will we turn
> To where the silver Thames first rural grows.
> There let the feasted eye unwearied stray;
> Luxurious, there, rove through the pendent woods
> That nodding hang o'er Harrington's retreat;
> And stooping thence to Ham's embowering walks,
> Beneath whose shades, in spotless peace retired,
> With Her the pleasing partner of his heart,
> The worthy Queensbury yet laments his Gay.
>   . . .
> Enchanting vale! beyond whate'er the Muse
> Has of Achaia or Hesperia sung!
> O vale of bliss! O softly-swelling hills!
> On which the Power of Cultivation lies,
> And joys to see the wonder of his toil!
> Heavens! what a goodly prospect spreads around,
> Of hills, and dales, and woods, and lawns, and spires,
> And glittering towns, and gilded streams, till all
> The stretching landskip into smoke decays!

And so on and so on, in effortless profusion, in a gracefully blended mixture of generality, precise location, well-chosen compliment, and patriotic self-congratulation. Another remarkable hilltop passage which Thomson inserted into 'Spring' after visiting the celebrated Hagley Park in Worcestershire in 1743 illustrates the same qualities. Hagley was thought by Horace Walpole to have been inspired by Milton's description of Eden, and Walpole himself praised it extravagantly, in a letter to Richard Bentley, as one of the most magnificent and enchanting parks in the country:

> It is a hill of three miles, but broke into all manner of beauty; such lawns, such woods, rills, cascades, and a thickness of verdure quite to the summit of the hill, and commanding such a vale of towns, and meadows, and woods extending quite to the Black Mountains in Wales, that I quite forgot my favourite Thames . . .

Thomson's version goes thus:

> Meantime you gain the Height, from whose fair Brow
> The bursting prospect spreads immense around;
> And snatch'd o'er Hill and Dale, and Wood and Lawn,
> And verdant Field, and darkening Heath between,
> And villages embosom'd soft in Trees,
> And spiry Towns by dusky Columns mark'd
> Of rising Smoak, your Eye excursive roams . . .
> To where the broken Landskip by degrees,
> Ascending, roughens into ridgy Hills;
> O'er which the Cambrian mountains, like far Clouds
> That skirt the blue horizon, doubtful, rise.

No wonder Thomson was a welcome guest: he delivered similar compliments to Bubb Dodington's Eastbury (designed by Vanbrugh) and to Stowe, was warmly received at Shenstone's Leasowes near Hagley, and repaid the Countess of Hertford's hospitality with panegyric. No wonder, also, that with such hosts, he found the world a smiling garden, a castle of indolence, in which he grew fat and idle; an anecdote relates that once while staying with George Lyttleton at Hagley he was seen eating a peach off a tree with both hands in his pockets. The Garden of Eden was, for him, almost a reality.

The popularity of Thomson's work was closely related to the new enthusiasm for landscape painting and landscape gardening – the first edition of *The Seasons* was appropriately adorned with designs by William Kent, and painters of succeeding generations attested to his influence by using quotations from his work in their catalogues and descriptions. J. M. W. Turner accompanied *Buttermere with a Rainbow* (1797–98) with a quotation which according to Kenneth Clark specifically anticipated the theories of Impressionism. Thomson had studied Newton's *Opticks*, and wrote in 'Spring':

> Meantime refracted from yon eastern cloud,
> Bestriding earth, the grand ethereal bow
> Shoots up immense; and every hue unfolds,
> In fair proportion running from the red
> To where the violet fades into the sky.
> Here, awful Newton, the dissolving clouds
> Form, fronting on the sun, thy showery prism;
> The various twine of light, by thee disclosed
> From the white mingling maze.

For Thomson was interested not only in the utility of beauty, and the free dinners he could obtain by flattering landlords: he also had a feeling for the Sublime, for colour and movement, for fiery sunsets and fierce tempests, for the grand and useless manifestations of nature. It would be unjust to present him as a paid and servile enthusiast, who worked up emotion for the occasion; his observations are original, his feelings profound, and although predominantly cheerful of spirit he can strike with conviction a melancholy note, foreshadowing generations of Romanticism. In 'Autumn' he describes the sobbing boughs, the 'leafy ruin' streaming through the sky, the blasted verdure, the naked tree:

Woods, fields, gardens, orchards, all around
The desolated prospect thrills the soul.

When Kent plants dead trees in Kensington Gardens for their picturesque, Salvator-Rosa effect, we smile, but Thomson is sincere: he
responds to the natural as well as to the artificial, and one of the proofs of
this lies in the fact that his successors looked to him not for his style but
for his truth. We may with Coleridge and Wordsworth find his style 'meretricious' or 'vicious', or, with Tennyson, 'hate it like poison', but Coleridge
admitted that he 'was a great poet, rather than a good one; his style was as
meretricious as his thoughts were natural'. Duck and Bloomfield, far
from objecting to his lordly perspective, admired him greatly, and Clare
was 'excited beyond his capacity for explanation' by the first lines of
'Spring', lines which may look vapid enough today, but which spoke
directly to Clare:

Come gentle Spring, ethereal Mildness come;
And from the bosom of yon dripping cloud,
While music wakes around, veil'd in a shower
Of shadowing roses, on our plains descend.

The case of John Clare is extraordinarily interesting. By the time his
first volume was published in 1820 the literary establishment had for
some time been pleased to discover, adopt, and educate the gifted
peasant and ploughman. The eighteenth-century invention of the noble
savage had caused patrons such as Hannah More, Shenstone and Capell
Lofft to encourage Duck, Bloomfield, Ann Yearsley, James Woodhouse
the cobbler, Robert Dodsley the weaver, Kirk White the butcher's son.
Many of these were, alas, undone by attention: Duck's poetry deterio-
rated as he learned pastoral conventions, Bloomfield died in poverty.
Clare too, as everyone knows, came to a sad end, in poverty and madness,
but before his death he had produced a remarkable body of poetry.
Unlike Duck and Bloomfield, he did not succumb to the humble, syco-
phantic line preferred by patrons: he was obstinate, confident of his own
judgment, defending his idiosyncratic use of dialect and punctuation

with articulate intelligence. His work cannot be dismissed as merely descriptive, or as imitative; it is subtle, original, varied, with a wholly personal command of language and a sophisticated metrical control. A poem like 'Remembrances' shows an organizing power more complex than Thomson's yet different in kind, evoking landscapes utterly different in nature.

Clare is the poet of the commonplace, the near at hand. Not for him the smoky distance and the glittering prospect; he apologizes several times in his poems for the lack of picturesque mountains, but maintains that to the knowing eye an overgrown stone quarry is just as beautiful. He was born in 1793, the son of a day labourer in the village of Helpston near Peterborough in Cambridgeshire, and happened to live through and record from the labourer's viewpoint one of the great historical changes in English landscape – the enclosure of the open field system. Enclosures of various kinds had been taking place for centuries – Sir Thomas More deplores their effects in his *Utopia* in 1516 – nor had the open field system ever been operated in the whole of Britain. Nevertheless Clare was present at and indeed helped to implement a lasting transformation of a characteristic English scene, for he worked as a member of a labouring gang planting the quick-set hedges which parcelled out the old open spaces, superimposing on them a new grid pattern of hedges, drains and ditches that now looks old and natural enough.

The economic effects of the enclosures have been long debated, and the traditional view, both of peasants and of historians such as Cobbett, was that they threatened the common birthright of the labourer and the small independent farmer. This is no longer so widely believed: the move towards drainage, land reclamation, greater efficiency was inevitable, and finally benefited everyone. Nor were all rural hardships connected with enclosure: some of the worst poverty in the eighteenth century preceded it. Nor were the open fields necessarily considered beautiful; in an extremely interesting discussion of Clare's attitude to landscape, John Barrell in *The Idea of Landscape and the Sense of Place* suggests that some may have found them unattractive, menacing in their boundless monotony, as Dr Johnson found Scotland; he quotes a Reverend James Tyley, also writing of Northamptonshire, in 1823, who described the unenclosed lands as sterile ground, distinguished by no beauty, a wide expanse of English soil; roughened by sluggish frost and strident winds the wide fields extended, and unbroken tracts strained and tortured the sight . . . I have seen neighbouring districts stretching out their fields successively for twenty miles with no division.

One can well imagine that such vast expanses, defying any organization into Claudian perspectives, might well have induced a sense of panic and agoraphobia in an unaccustomed traveller. Salisbury Plain seems to have had something of this effect on Wordsworth.

Clare, naturally, saw the landscapes of home with a different eye, and writes of a countryside which has found few poets. He shows his admiration for Thomson in conventional pastoral, in haymaking scenes, in descriptions of fields full of girls gathering cowslips, but he reserves his finest verse for a terrain of furze and ling and 'oddling thorns', of teazels and ragwort, of rabbit tracks and, of all things, molehills. Clare loves moles and molehills, and writes of them again and again. They are generally thought of as the enemy of gardener and farmer, blots on the landscape, but to Clare they seem to have represented some kind of anarchic primal freedom, the common freedom that private property and enclosure threatened. Let Dyer keep Grongar Hill and Thomson his view of the Cambrian mountains – a molehill would do for John Clare. With what rapture he sings of the kind of scruffy, brambly, thistly, hillocky, rabbit-mined common that one can still find in odd corners, either protected, or unnoticed, or simply not worth the trouble of cultivating – green England is still there, though Clare passionately laments its passing, and the passing of his own youth; the humbler one's concept of beauty, the more likely one is to find it:

> I love the muse who sits her down
> Upon the molehills little lap
> Who feels no fear to stain her gown
> And pauses by the hedgerow gap . . .

he says in 'The Flitting', praising in the same poem the weed shepherd's purse as an 'ancient neighbour', cheering him in his exile. The names – Royce

Wood, Langley Bush, Eastwell's Spring, Swordy Well, Round Oak Waters, Emmonsales Heath, Salter's Tree – pour forth like an incantation. In 'The Mores' (1822) Clare describes the open spaces that tortured Tyley's sight:

> Far spread the moorey ground a level scene
> Bespread with rush and one eternal green
> That never felt the rage of blundering plough
> Though centurys wreathed springs blossoms on its brow
> Still meeting plains that stretched them far away
> In uncheckt shadows of green brown and grey
> Unbounded freedom ruled the wandering scene
> Nor fence of ownership crept in between
> To hide the prospect of the following eye
> Its only bondage was the circling sky
> One mighty flat undwarfed by bush and tree
> Spread its faint shadow of immensity
>
> . . .
>
> But now alls fled and flats of many a dye
> That seemed to lengthen with the following eye
> Moors losing from the sight far smooth and blea
> Where swopt the plover in its pleasure free
> Are vanished now with commons wild and gay
> As poets visions of lifes early day . . .

Again and again, Clare compares the unenclosed land to Eden, from which the poet is expelled in adult life. It is an Eden not lush like Milton's or Marvell's, but wild, open, even bleak, full of weeds and lonely birds, brambles and ants and snail-shells. Brambles, in a traditional Eden, are a warning: to Clare they are one of nature's glories, and the word 'common', by an extraordinary shift of meaning, which shifts the meaning of man's relation to the whole world, comes to signify, in Clare's language, the wonderful, the rare, the vanishing, the highly prized, as here in 'Decay':

> The fields grow old and common things
> The grass the sky the winds a blowing

And spots where still a beauty clings
Are sighing 'going all a going'
O poesy is on the wane
I hardly know her face again.

Clare's language, which his editors tried to tidy and de-provincialize, embodies the specific nature of the land and his vision of it. It is intensely onomatopoeic: 'blea', 'cronk', 'rawky', 'croodle', 'pudge', 'oddling' – one hardly needs to consult a glossary to guess that these words mean 'exposed and cold', 'to croak or honk', 'misty', 'to shrink or huddle from the cold', 'a small puddle'; and as for 'oddling', one of Clare's favourite words – how could he have done without it, when the definition is 'one differing from the rest of a family, brood, or litter; generally applied to the smallest, or to one with a peculiarity'? And who has not felt the need for the word 'crumping', meaning 'making a crunching noise on frozen snow'?

His verse transcends the faithful and accurate note-taking verse so common in the nineteenth century, and his precise description of place, in his best poetry, produces an effect beyond the local; his poem 'To the Snipe', with its brilliant invocation of a flat, sedgy, treacherous, washy, pudgy, flaggy terrain, contains in its heart a moment of intense excitement:

And here mayhap
When summer suns hath drest
The moors rude desolate and spungy lap
May hide thy mystic nest

Mystic indeed
For isles that oceans make
Are scarcely more secure for birds to build
Then this flag hidden lake

Boys thread the woods
To their remotest shades

But in these marshy flats these stagnant floods
Security pervades

The use of the word 'mystic' here is wonderfully suggestive, and the parallel between the lonely poet and the lonely bird is unforced: Clare leaves well alone as only Wordsworth could leave it. One of his finest poems, 'Remembrances', is surely a worthy companion to Wordsworth's *Immortality Ode*, and it evokes a world of ordinary rural activity that Wordsworth, Cambridge-educated, a spirit apart, could never have entered:

> ... O I never call to mind
> Those pleasant names of places but I leave a sigh behind
> While I see the little mouldiwarps hang sweeing to the wind
> On the only aged willow that in all the field remains
> And nature hides her face while theyre sweeing in their chains
> And in a silent murmuring complains
>
> Here was commons for their hills where they seek for
>   freedom still
> Though every commons gone and though traps are set to kill
> The little homeless miners – O it turns my bosom chill
> When I think of old 'sneap green' puddocks nook and hilly snow
> Where bramble bushes grew and the daisey gemmed in dew
> And the hills of silken grass like to cushions on the view
> Where we threw the pismire crumbs when we'd nothing else
>   to do
> All leveled like a desert by the never weary plough
> All banished like the sun where that could is passing now
> And settled here for ever on its brow
>
> O I never thought that joys would run away from boys
> Or that boys should change their minds and forsake
>   mid-summer joys
> But alack I never dreamed that the world had other toys
> To petrify first feelings like the fable into stone

Till I found the pleasure past and a winter come at last
Then the fields were sudden bare and the sky got over cast
And boy hoods pleasing haunts like a blossom in the blast
Was shrivelled to a withered weed and trampled down and done
Till vanished was the morning spring and set the summer sun
And winter fought her battle strife and won

By Langley bush I roam but the bush hath left its hill
On cowper green I stray tis a desert strange and chill
And spreading lea close oak ere decay had penned its will
To the axe of the spoiler and self interest fell a prey
And crossberry way and old round oaks narrow lane
With its hollow trees like pulpits I shall never see again
Inclosure like a buonaparte let not a thing remain
It levelled every bush and tree and levelled every hill
And hung the moles for traitors – though the brook is
    running still
It runs a naked stream cold and chill . . .

Some have argued that Clare is lamenting the lost innocence of child-hood, 'Eden's garden', the intense joy that he, Traherne and Wordsworth, as boys found in nature; others that he is, more specifically, lamenting the death of green England. Either way, or both ways at once, the poem is a work of stunning originality: Clare's vision of the little homeless moles hung as traitors seems to capture in one image the tenderness, the rage, the helplessness of the labourer, oppressed through centuries, loving the land yet denied his rights to it. Wat Tyler, Jack Straw, John Ball, Piers Plowman, Robert Ket of Mousehold Heath strung up at Norwich Castle, and his brother William dangling from Wymondham steeple, the poach-ers whose hanging Cobbett so bitterly laments, the Rebecca rioters, the elusive Captain Swing – generations stretch behind and around Clare, finding in him a voice – a voice that is still largely unheard.

Clare's are not the only descriptions of the ancient common to survive, though they are perhaps the most eloquent: Raymond Williams in *The Country and the City* quotes Thomas Bewick the engraver, writing in the 1820s of a Northumberland common remembered from forty years earlier:

> On this common – the poor man's heritage for ages past, where he kept a few sheep, or a Kyloe cow, perhaps a flock of geese, and mostly a stock of bee-hives – it was with infinite pleasure that I long beheld the beautiful wild scenery that was there exhibited, and it is with the opposite feeling that I now find all swept away. Here and there on this common were to be seen the cottage, or rather hovel, of some labouring man, built at his own expense, and mostly with his own hands; and to this he always added a garth, or garden . . . These men . . . might truly be called – 'A bold peasantry, their country's pride.'

Williams continues,

> Again and again, down to our own day, men living in villages have tried to create just this kind of margin: a rented patch or strip, an extended garden, a few hives or fruit trees. When I was a child my father had not only the garden that went with the cottage, but a strip for potatoes on a farm where he helped in the harvest, and two gardens which he rented from the railway company from which he drew his wages.

Britain is still covered with allotments, increasingly in demand as the price of food rises and as suspicions about commercially grown, wastefully imported and supermarket-sized and shaped vegetables increases; we may still glimpse beehives on railway embankments. Allotment literature, both practical and poetic, remains a flourishing genre, often but not always tinged with nostalgia and regret. David Crouch and Colin Ward's *The Allotment: Its Landscape and Culture* (1988) offers a scholarly and sensitive appraisal of the growth and evolution of the allotment tradition, and is prefaced by a poignant poem by Charles Tomlinson, an emblematic portrait of his father in Stoke-on-Trent. Titled 'John Maydew, or The Allotment' (*A Peopled Landscape*, 1963), this elegiac piece evokes 'the ineradicable peasant in the dispossessed and half-tamed Englishman' with his watch-chained waistcoat and his rolled-back sleeves.

The poetry of Robert Burns offers an obvious comparison with that of Clare, and has proved lastingly popular with a much wider audience. Their backgrounds were not dissimilar. Burns's father was a gardener who took up farming, not very successfully, when Burns was six years old; the cottage in Alloway where Burns was born, now a museum, was built by William Burns with his own hands. The father encouraged his son's literary interests, and provided him with a good education; from his childhood Burns had more intellectual stimulus and companionship than Clare, a reflection of the higher value placed on education in Scotland. Nevertheless, Burns too was obliged to work as a labourer, and after some years of effort, and attempts to learn other trades, he published his first volume of poems in 1786, ostensibly to raise money for his fare to emigrate to Jamaica. His poems proved so successful that he stayed at home, though he never achieved financial security, and had to scratch a living for himself and his large family as farmer, exciseman, and poet.

His range is wider than Clare's: he writes as the Ayrshire ploughman, turning up the mouse in her nest, or turning down the daisy, but he also wrote drinking songs, satirical verse, verse epistles, and some of the most famous love songs ever written. Both poets enjoyed drinking, but Burns was of a more convivial, extrovert, flamboyant temperament. Although he recalls his years as 'a dextrous ploughman' with some bitterness, boiling with indignation at the insolent threats of the factor into whose hands the farm fell, he managed to attend dancing classes, engage in literary correspondences, debates and flirtations, and a friend recalls that 'he wore the only tied hair in the parish'. Burns himself was to complain of his own weakness for society: 'It is the private parties in the family way, among the hard drinking gentlemen of this country, that do me the mischief...'

His attitude to landscape was not that which came to be called Romantic, though he used the word often enough in his letters and in his more frigid anglicized verses. He has a tenant farmer's eye – the eye of one who knows hard labour, can appreciate prosperity and productivity.

On the way to Dunbar on an excursion he noted 'the most glorious corn country I ever saw', and makes a most interesting analysis of landscape in his diary for 25 August 1787:

> Linlithgow – a fertile improved country – West Lothian. The more elegance and luxury among the farms, I always observe, in equal proportion, the rudeness and stupidity of the peasantry. This remark I have made all over the Lothians, Merse, Roxburgh, etc. For this, among other reasons, I think that a man of romantic taste, a 'Man of Feeling', will be better pleased with the poverty, but intelligent minds of the peasantry in Ayrshire (peasantry they are all below the Justice of Peace), than the opulence of a club of Merse farmers, when at the same time he considers the vandalism of their plough-folks, etc. I carry this idea so far, that an unenclosed, half-improven country is to me actually more agreeable, and gives me more pleasure as a prospect, than a country cultivated like a garden.

Burns, here, is clearly admiring the moral qualities of the landscape, transferred to it by the independence of its farmers and labourers, as was Bewick in his description of the Northumberland common; his rejection of the beauty of the opulent, smiling, Augustan corn fields is as much moral as aesthetic. The farm that he and his brother Gilbert worked at Mossgiel was poor land, 'very high, and mostly on a cold wet bottom', with most of the top soil removed from the clay beneath by heavy rain and bad cultivation. Did he really find this more attractive than more fertile pastures? Certainly he does not fall into the later romantic habit of finding beauty in every barren deserted spot: of the Highlands he wrote to Robert Ainslie on 28 June 1787, 'I write you this on my tour through a country where savage streams tumble over savage mountains, thinly overspread with savage flocks, which starvingly support savage people . . . ' – a state of affairs in which he clearly saw little virtue. He thinks the 'Lammermoir hills miserably dreary, but at times picturesque', and remarks, 'the whole country hereabout, both on Tweed and Ettrick, remarkably stony'. He stirs himself to praise the ruins of Melrose and Jedburgh, the wild grandeur of the Pass of Killiecrankie, but is equally pleased with the 'fine, fruitful, hilly, woody country near Perth', and never mentions in prose or verse the peaks of Arran, familiar sights of his youth. Perhaps what we see here is an intermediate position, between Thomson and Jane Austen's gentleman, and the dispossessed Clare; a poet who can enter into the feelings both of the small tenant farmer and of the day labourer, being, as he was, a little of each, living in a half-way, 'half-improven' country.

It was impossible, in the eighteenth century, to avoid having views on landscape, and Burns was expected to respond as a man of feeling when taken to visit beauty spots. Sometimes he obliged, sometimes not. In early editions of Lockhart's *Life* there is a somewhat comic account of his crossing the bridge at Coldstream in 1787 for the sake of setting foot in England, whereupon his companion Mr Ainslie 'was surprised to see the poet throw away his hat, and thus uncovered, kneel down with uplifted hands, apparently in a fit of enthusiasm'. Ainslie waited silently to see what would happen next, and was rewarded with the sight of Burns praying for and blessing Scotland 'most solemnly', and then reciting two verses from his own poem, 'The Cotter's Saturday Night', starting

> Oh, Scotia! my dear, my native soil!
> For whom my warmest wish to Heaven is sent!
> Long may thy hardy sons of rustic toil
> Be blest with health, and peace, and sweet content!

Whether or not this is a true account, it was certainly the kind of behaviour Burns's admirers expected of him. He produced an equally acceptable response when visiting the Falls of Bruar at Blair; in Burns's day the hillside was unwooded, and Burns wrote a poem described as 'The Humble Petition of Bruar Water to the Noble Duke of Athole', requesting the noble duke to

> Let lofty firrs, and ashes cool,
> My lowly banks o'erspread,
> And view, deep-bending in the pool,

Their shadows' watery bed!
Let fragrant birks in woodbines drest
My craggy cliffs adorn
And, for the little songster's nest,
The close embowering thorn.

The duke responded, and the trees are now there, one of the most direct testimonies to a writer's influence on landscape: so, alas, are a good many cigarette packets and sweet wrappers, but that is hardly the fault of the poet or the duke, and even in Burns's day he found the 'scenes round Blair – fine, but spoiled with bad taste', of what sort he does not specify. Burns was exceptionally good at occasional verse: the celebrated 'Tam o'Shanter' was written in a day, as he walked by the river, to accompany a drawing of the dilapidated, roofless, haunted Alloway Kirk in Francis Grose's *Antiquities of Scotland*. But the poems that evoke Burns's landscape most powerfully are not the set pieces, describing specific places, but those songs that celebrate the nameless fields of corn rigs, barley and rye – verses like this, the first of 'The Holy Fair':

Upon a simmer Sunday morn,
When Nature's face is fair,
I walked forth to view the corn,
An' snuff the caller air.
The rising sun, owre Galston muirs,
Wi' glorious light was glintin;
The hares were hirplin down the furs,
And lav'rocks they were chanting
    Fu' sweet that day.

or the celebrated refrain –

Corn rigs, an' barley rigs,
An' corn rigs are bonnie:
I'll ne'er forget that happy night,
Amang the rigs wi' Annie.

Burns portrays a life in which happiness can be snatched from toil, in which natural good spirits can overcome 'the unceasing moil of the galley slave' which he endured in his early years. The Scottish peasant, as Burns portrays him, is hardy, independent, cheerful. Yet even Burns lapses into servility now and then, begging heaven to spare the poor from 'Luxury's contagion, weak and vile'. This was a convention of the pastoral: the virtuous poor, far from the city's wicked influence, were supposed to lead lives of simple contentment, and the virtuous rich praised their happiness and longed, though safely in vain, to join them. Dr Johnson, writing in 1756, stated the case fairly bluntly:

> Luxury, avarice, injustice, violence and ambition, take up their ordinary residence in populous cities; while the hard and laborious lives of the husbandmen will not admit of these vices. The honest farmer lives in a wise and happy state, which inclines him to justice, temperance, sobriety, sincerity, and every virtue that can dignify human nature.

In *The Wealth of Nations* Adam Smith praises in terms that Burns would have appreciated the superior intelligence and independence of the ploughman, whose work encourages judgment and discretion: 'his understanding . . . being accustomed to consider a greater variety of objects, is generally much superior to that of [the town mechanic] whose whole attention from morning to night is commonly occupied in performing one or two very simple operations'. These arguments appear reasonable enough, but as the eighteenth century wore on, an increasing poetic idealization of country life and values was accompanied by a real fear of their decline: raised rents, greedy landlords, and enclosures were blamed for the state of affairs which Oliver Goldsmith laments in his *Deserted Village*. Yet Goldsmith's lament for sweet Auburn looks back, as many historians have argued, to a Golden Age of Merrie England that never was, a far-off time 'when every rood of ground maintained its man', a time as unhistorical as Virgil's dream of grapes ripening on thorn trees. Goldsmith, like Johnson a true city dweller, sings tunefully enough of the lovely bowers of innocence and ease, the hawthorn bush with seats beneath the shade, the vanished charms of village life, but they are charms set firmly in the past – and even were they available, one feels that they would not have much attraction for Goldsmith himself. There is a melancholy poetic pleasure in his portrait of desolation:

> No more thy glassy brook reflects the day,
> But choked with sedges works its weedy way;
> Along thy glades, a solitary guest,
> The hollow-sounding bittern guards its nest;
> Amid thy desert walks the lapwing flies,
> And tires their echoes with unvaried cries.
> Sunk are thy bowers in shapeless ruin all,
> And the long grass o'ertops the mouldering wall . . .

Goldsmith claims to deplore this state of affairs, but he clearly gets aesthetic satisfaction from it, as Gray did from contemplating the fate of the inglorious dead in his country churchyard: both the golden past and the ruins of the present are distanced, idealized, bathed in a golden light of nostalgia.

Stephen Duck, John Clare and Burns all reacted against the idealizing pastoral, yet all of them were in part seduced by the pastoral tradition, its language and its vision. The most consistent of anti-pastoral poets was not a farm labourer but a clergyman, George Crabbe, whose work contains some of the harshest and most startlingly realistic landscapes in English literature. His dismissal of 'the tinsel trappings of poetic pride' that hide the real ills of the working man has been hailed as one of those fine moments in human consciousness that seem to lead us into a more humane, more dignified future. (A very different and challenging reading of his work may be found in John Barrell's *The Dark Side of the Landscape*, published in 1980, which sees Crabbe as a pessimistic conservative more anxious to encourage stoic acceptance of labour than a desire for progress or improvement. Barrell also offers a radical reinterpretation of Goldsmith.)

Crabbe's *The Village* is a work of intelligence, wit and close observation that appears to sweep away centuries of sanctimonious moralizing about the happy, sober, simple, industrious poor:

Fled are those times, when, in harmonious strains,
The rustic poet praised his native plains:
No shepherds now, in smooth alternate verse,
Their country's beauty or their nymphs' rehearse;

Yet still for these we frame the tender strain,
Still in our lays fond Corydons complain,
And shepherds' boys their amorous pains reveal
The only pains, alas! they never feel

. . .

Yes, thus the Muses sing of happy swains,
Because the Muses never knew their pains:
They boast their peasants' pipes; but peasants now
Resign their pipes and plod behind the plough . . .

Crabbe's eyes were opened to the grim realities of peasant life by the
Suffolk landscape into which he was born. He describes himself as 'cast
by Fortune on a frowning coast'; and his home town, Aldeburgh, was a
dying town. Indeed the whole coast was dying. In the sixteenth and early
seventeenth centuries Aldeburgh had flourished, but by Crabbe's birth in
the mid-eighteenth century its population had been halved, and the sea
was encroaching rapidly; whole streets had crumbled and been swept
away. The melancholy of the landscape not only emphasized the melancholy of the inhabitants – it was largely responsible for it. Crabbe's own
early years were poverty-stricken: his father was a warehouse-keeper and
collector of salt duties, and, although ambitious for his son, was unable to
provide adequately for him to pursue his apprenticeship as a doctor.
Crabbe struggled along, suffering terrible hardship when he decided to
abandon medicine for poetry; his sympathies with the poor were rooted
in experience. His descriptions of the landscape of his childhood, to
which he returned as curate, combine moral indignation with an acute and
scientific eye for detail. He was an enthusiastic student of botany and
zoology, and his poems are stacked with minute observations about the
colours of the lichen on his weathering church, about fossils, butterflies,
seaweed, jellyfish:

Those living jellies which the flesh inflame
Fierce as a nettle, and from that its name . . .

There is nothing conventional in his evocations, none of the tired language and predictable epithets of so much eighteenth-century verse. The landscapes he describes had rarely surfaced in literature before, so he was able to present them freshly, as though seen for the first time (here in 'The Village'):

Lo! where the heath, with withering brake grown o'er,
Lends the light turf that warms the neighbouring poor;
From thence a length of burning sand appears,
Where the thin harvest waves its wither'd ears;
Rank weeds, that every art and care defy,
Reign o'er the land, and rob the blighted rye:
There thistles stretch their prickly arms afar,
And to the ragged infant threaten war;
There poppies nodding, mock the hope of toil;
There the blue bugloss paints the sterile soil;
Hardy and high, above the slender sheaf,
The slimy mallow waves her silky leaf;
O'er the young shoot the charlock throws a shade,
And clasping tares cling round the sickly blade;
With mingled tints the rocky coasts abound,
And a sad splendour vainly shines around.

There is nothing here of Augustan plenty; life is a struggle, the faces of the poor display 'sullen woe'. The fault, he acknowledges, is partly the fault of nature, whose 'niggard hand / Gave a spare portion to the famished land'. The heath, unlike Clare's and Bewick's, will not support the independent peasant. Peter Grimes the fisherman lives in a desolate marshy waste:

Thus by himself compell'd to live each day,
To wait for certain hours the tide's delay;

At the same times the same dull views to see,
The bounding marsh-bank and the blighted tree;
The water only, when the tides were high,
When low, the mud half-cover'd and half-dry;
The sun-burnt tar that blisters on the planks,
And bank-side stakes in their uneven ranks

. . .

There anchoring, Peter chose from man to hide,
There hang his head, and view the lazy tide
In its hot slimy channel slowly glide;
Where the small eels that left the deeper way
For the warm shore, within the shallows play;
Where gaping muscles, left upon the mud,
Slope their slow passage to the fallen flood; –
Here dull and hopeless he'd lie down and trace
How side long crabs had scrawl'd their crooked race;
Or sadly listen to the tuneless cry
Of fishing gull or clanging golden-eye;
What time the sea-birds to the marsh would come,
And the loud bittern, from the bull-rush home,
Gave from the salt-ditch side the bellowing boom:
He nursed the feelings these dull scenes produce . . .

An unprofitable man, wasting time in an unprofitable landscape.
Crabbe was familiar with more productive terrain: he spent some years as
chaplain to the Duke of Rutland's household at Belvoir Castle in the rich
Vale of Belvoir, but he was unhappy there, ill at ease in a nobleman's
home, tormented by the domestics who made him drink glasses of salt
water because he would not join in their Tory toasts, and when he praises
the countryside he does so ironically, contrasting it with his own poorer
birthplace, as in *The Borough,* Letter I (1810):

Thy walks are ever pleasant; every scene
Is rich in beauty, lively, or serene;
Rich – is that varied view with woods around,

Seen from the seat, within the shrubb'ry bound;
Where shines the distant lake . . .

We scent the vapours of the sea-born gale;
Broad-beaten paths lead on from stile to stile,
And sewers from streets, the road-side banks defile;
Our guarded fields a sense of danger show,
Where garden-crops with corn and clover grow;
Fences are formed of wreck and placed around
(With tenters tipp'd) a strong repulsive bound . . .

The awareness of the interdependence of man and nature, of the formative power of landscape on the spirit, is something new, foreshadowing the Romantics; though Crabbe himself is so much a realist that he never forgets that even when Plenty smiles, as she did at Belvoir, 'she smiles for few'.

From Crabbe's poetry we get a sense of a precise and peculiar landscape, and a new and more compassionate awareness of the problems it presents to the labourer. We get something of the same compassion from William Cobbett, whose *Rural Rides* are one of the most celebrated records of rural working conditions in England in the nineteenth century. Unlike Crabbe, Cobbett was born into a land of plenty, and perhaps for this reason remained convinced that England had once been Merry England; for his native Surrey, and for many other regions, the late eighteenth century really was a time of prosperity, and in 1763, the year of his birth, according to his biographer James Sambrook,

the material conditions of the agricultural labouring poor in Cobbett's countryside were probably somewhat better than they had been fifty years earlier (and than they would be fifty years later), and they were quite probably better than those of the same class of people in every part of the world except North America. Contemporary observers would have called this a certainty rather than a probability . . .

Cobbett was not born to riches, but, as he tells us in *The Life and Adventures of Peter Porcupine*, at the plough-tail:

> I do not remember a time when I did not earn my living. My first occupation was, driving the birds from the turnip-seed, and the rooks from the peas . . . My next employment was weeding wheat, and leading a single horse at harrowing barley. Hoeing peas followed and hence, I arrived at the honour of joining the reapers in harvest, driving the team, and holding plough.

But he looked back on this life with nostalgia in *Advice to Young Men*:

> Born and bred up in the sweet air myself, I resolved that they [i.e. his children] should be bred up in it too. Enjoying rural scenes and sports, as I had done, when a boy, as much as any one that ever was born, I was resolved that they should have the same employments tendered to them. When I was a very little boy, I was, in the barley-sowing season, going along by the side of a field, near Waverley Abbey; the primroses and bluebells bespangling the banks on both sides of me; a thousand linnets singing in a spreading oak over my head; while the jingling of the traces and the whistling of the ploughboy saluted my ear from over the hedge . . . I was not more than eight years old; but this particular scene has presented itself to my mind many times every year from that day to this.

Cobbett's love of the land is intense: he loves the very soil, writing with passionate interest of the alternate chalk and sand near Guildford, the great chalk ridges of the South Downs, the 'pale yellow loam, looking like brick earth, but rather sandy', near East Grinstead, the 'poor miserable clayey-looking sand' near Crawley, the stiff loam upon chalk near Winchester, the land between Selborne and Thursley which was 'the very best barley-land in the kingdom; a fine, buttery, stoneless loam, upon a bottom of sand or sandstone. Finer barley or turnip land it is impossible to see.' He loves the sights of nature, and feels that they rejoice in their own flourishing: in the Vale of Pewsey 'the trees are everywhere lofty. They are generally elms, with some ashes, which delight in the soil that they find here. There are, almost always, two or three large clumps of trees in every parish, and a rookery or two (not a *rag*-rookery) to every parish.' At Eversley, staying at one of the pleasantest inns in England, he notes beyond the garden, 'a large clump of lofty sycamores, and in these, a populous rookery, in which, of all things in the world, I most delight'. He notes that the rooks, feasting on the stubble fields, 'rob the pigs; but, they have a *right* to do it. I wonder, upon my soul I do, that there is no lawyer, Scotchman, or Parson-Justice, to propose a law to punish the rooks for *trespass*' – a sentiment shared by Hardy's Jude the Obscure, who also started life as a bird-scarer, and who also felt sympathy with the birds, who had as great a right to life and food, in his view, as the farmer.

Cobbett's dislikes were as powerful as his enthusiasms. Certain tracts of land could in themselves stir him to rage: Windsor Forest is 'as bleak, as barren and as villainous a heath as ever man set his eyes on', and its soil is execrable; its beautiful roads he regards as a mockery.

A much more ugly country than that between Egham and Kensington would with great difficulty be found in England. Flat as a pancake, and, until you come to Hammersmith, the soil is a nasty stony dirt upon a bed of gravel. Hounslow Heath, which is only a little worse than the general run, is a sample of all that is bad in soil and villainous in look. Yet this is now *enclosed*, and what they call '*cultivated*.' Here is a fresh robbery of villages, hamlets, and farm and labourers' buildings and abodes!

His indignation is at heart moral: as he travels around, he takes as his measure of prosperity not the smiling cornfields, but the clothes and faces of the girls labouring in the fields, some of whom he finds as thin as herrings, as ragged as colts, as pale as ashes. He fulminates against the Game Laws, against landlords who hang poachers, against the changes that caused working men to die of hunger, with nothing but sour sorrel in their stomachs. He points out that, paradoxically, the better the land the worse the worker's lot, a point also made by Burns fifty years earlier.

In the corn country of Kent, in the Isle of Thanet, he writes angrily on 4 September 1823 in *Rural Rides*,

> I got to a little hamlet, where I breakfasted; but could get no corn for my horse, and no bacon for myself! All was corn around me. Barns, I should think, two hundred feet long; ricks of enormous size and most numerous; crops of wheat, five quarters to an acre, on the average, and a public house without either bacon or corn! The labourers' houses, all along through this island, beggarly in the extreme. The people dirty, poor-looking; ragged, but particularly *dirty*. The men and boys with dirty faces, and dirty smock-frocks, and dirty shirts; and good God! what a difference between the wife of a labouring man here, and the wife of a labouring man in the forests and woodlands of Hampshire and Sussex! Invariably have I observed, that the richer the soil, and the more destitute of woods; that is to say, the more purely a corn country, the more miserable the labourers. The cause is this, the great, the big bull frog grasps all. In this beautiful island, every inch of land is appropriated by the rich. No hedges, no ditches, no commons, no grassy lanes ... The rabbit countries are the countries for labouring men.

Rich land made poor labourers, and Cobbett could not wholeheartedly admire an exploited view, however lovely – but equally, he could not decide what kind of landscape stirred him most, so receptive was he to so many varying influences. His loyalty to the prosperous hop gardens of his native Farnham, and the sand-hills where he used to roll as a boy, appears to be much tested by rival beauties of the borders left by the plough round the fields of Hertfordshire: 'The hedges are now full of the shepherd's rose, honeysuckles, and all sorts of wild flowers; so that you are upon a grass walk, with this most beautiful of all flower gardens and shrubberies on your one hand, and with the corn on the other ... Talk of *pleasure*-grounds indeed!'

One of his finest descriptive passages, of the land near Winchester, shows loyalty and new affections in happy conflict, and deserves to be quoted at length for its wonderful grasp of the variety offered by the landscape, both to the eye and to the farmer. The tracts he here describes, in *Rural Rides* for 31 October 1825, span only a few miles, but he makes them sound limitless in extent and richness and individual oddities:

> There are not many finer spots in England; and if I were to take in a circle of eight or ten miles of semi-diameter, I should say that I believe there is not one so fine. Here are hill, dell, water, meadows, woods, corn-fields, downs; and all of them very fine and very beautifully disposed. This country does not present to us that sort of beauties which we see about Guildford and Godalming, and round the skirts of Hindhead and Blackdown, where the ground lies in the form that the surface-water in a boiling copper would be in, if you could, by word of command, *make it be still,* the variously-shaped bubbles all sticking up; and really, to look at the face of the earth, who can help imagining, that some such process has produced its present form? Leaving this matter to be solved by those who laugh at mysteries, I repeat, that the country round Winchester does not present to us beauties of *this sort*; but of a sort which I like a great deal better. Arthur Young calls the vale between Farnham and Alton *the finest ten miles in* England. Here is a river with fine meadows on each side of it, and with rising grounds on each outside of the meadows, those grounds having some hop-gardens and some pretty woods. But, though I was born in this vale, I must confess, that the ten miles between Maidstone and Tunbridge (which the Kentish folks call the *Garden of Eden*) is a great deal finer; for there, with a river three times as big and a vale three times as broad, there are, on rising grounds six times as broad, not only hop-gardens and beautiful woods, but immense orchards of apples, pears, plums, cherries and filberts, and these, in many cases, with gooseberries and currants and raspberries beneath; and, all taken together, the vale is really worthy of the appellation which it bears. But, even this spot, which I believe to be the very finest, as to fertility and diminutive beauty, in this whole world, I, for my part, do not like so well; nay, as a spot to *live on,* I think nothing at all of it, compared with a country where high downs prevail . . .

This is the variety we could still see if we travelled more slowly, and had, like Cobbett, a trained eye. It is amusing to note that he complains of the turnpike roads as we might of the motorway, though for slightly different reasons: 'Those that travel by turnpike roads know nothing of England . . . Against a *great road* things are made for *show*.' Cobbett knew England better than almost any of his contemporaries, and although his analysis of social problems was at times wildly inaccurate, it was always inspired by love, a love not for the past, but for the temperamental, perplexing, peculiar land itself.

Rural change was a theme that preoccupied the great nineteenth-century novelists. Elizabeth Gaskell, George Eliot, Anthony Trollope and Thomas Hardy have all left magnificent accounts of country life and manners: all of them are aware that they live in an age of transition, and look back, with varying degrees of regret and nostalgia, to the apparently eternal worlds of their own childhood, to the order that had seemed so stable. Even while presenting ideas that were socially or politically progressive, they cannot avoid a note of regret for a lost Golden Age: Reform Bills, railways, and improved agricultural methods were, as they wrote, in the process of creating changes that Cobbett, who died in 1835, foretold but did not live to see, and could never have fully imagined.

George Eliot was born in Warwickshire, in what Henry James in *English Hours* called 'the core and centre of the English world; midmost England, unmitigated England . . . the genius of pastoral Britain'. In another essay in the same book he remarks, 'The landscape indeed sins by excess of nutritive suggestion; it savours of larder and manger; it is too ovine, too bovine, it is almost asinine . . .' Cobbett, less preciously, agrees. Writing of the same countryside while travelling towards Liverpool to take ship for America in 1817, he had seen in it a plenty that could surely be shared even with the eight thousand miserable paupers of nearby Coventry. His account was published in *The Political Register* on 12 July 1817:

> The road very wide and smooth; rows of fine trees on the sides of it; beautiful white-thorn hedges, and rows of ash and elm dividing the fields; the fields so neatly kept; the soil so rich; the herds and flocks of fine cattle and sheep on every side . . . Here is wealth! Here

are all the means of national power, and of individual plenty and happiness! . . . The beautiful country . . . never can be destined to be inhabited by slaves.

George Eliot's father was a man of the land, but, like Wordsworth's father, he was a middleman, not a labourer. He was agent to the Newdigate family of Arbury Hall, and his daughter would travel around with him on business, making the acquaintance of tenant farmers, of servants in the kitchens of the big houses, of labourers, observing from afar the country house life she was to describe in *Middlemarch* and *Daniel Deronda*, learning about mortgages, land values and the problems of bad debts – knowledge she was to put to good use in *The Mill on the Floss*. Like Cobbett, she had a surveyor's eye for good land, and a surveyor's view of a wide provincial scene. Her work is coloured both by her personal knowledge and memories, and also by the progressive political and social views she developed; it is at once deeply local, and extremely well informed. Her childhood was, as for most writers, a period of profound and lasting significance, and many of her mature novels are set back in the period of her infancy: both *Felix Holt* and *Middlemarch*, published at the time of the second Reform Act of 1867, are concerned with the period preceding the first Reform Bill of 1832, when she was a child of ten or eleven, and *The Mill on the Floss* looks back to a time of rick burning, as well as to the golden pastoral of the red-fluted roofs and warehouse gables of the seemingly unchanging St Ogg's, 'one of those old, old towns which impress one as a continuation and outgrowth of nature', and the white ducks among the withies at Dorlcote Mill. Change flows through the countryside like the river Floss itself, sweeping away both good and bad; only in art can George Eliot arrest the current, and paint things as they seemed to her as a child, immemorial, eternal.

Her earliest impressions inspired some of her most intense writing. 'These are the things that make the gamut of joy in landscape to midland-bred souls – the things they toddled among, or learned by heart, standing between their father's knees, while he drove leisurely', she says in Chapter 12 of *Middlemarch*, of the landscape through which Fred and Rosamond Vincy ride on their way to Stone Court:

The pool in the corner where the grasses were dank and trees leaned whisperingly; the great oak shadowing a bare place in mid-pasture; the high bank where the ash-trees grew; the sudden slope of the old marl-pit making a red background for the burdock; the huddled roofs and ricks of the homestead without a traceable way of approach; the grey gate and fences against the depth of the bordering wood; and the stray hovel, its old, old thatch full of mossy hills and valleys . . .

And again:

There is no sense of ease like the ease we felt in those scenes where we were born, where objects became dear to us before we had known the labour of choice . . . One's delight in an elderberry bush overhanging the confused leafage of a hedgerow bank, as a more gladdening sight than the finest cistus or fuchsia spreading itself on the softest undulating turf, is an entirely unjustifiable preference to a nursery-gardener . . . And there is no better reason for preferring this elderberry bush than that it stirs an early memory – that it is no novelty in my life, speaking to me merely through my present sensibilities to form and colour, but the long companion of my existence, that wove itself into my joys when joys were vivid.

Arbury Hall reappears in her first published work, *Scenes of Clerical Life*, as Cheverel Manor:

A charming picture Cheverel Manor would have made that evening, if some English Watteau had been there to paint it: the castellated house of grey-tinted stone, with the flickering sunbeams sending dashes of golden light across the many-shaped panes in the mullioned windows, and a great beech leaning athwart one of the flanking towers, and breaking, with its dark flattened boughs, the too formal symmetry of the front; the broad gravel-walk winding on the right, by a row of tall pines, alongside the pool – on the left branching out among swelling grassy mounds, surmounted by clumps of trees, where the red trunk of the Scotch fir glows in the descending sunlight against the bright green of limes and acacias ...

In such a garden Dorothea Casaubon was to wander disconsolate, and Gwendolen Harleth to captivate Mr Grandcourt with her skill at archery; from such windows Mrs Transome gazes sadly at the same Scotch fir. Equally evocative are George Eliot's portraits of ordinary domestic country activities – Hetty Sorrel in the dairy, Hetty gathering currants, Adam Bede at his carpentry with a shepherd dog asleep on a pile of soft shavings by his side, Mrs Garth peeling apples. One is reminded of the Dutch masters, who painted the bourgeois scene with such calm and glowing passion: the dairy is composed for us, and as George Eliot remarks in *Adam Bede*, is

> certainly worth looking at ... such coolness, such purity, such fresh fragrance of new-pressed cheese, of firm butter, of wooden vessels perpetually bathed in pure water; such soft colouring of red earthenware, and creamy surfaces, brown wood and polished tin, grey limestone and rich orange-red rust on the iron weights and hooks and hinges.

George Eliot wrote her novels when she was in a sense exiled from the landscapes of her youth, and she remembers with the clarity of regret. Clare and Wordsworth were exiled too, by age and change, but George Eliot, having quarrelled with her family, could never return. Her relationship with her brother Isaac, beautifully enacted and exorcized in the tragic drama of *The Mill on the Floss*, gathers around remembered places – the Round Pond, framed in with willows and tall reeds, was for her what Swordy Well was for Clare, but she is keenly aware that it is she and Isaac that have changed, not the pond:

> It was one of their happy mornings. They trotted along and sat down together, with no thought that life would ever change much for them. They would only get bigger and not go to school, and it would always be like the holidays; they would always live together

and be fond of each other. And the mill with its booming; and the great chestnut tree under which they played at houses; their own little river, the Ripple, where the banks seemed like home, and Tom was always seeing the water rats, while Maggie gathered the purple plumy tops of the reeds, which she forgot, and dropped afterwards; above all the great Floss, along which they wandered with a sense of travel, to see the rushing spring-tide, the awful Eagre, come up like a hungry monster, or to see the Great Ash which had once wailed and moaned like a man; – these things would always be the same to them. Tom thought people were at a disadvantage who lived on any other spot of the globe; and Maggie, when she read about Christiania passing 'the river over which there is no bridge', always saw the Floss between the green pastures by the Great Ash.

George Eliot's vision is essentially a mature vision; as here in Chapter 5 of *The Mill on the Floss*, the child's memories are qualified by the woman's knowledge. Like Jane Austen, she has little time for the merely picturesque or Romantic, which, as she knows, are usually associated with poverty. In *Middlemarch* her heroine Dorothea, although guiltily sorry to be deprived of the opportunity for improvement, is pleased by the sight of her future husband's tenants: 'Everybody, he assured her, was well off in Lowick: not a cottager in those double cottages at a low rent but kept a pig, and the strips of garden at the back were well tended . . . ' In *The Mill on the Floss*, she gives a sympathetic account of Aunt Moss's poor farm, with its tumbledown buildings, foul land, muddy lanes, and damp and dirty farmyard, lying at an unprofitable distance from the nearest market town. She shows a keen eye for mismanagement in describing Mr Brooke's visit to Dagley's farm, Freeman's End, in Chapter 39 of *Middlemarch*:

It is true that an observer, under that softening influence of the fine arts which makes other people's hardships picturesque, might have been delighted with this homestead called Freeman's End: the old house had dormer-windows in the dark-red roof, two of the chimneys were choked with ivy, the large porch was blocked up with bundles of sticks, and half the windows were closed with grey worm-eaten shutters about which the jasmine-boughs grew in wild luxuriance; the mouldering garden wall with hollyhocks peeping over it was a perfect study of highly-mingled subdued colour, and there was an aged goat (kept doubtless on interesting superstitious grounds) lying against the open back-kitchen door. The mossy thatch of the cowshed, the broken grey barn-doors, the pauper labourers in ragged breeches who had nearly finished unloading a waggon of corn into the barn ready for early thrashing; the scanty dairy of cows being tethered for milking and leaving one half of the shed in brown emptiness; the very pigs and white ducks seeming to wander about the uneven neglected yard as if in low spirits from feeding on a too meagre quality of rinsings – all these objects under the quiet light of a sky marbled with high clouds would have made a sort of picture which we have all paused over as a 'charming bit', touching other sensibilities than those which are stirred by the depression of the agricultural interest, with the sad lack of farming capital, as seen constantly in the newspapers of that time. But these troublesome associations were just now strongly present to Mr Brooke, and spoiled the scene for him. Mr Dagley himself made a figure in the landscape, carrying a pitchfork and wearing his milking-hat – a very old beaver flattened in front. His coat and breeches were the best he had . . .

Her vision of the landscape and its inhabitants is practical, inclusive, benign: much as she loves the beauty of 'old, old' trees and buildings, her heart is with the future, with Reform, with a greater sharing. Dorothea, after a night of weeping, is brought back to life and action in Chapter 80 by a sight that seems as old as the land itself:

She opened her curtains, and looked out towards the bit of road that lay in view, with fields beyond, outside the entrance-gates. On the road there was a man with a bundle on his back and a woman carrying her baby; in the field she could see figures moving – perhaps the shepherd with his dog. Far off in the bending sky was the pearly light; and she felt the largeness of the world and the man-ifold wakings of men to labour and endurance. She was a part of that involuntary, palpitating life, and could neither look out on it from her luxurious shelter as a mere spectator, nor hide her eyes in selfish complaining.

Elizabeth Gaskell's love of the countryside was as deep as George Eliot's, though she too was exiled: her conscience obliged her to spend most of her adult life in smoky Manchester, and to use the industrial scene as material. But both in life and in her work she would escape into the rural idyll of childhood, remembering and vividly recreating the happy days she spent in the small town of Knutsford in Cheshire, and particularly at her grandfather's farm at Sandlebridge, four miles away. Her knowledge of farming is displayed in many of her books: *Wives and Daughters* contains knowledgeable discussions of land drainage, and much of the plot revolves round the conflict between the old Tory Hamley and the Whig landlord and his agent, who sees Hamley as 'a beg-garly squire – a man who did turn off his men just before winter, to rot or starve, for all he cared – it's just like a venal old Tory'. The heroine of *Sylvia's Lovers*, at the little farm of Haytersbank near Whitby, is at home in the cowshed watching the cows being milked while 'pretending to knit at a grey worsted stocking, but in reality laughing at Kester's futile endeav-ours, and finding quite enough to do with her eyes in keeping herself untouched by the whisking tail, or the occasional kick' – and when her lover calls she is vexed with her friend the cowman for not mentioning that she too can milk: 'Why,' she says, 'when we're throng, I help Kester; but now we've only Black Nell and Daisy giving milk. Kester knows I can milk Black Nell quite easy . . . '

Perhaps the most lyrical descriptions of country life are to be found in *Cousin Phillis*; here Sandlebridge is renamed Hope Farm, and Elizabeth Gaskell gives a most tender account of her grandfather, who was both farmer and lay preacher: 'He spends Saturday and Sunday a-writing sermons and a-visiting his flock at Hornby; and at five o'clock on Monday morning he'll be guiding his plough in the Hope Farm yonder just as well as if he could neither read nor write.' Appropriately, the minister at one point quotes Virgil's *Georgics* with approval: 'It's wonderful how exactly Virgil has hit the enduring epithets, nearly two thousand years ago, and in Italy; and yet how it describes to a T what is now lying before us in the parish of Heathbridge, county –, England.'

The ripe and golden world of Hope Farm, as Elizabeth Gaskell well knew, was not for everyone. Her work is full of compassion for the working people of Manchester, crammed into dark tenements and stinking cellars, deprived of the light itself. She had great faith in the restorative power of nature and natural surroundings; Dunham Park, near Manchester, was one of the scenes for excursions, and she describes it in *Libby Marsh*: 'Its scenery . . . presents such a complete contrast to the whirl and turmoil of Manchester: so thoroughly woodland, with its ancestral trees . . . ' In *Mary Barton*, the city dwellers love to stroll to Green Heys Fields:

> There is a charm about them which strikes even the inhabitant of a mountainous district, who sees and feels the effect of contrast in these commonplace but thoroughly rural fields, with the busy, bustling manufacturing town he left but half an hour ago . . . Here in their seasons may be seen the country business of haymaking, ploughing, etc. . . . here the artisan, deafened with noise of tongues and engines, may come and listen awhile to the delicious sound of rural life: the lowing of cattle, the milkmaid's call, the clatter and cackle of poultry in the old farm yards.

It is as though Gaskell feels that the pursuits of country life are in themselves so delightful, so natural, that the mere sight of them can revive the wilting machine operative: the country landscape has become a holiday resort for the common working man, not merely an agricultural prosperity-machine for the landowner. As industrialization and overpopulation made working and living conditions in the cities increasingly intolerable, there was a natural – though, as we have seen, by no means new – tendency to idealize country labour. By the middle of the century, the wretched of the earth included starving artisans as well as starving ploughmen; the ploughman's lot, in comparison, may have seemed idyllic.

The modern concept of the holiday seems to have arisen in mid-Victorian England, and with it, the concept of nature as a healing respite from labour, the country as a rest from the dirt and grind of the city. Farm holidays, now so popular, would have seemed an odd concept in a pre-dominantly rural economy, but we, like Elizabeth Gaskell, enjoy the opportunity of watching other people at work, particularly when the work is so different from and apparently so much pleasanter than our own. Gaskell had a rare capacity for enjoying holidays and change of scene; she retreated to Sandlebridge as an adult, but also to other places – to Wales, and to Silverdale in Morecambe Bay. She had family connections in Wales, at Portmadoc, and visited Snowdonia as a girl; she returned there for her honeymoon, staying at Aber near Bangor, and visiting Conway, Caernarvon, Llanberis and Beddgelert, – scenes that she incorporated into *Ruth*. The setting of a novel was always of great importance to her, and she took great care over local detail, even over local dialect. In *Ruth* she also describes Silverdale, and its landscape, which she loved for 'the expanse of view . . . such wide plains of golden sands with purple hill shadows – or fainter wandering filmy cloud-shadows, and the great dome of sky'. Ruth meets her former lover on 'the level sands . . . where the wet sands were glittering with the receding waves . . . perhaps half a mile or more from the grey, silvery rocks, which sloped away into brown moorland, interspersed with a field here and there of golden, waving corn. Behind were purple hills, with sharp, clear outlines, touching the sky . . .'

Her love of the inland Midlands came from her mother's family, but her love of the sea from her father's: he was from Berwick-on-Tweed, from a seafaring family, and one of her own brothers, lost at sea, re-appears in many of her novels. She set a whole novel, *Sylvia's Lovers*, on the North Yorkshire coast, and although she only visited Whitby briefly for a fortnight in 1859, she seems to have some hereditary affinity with the landscape, so powerfully does she evoke it: Haytersbank may be modelled on memories of Sandlebridge, but its setting is distinctive and particular, very different from the warm sunny court of Hope Farm:

> The farm-house lay in the shelter of a very slight green hollow, scarcely scooped out of the pasture field by which it was sur-

rounded; the short crisp turf came creeping up to the very door and windows, without any attempt at a yard or garden . . . The buildings were long and low, in order to avoid the rough violence of the winds that swept over that wild, bleak spot, both in winter and summer.

The moorland terrain is described in detail in the opening chapter:

High above the level of the sea towered the purple crags, whose summits were crowned with green sward that stole down the sides of the scaur a little way in grassy veins. Here and there a brook forced its way from the heights down to the sea, making its channel into a valley more or less broad in long process of time. And in the moorland hollows, as in these valleys, trees and underwood grew and flourished; so that, while on the bare swells of the high land you shivered at the waste desolation of the scenery, when you dropped into these wooded 'bottoms' you were charmed with the nesting shelter which they gave. But above and around these rare and fertile vales there were moors for many a mile, here and there bleak enough, with the red freestone cropping out above the scanty herbage; then, perhaps, there was a brown tract of peat and bog, uncertain footing for the pedestrian who tried to make a short cut to his destination; then on the higher sandy soil there was the purple ling, or commonest species of heather growing in beautiful wild luxuriance . . .

Poor though the sheep and cattle are, compared with those of the Midlands, Gaskell notes on their faces 'an odd, intelligent expression . . . which is seldom seen in the placidly stupid countenances of well-fed animals' – another tribute to the stimulating effect of the northern climate.

Like most of George Eliot's novels, Gaskell's *Sylvia's Lovers* is set back in time. It was partly the attraction of remembered landscapes that drew these writers to the past, but both were also aware of the accelerating rate of change, and of the need to record dying graces, dying customs. Gaskell looks back to the days when there was more time, a complaint as old as time itself; she describes farmers' wives and daughters selling their own milk and butter, and bargaining over prices, and says nostalgically, 'There was leisure for all this kind of work in those days . . . ' It seems as though any description of rural life, from Virgil onwards, has contained within it the seeds of its own ruin: the old order, which seems to stretch back forever into an unchanging past, is grasped as ephemeral even in the moment of description. The fate of Haytersbank Farm expresses the relentless inevitability of change better than Goldsmith's deserted village. In Chapter 33 Sylvia, now a married woman, goes back to her old home to pick balm, and finds it empty and tenantless:

> There were no shutters to shut; the long low window was blinking in the rays of the morning sun; the house and cow-house doors were closed, and no poultry wandered about the field in search of stray grains of corn, or early worms . . . Only a thrush in the old orchard down in the hollow, out of sight, whistled and gurgled with continual shrill melody.
>
> Sylvia walked slowly past the house and down the path leading to the wild, deserted bit of garden. She saw that the last tenants had had a pump sunk for them, and resented the innovation, as though the well she was passing could feel the insult. Over it grew two hawthorn trees; on the bent trunk of one of them she used to sit, long ago: the charm of the position being enhanced by the possible danger of falling into the well and being drowned. The rusty unused chain was wound round the windlass; the bucket was falling to pieces from dryness . . .

Trollope's picture of rural England is both more conservative and more cynical than George Eliot's or Elizabeth Gaskell's. Admirers of his novels usually have a very clear picture of his fictional county of Barsetshire, 'a pleasant green tree-becrowded county, with large bosky hedges, pretty damp lanes, and roads with broad grass margins running along them', and of the close at Barchester, with its plump clerics and worldly wives. Yet Trollope's style is less minutely descriptive than that of Eliot and Gaskell; he relies heavily on preconceived pictures, old associations, vague emotive phrases. When he chooses to describe a comfortable country house, he rarely descends to detail: the windows are mullioned, the architectural styles mixed and irregular, the general impression one of comfort rather than grandeur. Yet we can hardly doubt that these houses are grand enough. They have an avenue of chestnuts or limes, a fine lawn, an adjacent church, again of mixed periods, and a farmyard. But far beyond this Trollope does not venture, though he spent years of his life riding round the English countryside on behalf of the Post Office, and knew the western counties village by village. His interest in the landscape is not predominantly aesthetic. For him, land represents wealth and the plots of most of his novels revolve around inheritance of property.

He also had a good eye for hunting country, for he was himself a keen hunter, and spends more words describing a horse or a cover for foxes than a view. When he attempts the picturesque, as in his description of The Cleeve in Orley Farm, he includes the right ingredients – a waterfall, rocks, moss, overhanging trees – but there is nevertheless something oddly sportsmanlike about the passage, which ends:

> There was a spot in the river from whence a steep path led down to the park from the water, and at this spot deer would come to drink. I know of nothing more beautiful than this sight, when three or four of them could be so seen from one of the wooden bridges towards the hour of sunset in the autumn.

The deer seem to be waiting for the hunter, as in so many of Landseer's paintings, and there is nothing Trollope deplores more in a landscape than absence of foxes.

Trollope tells us the deer are beautiful, and leaves it at that. Similarly, he leaves Barchester largely to our imagination, conjuring it up by a few phrases, which we can each relate to our own impressions or memories of Salisbury, Winchester or Wells. Occasionally he launches into longer descriptions, reserving his highest praise for an impression of antiquity; in his novels, the strife between old ways and new is usually won, without much effort, by the old – even while Trollope is making it quite clear that in reality the new ways are vanquishing, old estates are being broken up, and falling into the hands of money-lenders, bankers, and horror of horrors, Jewish tailors. Despite his apparent respect for tradition, and for the old unostentatious pre-Victorian country life, his pictures of those working on the land are suffused with a Victorian snobbery rarely detectable in Elizabeth Gaskell or George Eliot: servile gardeners, country bumpkins, gullible maidens and knowing grooms provide comic relief, relegated to inferior background roles, giving the impression that ploughmen, in his own words, were still painted with ruddle, and milkmaids covered with skins. Instead of advancing with Reform Bills, the labourers recede into an unknown hinterland. Trollope's father was a failed barrister and failed farmer; his boyhood was marked by poverty and bitter social humiliation, which may explain his almost religious reverence for land and heredity. One of the greatest crimes, in Trollope's book, is to lose or squander one's inheritance. Yet there is a great deal of double-thinking in Trollope, as in most Victorians, who had difficulty in adjusting to the world of new money, and who were not sure whether they admired or despised those who had made their own fortunes.

The Thornes of Ullathorne represent the old order, and their home, Ullathorne Court, embodies a traditional way of life that Trollope tries to represent as plain, homely, unpretentious. It is, clearly, by modern standards, and by Trollope's own standards, a very fine house indeed, yet in *Barchester Towers*, Chapter 22, he describes it, curiously, in negatives: 'It was not a large house, nor a fine house, nor perhaps to modern ideas a very convenient house; but by those who love the peculiar colour and peculiar ornaments of genuine Tudor architecture it was considered a perfect gem.' He goes on to tell us that this ordinary home for 'ordinary homely folk' (!) is built on two sides of a court, has a great hall hung with portraits by Lely and Kneller, a garden full of urns, nymphs and satyrs, a magnificent avenue of limes, and a wall about twenty feet high completing the two sides of the court:

> This wall was built of cut stone, rudely cut indeed, and now much worn, but of a beautiful rich tawny yellow colour, the effect of that stonecrop of minute growth, which it had taken three centuries to produce. The top of this wall was ornamented by huge round stone

balls of the same colour as the wall itself. Entrance into the court was had through a pair of iron gates, so massive that no one could comfortably open or close them . . . With those who are now adepts in contriving house accommodation, it will militate much against Ullathorne Court, that no carriage could be brought to the hall-door.

Trollope's respect for antiquity is hard to analyse. The moment one decides it is based on a respect for power, property and status, one turns up some passage which seems to indicate that his feeling for it is largely aesthetic. He is lyrical about the colour of Ullathorne,

that delicious tawny hue which no stone can give, unless it has in it the vegetable richness of centuries. Strike the wall with your hand, and you will think that the stone has on it no colouring, but rub it carefully, and you will find that the colour comes off upon your finger. No colourist that ever yet worked from a palette has been able to come up to this rich colouring of years crowding themselves upon years.

The large straggling trees at Orley Farm 'do not delight the eyes of modern gardeners; but they produced fruit by the bushel, very sweet to the palate, though probably not so perfectly round, and large, and handsome as those which the horticultural skill of the present day requires'. Again, moral and aesthetic judgements are combined and contrasted, to the benefit of the old. Yet Trollope was a new man, a self-made man. Did he respect the ancient patina because of the grim years at Harrow and Winchester and as a clerk in London when he was penniless, neglected, shabby, despised? Did he comfort himself by thinking that the less striking, less ostentatious gifts hidden within him might prove sweeter and more fruitful in the long run?

Thomas Hardy is perhaps the greatest writer of rural life and landscape in the language. Accidents of time, place and family background combined to endow him with a uniquely articulate view of agricultural life, and his novels and poems span a vast range of rural experience and change. Each novel has its own atmosphere, its own world of landscape, even though most are set within a fairly narrow compass in Dorset. Like Cobbett, Hardy observed and described the smallest details of soil, contour, crop and vegetation, and he adds to this knowledge an antiquarian interest in topography, and a poet's use of language: his ear was as keen as his eye, and he could hear the wind whispering in the dried harebells, and tell each tree from the distinct rustling of its leaves. His novels contain the most precise and informed descriptions of country tasks, and of man's relation to the land. Other writers, observing from a distance, tend to see small farmers, labourers and day labourers lumped together in one undifferentiated mass, but Hardy's plots turn on the small distinctions, the rises and falls of country fortunes: Tess's father Jack Durbeyfield is at the beginning of the novel a 'haggler' or carrier with a horse, albeit an old one, and ends as a foot haggler; Gabriel Oak starts as a shepherd, becomes a bailiff, then a small independent peasant farmer, then sinks again to the role of hired man.

His knowledgeable descriptions of country labour are unrivalled. In *The Woodlanders*, we enter a world of cider-making, of planting and barking and spar-making; trees dominate the novel, and the weather seems always to be wet – it is the steady rain that finally kills Giles. Little Hintock House is overgrown by heavy-armed ivy, enclosed by trees and shrubs, 'vegetable nature's own home'. The woods are so dense that even Grace, who knows them well, loses her way. The evocation of woodland in Chapter 7 is superb:

> They went noiselessly over mats of starry moss, rustled through interspersed tracts of leaves, skirted trunks with spreading roots whose mossed rinds made them like hands wearing green gloves; elbowed old elms and ashes with great forks, in which stood pools of water that overflowed on rainy days, and ran down their stems in green cascades ... they dived amid beeches under which nothing grew, the younger boughs still retaining their hectic leaves, that rustled in the breeze with a sound almost metallic, like the iron-sheet foliage of the fabled Jarnvid wood ...

Yet the descriptions are not inserted for picturesque effect, picturesque though they are: this is a working landscape, and we see Giles and Marty South planting young firs 'with a gentle conjuror's touch', and Melbury's men, helped by Marty, barking doomed trees with billhooks. Even here there is variety: the wet dense woodland is contrasted with the cider valley where 'the air was blue as sapphire – such a blue as outside that apple valley was never seen. Under the blue the orchards were in a blaze of pink bloom . . .' Fitzpiers rides through the

> gorgeous autumn landscape of White-Hart Vale, surrounded by orchards lustrous with the reds of apple-crops, berries and foliage, the whole intensified by the gilding of the declining sun . . . In the poorest spots the hedges were bowed with haws and blackberries; acorns cracked underfoot, and the burst husks of chestnuts lay exposing their auburn contents as if arranged by anxious sellers in a fruit-market.

No wonder, in this world, that Giles appears to Grace as

> the fruit-god and the wood-god in alternation; sometimes leafy and smeared with green lichen, as she had seen him among the sappy boughs of the plantations: sometimes cider-stained and starred with apple pips, as she had met him on his return from Blackmoor Vale, with his vats and presses beside him . . .

The man is the essence of the landscape: he grows out of it as naturally as a tree.

The more conventionally pastoral life of sheep and dairy farming is described in *Far from the Madding Crowd* and *Tess*. These are true modern pastorals; none of the real problems are ignored, for sheep suffer from wind, ricks burn, sheepdogs run amok, cows are stubborn and hard to milk, milkmaids are seduced and break their hearts and take to drink. Yet there are passages that cannot but recall Virgil's Golden Age: in *Tess*, Chapter 16, for instance, in the beautiful valley of the Frome, the cows that were spotted with white reflected the sunshine in dazzling brilliancy, and the polished brass knobs on their horns glittered with something of military display. Their large-veined udders hung ponderous as sandbags, the teats sticking out like the legs of a gipsy's crock; and as each animal lingered for her turn to arrive, the milk oozed forth and fell in drops to the ground.

The milking sheds, 'their slopes encrusted with vivid green moss, and their eaves supported by wooden posts rubbed to a glossy smoothness by the flanks of infinite cows and calves of bygone years, now passed to an oblivion almost inconceivable in its profundity', are reminders of that vanished world. The Great Barn used for shearing in *Far from the Madding Crowd* represents the seemingly eternal, and in Chapter 22 Hardy allows nature a passage of total benevolence:

It was the first day of June, and the sheep-shearing season culminated, the landscape, even to the leanest pasture, being all health and colour. Every green was young, every pore was open, and every stalk was swollen with racing currents of juice. God was palpably present in the country, and the devil had gone with the world to town. Flossy catkins of the later kinds, fern-sprouts like bishops' croziers, the square-headed moschatel, the old cuckoo-pint – like an apoplectic saint in a niche of malachite – snow-white ladies's smocks, the toothwort, approximating to human flesh, the enchanter's nightshade, and the black-petaled doleful-bells, were among the quainter objects in and around Weatherbury at this teeming time . . . They sheared in the Great Barn, called for the nonce the Shearing-barn, which on ground-plan resembled a church with transepts. It not only emulated the form of the neighbouring church of the parish, but vied with it in antiquity . . . The dusky, filmed, chestnut roof, braced and tied by huge collars, curves, and diagonals, was far nobler in design, because more wealthy in material, than nine-tenths of those in our modern churches. [Hardy, one remembers, was also an architect and church restorer.] Today the large side doors were thrown open towards the sun to admit a bountiful light to the immediate spot of the shearers' operations, which was a wooden threshing-floor in the centre, formed of thick oak, black with age and polished by the beating of flails for many generations, till it had grown as slippery and as rich in hue as the state-room floors of an Elizabethan mansion. Here the shearers knelt, the sun slanting in upon their bleached shirts, tanned arms, and the polished shears they flourished, causing them to bristle with a thousand rays strong enough to blind a weak-eyed man. Beneath them the captive sheep lay panting, quickening its pants as misgiving merged in terror, till it quivered like the hot landscape outside.

This picture of today in its frame of four hundred years ago did not produce that marked contrast between ancient and modern which is implied by the contrast of date. In comparison with cities, Weatherbury was immutable . . . Five generations hardly modified the cut of a gaiter, the embroidery of a smock-frock, by the breadth of a hair. Ten generations failed to alter the turn of a single phrase. In these Wessex nooks the busy outsider's ancient times are only old; his old times are still new; his present is futurity.

So the barn was natural to the shearers, and the shearers were in harmony with the barn.

Yet Hardy knew quite well that this harmony was preserved only in nooks, and that God was not always present in the country. Nature in his novels is often indifferent, occasionally actively malevolent. Egdon Heath is sombre and severe: in *The Return of the Native* Clym Yeobright's adopted calling of furze cutter blisters his hands; a walk across the heath in the heat of the day kills his mother; Eustacia, in her flight towards Rainbarrow, stumbles over 'twisted furze-roots, tufts of rushes, or oozing lumps of fleshy fungi, which at this season lay scattered about the heath like the rotten liver and lungs of some colossal animal'. Hardy seems to take a gloomy satisfaction in describing the bleaker features of the landscape: monuments like the Cross-in-Hand on Batcombe Down, 'site of a miracle, or murder, or both', fascinated him, as did Stonehenge itself and the gloomy stone circle near Casterbridge (Maumbury Rings, at Dorchester) where in *The Mayor of Casterbridge* Henchard arranges to meet his estranged wife. 'Melancholy, impressive, lonely, yet accessible from every part of the town, the historic circle was the frequent spot for appointments of a furtive kind . . . though close to the turnpike-road, crimes might be perpetrated there unseen at mid-day', he says, and describes in detail its lurid history of executions. The prehistoric burial mound called Rainbarrow features prominently in *The Return of the Native*, adding a sense of ancient horror – Eustacia's figure, seen rising from it by the reddleman, might have been the Celt who built the barrow, 'a sort of last man among them, musing for a moment before dropping into eternal night with the rest of his race'; and the fatal associations are reinforced by references to death – the beacon lit on the summit shows up the pits of the heath 'like the eye-sockets of a skull'. Norecombe Hill in *Far from the Madding Crowd* (Chapter 2) is also sinister:

> Norecombe Hill – not far from lonely Toller-Down – was one of the spots which suggest to a passer-by that he is in the presence of a shape approaching the indestructible as nearly as any to be found on earth. It was a featureless convexity of chalk and soil – an ordinary specimen of those smoothly-outlined protuberances of the globe which may remain undisturbed on some great day of confusion, when far grander heights and dizzy precipices topple down.
>
> The hill was covered on its northern side by an ancient and decaying plantation of beeches, whose upper verge formed a line over the crest, fringing its arched curve against the sky, like a mane. Tonight these trees sheltered the southern slope from the keenest blasts, which smote the wood and floundered through it with a sound as of grumbling, or gushed over its crowning boughs in a weakened moan. The dry leaves in the ditch simmered and boiled in the same breezes, a tongue of air occasionally ferreting out a few, and sending them spinning across the grass. A group or two of the latest in date amongst the dead multitude had remained till this very mid-winter time on the twigs which bore them, and in falling rattled against the trunks with smart taps.
>
> Between this half-wooded, half-naked hill, and the vague, still horizon that its summit indistinctly commanded, was a mysterious

sheet of fathomless shade – the sounds from which suggested that what it concealed bore some reduced resemblance to features here. The thin grasses, more or less coating the hill, were touched by the wind in breezes of differing powers, and almost of differing natures – one rubbing the blades heavily, another raking them piercingly, another brushing them like a soft broom. The instinctive act of humankind was to stand and listen, and learn how the trees on the right and the trees on the left wailed or chanted to each other in the regular antiphonies of a cathedral choir...

So well does Hardy catch the ancient, prehistoric nature of the landscape that it comes as a surprise to note that the clump of beeches was in fact a plantation, not a natural outcrop: a similar hill, the familiar Chanctonbury Ring on the South Downs, was planted with beech saplings in 1760 by a lad named Charles Goring, heir to the estate, and looks now as though it must have been so crowned throughout history.

The contrast between harsh and fruitful landscapes runs through Hardy's work: no wonder he admired Crabbe, with whom he has much in common. Its effect on the lives of men is woven into the events of the novels. The starkest and least pastoral of the novels, *Jude the Obscure*, is set in the stoniest ground; there are no descriptions of rural happiness and fruitfulness. Nature here is brutal: it is a world where men stone birds, stick pigs, and torture rabbits in gin traps.

Tess also contains, as well as the idyllic valleys of the Little and Great Dairies (carefully distinguished from one another in description), the chalk plateau of Flintcomb-Ash and Chalk-Newton, where rough labour only was in demand; there Tess worked as a swede-hacker with her old friend Marian, 'the single fat thing on the soil'. Flintcomb-Ash was so near 'greeny, sunny, romantic Talbothays', where Tess had worked as dairymaid, that Marian says, 'You can see a gleam of a hill within a few miles o' Froom Valley from here when 'tis fine'; yet the character of the land and work is utterly different. Hardy writes, in Chapter 43:

The swede field in which she and her companion were set hacking was a stretch of a hundred odd acres, in one patch, on the highest ground of the farm, rising above stony lanchets or lynchets – the outcrop of siliceous veins in the chalk formation, composed of myriads of loose white flints in bulbous, cusped and phallic shapes. The upper half of each turnip had been eaten off by the livestock, and it was the business of the women to grub up the lower or earthly part of the root with a hooked fork called a hacker, that it might be eaten also. Every leaf of the vegetable having already been consumed, the whole field was in colour a desolate drab; it was a complexion without features, as if a face, from chin to brow, should be only an expanse of skin. The sky wore, in another colour, the same likeness; a white vacuity of countenance with the lineaments gone. So these two upper and nether visages confronted each other all day long, the white face looking down at the brown face, and the brown face looking up at the white face, without anything standing between them but the two girls crawling over the surface of the former like flies.

It is not merely poetic justice and artistic irony that brings Tess to this desolate spot; she is a victim of Alec D'Urbeville's sensuality and Angel Clare's puritanism, but she is also a victim of a much larger process of rural change, which was destroying traditional ways of life. The monotonous and rough work is all that she can find: female labour is cheap, the villages are emptying, machinery is taking over, trains are invading the countryside. We are told in Chapter 51:

A depopulation was also going on. The village had formerly contained, side by side with the agricultural labourers, an interesting and better-informed class, ranking distinctly above the former – the class to which Tess's father and mother had belonged – and including the carpenter, the smith, the shoemaker, the huckster, together with other nondescript workers other than farm labourers . . . These families, who had formed the backbone of village life in the past, had to seek refuge in the large centres; the tendency, humorously designated by statisticians as 'the tendency of the rural population towards the large towns', being really the tendency of water to flow uphill when forced by machinery.

Actual machinery is seen not so much as an alleviation of toil, but as a threat to the individual labourer: the threshing machine is 'the red tyrant the women had come to serve' – and it keeps up a 'despotic demand upon the endurance of their muscles and nerves'. Its engineer (in Chapter 47) looks like

> a creature from Tophet, who had strayed into the pellucid smoke-lessness of this region of yellow grain and pale soil . . . He served fire and smoke; these denizens of the fields served vegetation, weather, frost and sun . . . The long strap which ran from the driving wheel of his engine to the red thresher under the rick was the sole tie-line between agriculture and him.

He is the man of the future: we glimpse a time when even hard manual labour in the fields will be remembered with a certain nostalgia. The unbroken centuries of tradition are about to be disrupted forever.

At times, Hardy seems keenly aware of this imminent dissolution, which would transform both labour and landscape. At others, he seems to believe – to hope? – that old ways will survive. In 1915 he wrote a poem, 'In Time of "The Breaking of Nations,"' which affirms continuity:

> Only a man harrowing clods
> In a slow silent walk
> With an old horse that stumbles and nods
> Half asleep as they stalk.

> Only thin smoke without flame
> From the heaps of couch-grass;
> Yet this will go onward the same
> Though Dynasties pass.

> Yonder a maid and her wight
> Come whispering by:
> War's annals will cloud into night
> Ere their story die.

Hardy, of course, was wrong: this did not go onward the same, for there are now no horses to harrow, and this is a scene, familiar throughout dynasties, that could no longer be photographed in this country. Change was sudden, irreversible, total. It was so total that it is astonishing that so many landscapes of the past, described by writers, should still remain recognizable. Farming methods have as we know been altered out of all recognition: tractors have replaced horses, machines perform most age-old customary chores, cattle and poultry live in factory farms. Yet we can still see the fields and hedgerows and herds of cows – and if we drive past factory farms, we do not recognize them for what they are. The agrarian revolution has left us with more than we might have expected, though less than Hardy might have foretold.

Since Hardy, pastorals and anti-pastorals have been produced in quantity. D. H. Lawrence in *The Rainbow* writes of haymaking and farmyards, cowsheds and lambing. The landscapes of Lawrence are interpenetrated by canals and railways, and scarred by mining, but Anna and Will Brangwen still set up sheaves of corn by hand in the moonlight, and horses still work on the farm – though these scenes, so natural and inevitable in Hardy, are made to bear a heavy weight of symbolism, foreshadowing the sexual melodramas of Mary Webb and their parody in Stella Gibbons's *Cold Comfort Farm*. *Cold Comfort Farm* is in its own way a significant work, pointing out as it does the ludicrous irrelevance of an artistic and literary convention, as Jane Austen did in *Northanger Abbey*. It has lasted so well not merely because it is funny, but because it says something true about change and nostalgia. It is hardly possible, now, to write a pastoral without a degree of self-consciousness that invokes satiric laughter. Self-supporting communes and simple-lifers have long been the subject of comedy, although the situation that has inspired them is grave enough. We are all aware of something comic and unnatural in our relationship to the land and its produce, and those who are brave enough to face the derision of their contemporaries by sticking to their principles are perhaps too removed from the mainstream of life to produce mainstream literature.

The exceptions are interesting: R. S. Thomas in Wales and Alasdair Maclean in Scotland both produced poetry that draws its strength from traditional imagery and a traditional way of life – and both lived in regions that have, in fact, seen less change and 'progress' than more prosperous agricultural regions. Thomas (who died in 2000) was another clergyman poet, who wrote of the people and landscapes of Wales, of the 'negligible men from the village, from the small holdings' who 'bring their grief sullenly to my back door'. His poems are full of compassion and bitterness, for a land with a tragic past and present: in 'Reservoirs' he says

> There are places in Wales I don't go:
> Reservoirs that are the subconscious of a people
>
> . . .
>
> . . . There are the hills,
> Too; gardens gone under the scum
> Of the forests; and the smashed faces
> Of the farms with the stone trickle
> Of the tears down the hills' side.
> Where can I go, then, from the smell
> Of decay, from the putrefying of a dead
> Nation? I have walked the shore
> For an hour and seen the English
> Scavenging among the remains
> Of our culture . . .

In 'Tenancies' he writes of the simple and speechless, with hard hands:

> This is pain's landscape.
> A savage agriculture is practised
> Here . . .

The terrain of the Lleyn peninsula where he lived and wrote is beautiful to the tourist, but bleak to the farmer: beauty is glimpsed only fitfully, beyond the harsh realities of plough and tractor, of fluke and foot-rot and fat maggot. Poem after poem celebrates the labourer, who

. . . wades in the brown bilge of earth
Hour by hour, or stoops to pull
The reluctant swedes . . .

and the peasant

Who pens a few sheep in a gap of cloud.
Docking mangels, chipping the green skin
From the yellow bones with a half-witted grin
Of satisfaction, or churning the crude earth
To a stiff sea of clods that glint in the wind . . .

This is a country of hard labour, like Tess's in the flint uplands, of labour
without dignity or grace – yet through the toil moments of joy speak.
Cynddylan on his tractor is 'a new man now, part of the machine'; the old
look that yoked him to the soil is gone. And in this poem, 'The Hill
Farmer Speaks':

I am the farmer, stripped of love
And thought and grace by the land's hardness;
But what I am saying over the fields'
Desolate acres, rough with dew,
Is, Listen, listen, I am a man like you.

The wind goes over the hill pastures
Year after year, and the ewes starve,
Milkless, for want of the new grass.
And I starve, too, for something the spring
Can never foster in veins run dry.

The pig is a friend, the cattle's breath
Mingles with mine in the still lanes;
I wear it willingly like a cloak
To shelter me from your curious gaze.
The hens go in and out at the door

From sun to shadow, as stray thoughts pass
Over the floor of my wide skull.
The dirt is under my cracked nails;
The tale of my life is smirched with dung;
The phlegm rattles. But what I am saying
Over the grasses rough with dew
Is, Listen, listen, I am a man like you.

For such men, agricultural progress has brought little change, and Thomas can still write of their lives in age-old language, in terms that Hardy would have understood.

Alasdair Maclean, born in 1926, also writes of a hard life on a bleak promontory – in his case the peninsula of Ardnamurchan. He comes from a crofting family, and his poems celebrate and lament a way of life that is dying rather than changing: he writes of deserted houses with the skeletons of small trapped birds in the lofts, of old women dying alone and hungry with a mouth full of raw potato, of old dogs and dying hens, of peat cutting, fishing, of violence of man and nature. In 'At the Peats' he describes the tourists who photograph himself and his father as they dig into the peat bog – 'They prod us with their cameras, making us aware of what we do . . . ' The age-old scene has become a set piece, preserved in copies of *Scottish Field* as a memento of the past, even while he and his father are still living it. It is, he says, 'a bleak, inhuman, fearful landscape', and its inhabitants are old or mad: James Mackenzie is simple, but 'could point the churchyard where the headstones tell how much inbreeding dribbles from his lips'. This is the tragedy of the Western Highlands, and Maclean's descriptions (as here in 'Stone') recall Crabbe's:

A long peninsula of solid rock,
upholstered every year in threadbare green.
Stones everywhere, ambiguous and burgeoning.
In Sanna ramparts of them
march around our crofts
but whether to keep cattle out or other stones
no man can say.

And at Kilchoan there were three houses
cropped from one field.
That was when I was a boy.
The masons left the pebbles
and there's a castle now, waiting to be harvested.
God was short of earth when He made Ardnamurchan.

Such stony land is beyond development, immune from culture: in the
summer, the beach is 'civilized by deckchairs', but in winter the landscape
returns to its timeless, wind-flayed desolation. Maclean takes a grim satisfaction in this indestructibility, for, as he has said, nature is the source of
imagery and of poetry, and although it has retreated to the fruitless edges
of Britain, it is still there, biding its time, waiting for the oil rigs. Pastorals
in the twentieth century have become cold indeed.

LANDSCAPE AS ART

The British have a fine reputation as gardeners, and English literature is full of writing about gardens – descriptive, instructional, polemical and symbolic. We have already referred to the legend of the garden of Eden, and Milton's account of the wild garden of Paradise. Until Milton's day and later, however, real gardens were not wild but formal, and as unlike uncontrolled nature as possible. The gardens evoked by Chaucer in the fourteenth century are highly artificial: they were walled, with raised flower beds, mounts, lawns planted with flowers, fountains, arbours and orchards. There was nothing particularly English about them, either; gardens at this period were much the same all over Europe, and some essential features, such as fountains, might be thought more appropriate to a dryer climate. I cannot be the only English visitor to have discovered, in the gardens of the Alhambra at Granada, the significance of the sight and sound of water in gardening. The fountains at Chatsworth are impressive, but they serve a different purpose. They are not in the same way necessary; the landscape can survive without them.

Chaucer's descriptions are of nature carefully ordered, cultivated and protected. The flowery mead in *The Romaunt of the Rose* (lines 1431–38) recalls the embroidered flowers of medieval tapestries:

> Ther sprang the violet al newe
> And fresshe pervinke rich of hewe,
> And floures yelowe, whyte and rede:
> Swich plentee grew ther never in mede,
> Ful gay was al the ground and queynt
> And poudred, as men had it peynt,
> With many a fresh and sondry flour
> That casten up a ful savour.

'As men had it peynt' – the comparison of nature with art is characteristic, and the medieval poet, when wishing to praise the beauties of nature, implied that they were as fine as the works of man. Elsewhere, Chaucer refers to spring as a garment, as a 'newe shroude', as an embroidered robe. In the anonymous poem, 'The Flower and the Leaf', the poet compares grass, as a compliment, to green wool, and a hedge to a wall:

> Thought I, this path, some whider goth, parde,
> And so I followed, till it me brought
> To a right pleasaunt herber well y wrought,
> That benched was and with turfes new
> Freshly turved, whereof the grene gras,
> So small, so thicke, so short, so fresh of hew
> That most like unto green wool I wot it was.
> The hegge also that yede in compas
> And closed in all the greene herbere
> With sicamour was set and eglatere.
>
> And shapen was this herber roof and all
> As a pretty parlour: and also
> The hegge as thicke as a castle wall . . .

The garden was charged with allegorical significance and sexual innuendo: the lover in *The Romaunt of the Rose* falls in love with the reflection of a rosebud mirrored in the waters of the Fountain of Narcissus, and his attempts to pluck it are aided and hindered by various allegorical personages – Danger, Shame, Bel-Accueil, and so forth. Flowers, similarly, have allegorical meanings, which play as prominent a role in medieval and Elizabethan literature as do their appearances. Shakespeare's Perdita chooses her gifts carefully for their symbolic meaning, as does Ophelia, and Sir Thomas More wrote, 'As for rosemarie I lette it runne all over my garden walls, not onlie because my bees love it, but because it is the herb sacred to rememberance and to friendship, whence a sprig of it hath a dumb language.'

The allegory of the rose garden was one of the central allegories of medieval literature, and could be invested with profane or sacred significance: most commonly however, gardens were associated with amorous dalliance. There lovers met, or observed one another secretly; there they retired to weep their fate. In 'The Knight's Tale' Chaucer describes Palamon and Arcite catching sight of bright Emily as she wanders in the garden beneath their prison walls, gathering red and white flowers for a garland; both fall in love with her, and worship her from their distant proximity. This story may even have taken on a little reality in the case of James I of Scotland, who was imprisoned at Windsor for nine years by Henry V, in what seem to have been very comfortable circumstances. In his poem *The Kingis Quair* his hero falls in love with 'Cupid's own princess', thought by some scholars to be Jane Beaufort, whom he was to marry in 1424, to whom the poem may be addressed. The poet first sees her as she walks in the garden, which he describes charmingly:

> Now was there maid, fast by the towris wall,
> A gardin fair, and in the corneris set
> Ane herbere grene:– with wandis long and small
> Railit about; and so with treis set
> Was all the place, and hawthorne hegis knet,
> That lif was none walking there forby,
> That might within scarce ony wight aspye.
>
> So thik the bewis and the leves grene
> Beschadit all the aleyes that there were,
> And middis every herbere might be sene
> The scharpe grene swete jenepere . . .

When he sees the maiden, he exclaims to her:

> Or are ye god Cupidis owin princesse,
> And cummin are to loose me out of band?
> Or ar ye verray Nature the goddesse,
> That have depainted with your hevinly hand
> This gardin full of flowris, as they stand?

If the maiden was Jane Beaufort herself, it is good to note one romance of courtly love that reached a satisfactory fulfilment, in marriage and release from bondage.

Many later lovers have rejoiced and suffered in gardens. John Donne went to Twicknam Garden, blasted with sighs and surrounded with tears, and found the trees laughed and mocked him to his face. Andrew Marvell writes, in 'Eyes and Tears':

> I have through every Garden been,
> Amongst the red, the white, the green,
> And yet, from all the flowers I saw,
> No honey, but these tears could draw.

Shakespeare's heroines are tricked into love in arbours; Jane Austen's are wooed in shrubberies. Perhaps Galsworthy's choice of the Botanical Gardens for the stolen meetings of his courtly and adulterous lovers, Irene Soames and Bosinney, in *The Forsyte Saga*, was animated by some faint memory of *The Romaunt of the Rose*, though in deference to a change of taste the season here is not spring but autumn, with its red and yellow leaves, with 'that slow and beautiful decay that flings crowns underfoot to star the earth with fallen glories, whence, as the cycle rolls, will leap again wild spring'.

The habit of seeing the natural world in terms of its allegorical significance has largely vanished, and so have the formal gardens themselves. Jolyon, overseeing by chance the tryst of Irene and Bosinney, has deliberately chosen a corner where the tidy brooms of the gardeners cannot reach, for he prefers the disorder of the leaves. We no longer praise nature by comparing it to art: we do the reverse. We praise a painter for his skill in evoking nature, a landscape gardener for his artful concealing of art. So deeply has this way of looking at the world infected us in this country that many of us have little feeling for highly organized gardens: we tend to despise ornamental flowerbeds with clocks and heraldic devices as the fantasies of civic gardening departments; we look upon topiary as charming but quaint, and the average English garden enthusiast's recoil from the little box hedges and symmetrical avenues of Versailles is still very much as it might have been in the days of Thomas Gray and Horace Walpole: their response to its 'sugar loaves and minced pies of yew; scrawl work of box and little squirting jets-d'eau . . . not to mention the silliest of all labyrinths' as Gray wrote to Richard West (22 May 1739) is now common enough. The geometric patterns of *Last Year in Marienbad* are as foreign to our eye as its romantic encounters were puzzling to the literal-minded viewer, and the geometry of clipped trees and shadows required a sharpness and brightness of sun rare in our climate.

Yet these early English gardens were beautiful in their way, and we can catch glimpses of them here and there, through the poetry of Marvell, through descriptions in Celia Fiennes's books of travels, through Sir Thomas Browne's curious dissertations. Several still remain, or have been restored. In the 1950s, the National Trust for Scotland recreated (and has maintained) an elaborate seventeenth-century parterre garden at Pitmedden, near Aberdeen. There are seventeenth-century restorations at Little Moreton Hall in Cheshire, at Moseley Old Hall near Wolverhampton (with knot gardens and nut walk), and at Ham House near Richmond, which has lavender parterres. Kew House has a seventeenth-century pastiche garden with a mount, a turf seat, and a knot garden with authentic plants; Hampton Court has a sunken pond garden laid out by Henry VIII and a later sunk garden in formal seventeenth-century style, as well as William III's formal gardens. A former world lives on in the Early Tudor courtyard house at Compton Wynyates in Warwickshire, which strikes Shakespearean pilgrims as the perfect setting for *Twelfth Night* or *A Midsummer Night's Dream*, and which moved Walter Scott and Henry James to rapture. On a smaller but even more resonantly historic scale, the garden at New Place in the centre of Stratford-upon-Avon has a beautiful replica of an Elizabethan sunken knot garden, filled with brightly coloured flowers, little box hedges, and herbs of the period. This site once belonged to Shakespeare himself, and is now administered by the Shakespeare Birthplace Trust. (Anne Hathaway's Cottage, which also belongs to the SBT, provides an interesting contrast in informal gardening style.)

Marvell's poem 'The Garden' offers an interesting mixture of the natural and the formal; the first eight stanzas evoke a 'delicious solitude' of fruit trees and fountains, but the last is pure seventeenth-century formality, and describes a living sundial, planted by gardeners:

How well the skilful gardener drew
Of flowers and herbs this dial new!
Where, from above, the milder sun
Does through a fragrant zodiac run;
And, as it works, the industrious bee
Computes its time as well as we.
How could such sweet and wholesome hours
Be reckoned but with herbs and flowers!

One has to agree with Robert Southey, who deplored the disappearance of 'a sundial in box, set round with true lovers' knots' at New College in Oxford. Of such works, he says, 'These have been destroyed more easily as well as more rapidly than they were formed, but as nothing beautiful has been substituted in their places, it had been better if they had suffered these old oddities to have remained.' Nice knots, which Milton would not admit into his Eden, were fancy-shaped flowerbeds, carefully planted with various coloured flowers. The king's herbalist John Parkinson described the art of planting them in *Paradisi in Sole Paradisus Terrestris* (1629):

> You may first observe the several kinds of them that do flower at one and the same time, and then place them in such order and so near one to another, that their flowers appearing together of several colours, will cause the more admiration in beholders, thus: the vernal crocus or saffron flowers of the spring, white, purple, yellow and striped, with some vernal colchicum or meadow saffron among them; some Dens Canis or dog's teeth, and some of the small early leucojum or bulbous violet, all planted in some proportion as near one to another as is fit for them, will give such grace to the garden, that the place will seem like a piece of tapestry of many glorious colours, to increase everyone's delight.

Such art would not seem to deserve Milton's scorn. Less attractive, perhaps, sounds the custom of edging the beds with the jawbones of sheep, but this Parkinson himself condemns as 'grosse and base'. He is particularly enthusiastic about the qualities of the tulip, a recent and dramatic import – it was first introduced to this country in 1582:

> Tulips may be so matched, one colouring answering and setting off another, that the place where they stand may resemble a piece of curious needlework or a piece of painting, and I have known in a garden, the Master as much commended for this artificial form in placing the colours of Tulips, as for the goodnesse of his flowers ...

One notes that Parkinson praises the very artificiality of such designs as their greatest virtue. We have become so accustomed to the idea that nature abhors a straight line that we find it hard to see the qualities that Celia Fiennes praised in her travels round the countryside. She likes to see a straight avenue, 'even' and 'smooth' and 'neat' are invariably terms of praise with her, whereas we are offended by the sight of a hillside planted in straight rows by the Forestry Commission. Yet her descriptions of gardens such as Patshull Park, near Shrewsbury (in *My Great Journey to Newcastle and to Cornwall, of* 1698), are very attractive:

> The grove I mentioned is the finest I ever saw, there are six walks thro' it and just in the middle you look twelve ways which discovers as many several prospects either to the house or entrance or fountaines or gardens or fields; the Grove itself is peculiar, being composed of all sorts of greens that hold their verdure and beauty all the yeare, and flourishes most in the winter season, when all other garden beautys fades, for Firrs (both Silver Scots and Noroway) Cyprus Yew Bays, etc., the severall squares being set full of these like a Maze; they are compassed round each square with a hedge of Lawrell about a yard high cut exactly smooth and even, there are also Box trees in the middle; there are two other large Gardens with gravell walkes and grass-plotts full of stone statues; the stone is taken out of the quarrys about this country which is not a very firm stone and so the weather cracks them.

A strange insight into the view that nature is ordered by mystic and mathematical laws (a view that would correspond with a geometric approach to gardening) can be found in Sir Thomas Browne's extraordinary essay on the quincunx, 'The Garden of Cyrus'. (The word 'quincunx' means 'a disposition of five objects so placed that four occupy the corners, and the fifth the centre of a square or rectangle', and was applied to a group of trees so planted in the seventeenth century.) Browne modestly asserts that he 'was never Master of any considerable Garden', yet we know he was a keen gardener, for his garden in Norwich was admired by the connoisseur John Evelyn in 1672, and Browne's essay displays a deep interest in botany and natural history, as well as a bizarre fascination with the number 5, with rhomboidal decussations, with 'the mystical mathematics of the City of Heaven', and with 'Quincunciall order'. In the appearances and ordering of nature, Browne detects a pattern mysteriously connected with the figure 5 – which is repeated in the leaves of the rose, in the specks on the top of the 'Miscle-berry', in the head of the common or prickled artichoke, in 'the remarkable disposure of those yellow fringes about the purple Pestill of Aaron, and elegant clusters of dragons, so peculiarly secured by nature, with an umbrella or skreening leaf about them'. In such manifestations, he notes 'how the needle of nature delighteth to work, even in low and doubtful vegetations'. Such an obsession with numbers lends itself naturally to an artificial style of gardening, where a certain pattern of tiles laid in a field can charm away dodder and tetter; he sees a hidden correspondence between the 'Quintuple section of a Cone of handsome practise in Ornamentall Garden-plots' and the five fingers and toes on the hand and foot, not to mention the crystalline humour in the eye of the cuttlefish.

Yet a more natural approach to nature and gardening certainly predated the great revolution of taste in the eighteenth century. As early as 1610 we find Perdita in *The Winter's Tale* rejecting carnations and streaked gillyflowers because they are nature's unnaturally bred bastards. She says:

> For I have heard it said
> There is an art which in their piedness shares
> With great creating nature.

The point here, it is true, is a moral and dramatic one, rather than an aesthetic one, yet it reflects the Renaissance debate on nature versus art. Marvell raises the same points in 'The Mower against Gardens', in which the mower objects to man's deformation and enclosing of nature:

> Luxurious man, to bring his vice in use,
>   Did after him the world seduce,
> And from the fields the flow'rs and plants allure,
>   Where Nature was most plain and pure.
> He first enclos'd within the gardens square
>   A dead and standing pool of air,
> And a more luscious earth for them did knead,
>   Which stupifi'd them while it fed. ....

Long before William Kent with his winding walks and serpentine lakes, Francis Bacon was condemning (in 'Of Gardens', 1597) knots as 'but toys; you may see as good sights many times in tarts', and sneering at 'images cut out in juniper or other garden stuff – they be for children'. His ideal garden contained a heath, or 'natural wildness':

> Trees I would have none in it; but some Thickets, made onely of Sweet-Briar, and Honeysuckle, and some Wilde Vine amongst; and the ground set with Violets, Strawberries, and Prime-Roses. For these are sweet, and prosper in the Shade. And these to be in the Heath, here and there, not in any Order. I like also little Heaps, in the Nature of Mole-hills, (such as are in Wilde Heaths) to be set, some with Wilde Thyme; some with Pinks: some with Germander...

The word 'wilderness' began to be used of wild gardens in the mid-seventeenth century, and Marvell's nymph complaining of the death of her faun says:

> I have a garden of my own
> But so with roses overgrown

And lilies, that you would it guess
To be a little wilderness . . .

Yet it would probably be a mistake to imagine such wildernesses as truly natural; the quotations used in the *Oxford English Dictionary* make it clear that they were planted and laid out in walks, 'often in the form of a maze or labyrinth' – and Bacon was enough a child of his time to consider a square the best shape for the garden, and to like 'little low hedges round like welts, with some pretty pyramids'. The wild gardens recommended by William Robinson in the late nineteenth century were still undreamed of.

The idea that too much interference with nature is somehow immoral has been with us for a long time: Perdita's dislike of carnations is echoed by many who take a particular dislike to particular varieties of plants, or methods of cultivating them. Exotic orchids and un-British cacti displease many; some gardeners prefer species to hybrids, and Angus Wilson writes wittily in *The Middle Age of Mrs Eliot* of snobbish contempt for the 'vulgar calceolaria'. William Morris, in *Hopes and Fears for Art* (1882), defends the garden rose against the wild rose – but only up to a certain point. He claims that florists are overdeveloping blooms, and missing 'the very essence of the rose's being', and goes on to warn the gardener:

> Be very shy of double flowers; choose the old columbine where the clustering doves are unmistakable and distinct, not the double one, where they run into mere tatters. Choose (if you can get it) the old china-aster with the yellow centre, that goes so well with the purple-brown stems and curiously coloured florets, instead of the lumps that look like cut paper, of which we are now so proud. Don't be swindled out of that wonder of beauty, a single snowdrop; there is no gain and plenty of loss in the double one . . . There are some flowers (inventions of men, i.e. florists) which are bad colour altogether, and not to be used at all. Scarlet geraniums, for instance, or the yellow calceolaria, which indeed are not uncommonly grown together profusely, in order, I suppose, to show that even flowers can be thoroughly ugly . . .

Despising other people's taste in flowers, gardens and shrubberies has long been part of the comedy of our literature, but these feelings are not wholly trivial or superficial; they reflect in some a deep preoccupation with notions of natural goodness and original sin. A craving for the exotic and expensive can reasonably enough be regarded as corrupt, as Marvell, a defender of Cromwell and the Commonwealth, implies. Why is not man satisfied with nature as God made it, why must he seek to improve it and cultivate it? The love of the natural for its own sake undoubtedly played a part in the concept of the garden wilderness and the wild garden, which are associated in the mind with a desire to return to the innocence of Eden. Nature, seen in the early Middle Ages as in itself corrupt, has been increasingly accepted as a standard of the good contrasted with the potential wickedness of man; and if nature is good, is it not *hubris* to seek to improve it? In these days of cloning and genetic engineering, such questions have acquired a new significance. Compared with the grafting of human beings, the grafting and interbreeding of plants seem innocent enough, yet they have always caused alarm to some, and the invasion of new types of vegetation from the New World may even have had its threatening as well as its delightful aspects – Britain was certainly made brighter by successive waves of imports, from tulips, lilacs, laburnums, nasturtiums, golden rod and Michaelmas daisies to maples, acacias, azaleas and magnolias, but she was also changed out of all recognition. Even the humble candytuft and love-in a-mist, so faithfully responsive to the youngest of gardeners, are apparently not indigenous. It is said that if a patch of woodland is left undisturbed by human interference, such trees as were naturally indigenous will eventually win the struggle for survival, thereby demonstrating their superior adaptation to the climate and the land. Whether or not this is true, the fact that the concept is so pleasing indicates that we have a natural liking for the naturally produced. And if it is true, might one not reasonably suppose that indigenous trees and plants have an affinity with the landscape that later interlopers lack? Our ancient trees – the beech, the oak, the hawthorn – certainly appear in our litera- ture accompanied by solemn and almost sacred associations; their very names evoke a sense of England. The British genius has been produced by thousands of years of interbreeding, but it is haunted by memories that may be summoned up more readily by the ghost of a rose than by the ghost of a tulip.

The movement towards a more natural style of gardening in the eighteenth century was accompanied by a growing appreciation of landscape for its own sake, and for the sake of Claude and Poussin. Ironically, the cult of landscape gardening resulted in far more derangement of earth, transformation of natural scenery, expensive and grandiose projects than previous gardening theories had done, although the great works of the immediately preceding style, Chatsworth and Blenheim, were on a grand enough scale; and even before the new wave, Aubrey remarked, 'There is now in 1691 ten times as much gardening about London as there was in 1660,' an assessment echoed by Defoe's praise of 'wonderful alteration', especially in Middlesex and Surrey. But the new passion carried such enthusiasm to unprecedented lengths, uprooting and replanting villages, flooding valleys, heaping up mounds and levelling hills. Maps showing the quantity and distribution of parks improved by Bridgeman, Kent, Capability Brown and Repton display their formidable energy. Many of the formal gardens of the seventeenth century were destroyed or 'improved' by the new zeal: another irony is that the lament for fallen avenues so often heard from this period onwards was a lament for the destruction of formality in the name of nature.

Much has been written on the art of landscape gardening, on the battles of taste waged by its arbiters, and by the later connoisseurs of the Picturesque. The admirers of the new style were articulate and opinionated, and many of them expressed their opinions in verse. It is a specialized subject, and I shall not attempt even to offer a précis of the views of those who have written on it so brilliantly – Christopher Hussey, Elizabeth Manwaring, John Dixon Hunt, Edward Malins and John Barrell, to name but a few. It is a subject that engrosses those who become involved in it, and the violent disagreements of the eighteenth century are in themselves so entertaining that the specialist tends to forget the fact that a good deal of landscape theory in verse is, as poetry, very dull. Who save the addict picks up William Mason's *The English Landscape*, Shenstone on *The Progress of Taste*, or Richard Payne Knight's *The Landscape*? Their passions have been immortalized by Jane Austen, by Peacock in *Headlong Hall*, by Walpole in his letters, but they have been forgotten. Daunted by the vast body of work, I shall take the coward's way out, and try to give an account only of those writers who seem to me to be interesting in their own right, and who have contributed to our common legacy of landscape sentiment, rather than try to follow the points and scores of particular debates.

Any such account could hardly omit the name of Alexander Pope, who serves as a guide to the changes in taste between the seventeenth and eighteenth centuries. He was passionately interested in gardening, corresponding on the subject with many of his contemporaries and regarded by them as an expert; he was also a great satirist, and the topic certainly invited satire. The first literary landscapes he produced were conventional, idealized, and almost wholly literary pastorals, smooth-flowing Virgilian imitations with the merest pretence at local colour. Here is a typical stanza from 'Spring':

> O'er golden sands let rich Pactolus flow,
> And trees weep amber on the banks of Po!
> Blest Thames's shores the brightest beauties yield,
> Feed here my lambs, I'll seek no distant field . . .

While nobody could doubt Pope's patriotic devotion to the Thames, it could hardly be claimed that he had described it very accurately or appeared to have observed it very precisely. Dr Johnson wrote, 'To charge these pastorals with want of invention is to require what was never intended', but a modern reader is perhaps more inclined to agree with Joseph Warton, writing in 1756, who complained that they contained 'not a single rural image that is new', and that their ideas were trite and common. Even Johnson agreed that they showed 'not a single new thought'. Indeed, Pope himself came to share this view, apologizing in later verses (as here in the 'Epistle to Dr Arbuthnot') for the emptiness of his early ones:

> Soft were my Numbers, who could take offence
> When pure description held the place of Sense?

Pope took the pastoral seriously enough to write a satire on his rival pastoralist Ambrose Philips, making fun of him for introducing wolves into the English landscape, and for making 'roses, lilies and daffodils blow in the same season', but his own efforts were little more than five-finger exercises. A more serious attempt to create landscape emerges in *Windsor Forest*, but even this is not strongly visualized, despite the fact that he knew and loved the forest, and spent many happy hours of his boyhood riding through it; his family lived at Binfield near Windsor, so the forest was familiar from his earliest years. He spent the exceptionally harsh winter of 1712 polishing and revising this poem: while his 'very imagination' was shivering with the cold, he attempted 'to raise up round about me a painted scene of woods and forests in verdure and beauty . . . while my trembling body is cowering o'er a fire, my mind is expatiating in an open sunshine'. Like a medieval poet, Pope still sees nature as 'a painted scene', and speaks in the poem of the enamelled ground, painted by blushing Flora. He nowhere approaches the organized views that James Thomson was to master, and the poem is strewn with gods and goddesses, with compliments to Queen Anne and an optimistic rhapsody on the signing of the Treaty of Utrecht. Yet there are acute observations, particularly of hunting scenes (Queen Anne was herself a keen follower of the chase). The pheasant who 'flutters in blood, and panting beats the ground' is seen with brilliant precision, as is this cold winter scene:

> With slaughtering guns the unwearied fowler roves,
> And frosts have whiten'd all the naked groves;
> Where doves in flocks the leafless trees o'ershade,
> And lonely woodcocks haunt the watery glade.
> He lifts the tube, and levels with his eye;
> Straight a short thunder breaks the frozen sky:
> Oft, as in airy rings they skim the heath,
> The clamorous lapwings feel the leaden death:
> Oft, as the mounting larks their notes prepare,
> They fall, and leave their little lives in air.

One looks, however, in vain for any vivid details about trees and glades, for any sense of the forest as a particular forest, different from all others.

We are offered bowery mazes, towering oaks, russet plains, fruitful fields, quivering shades and pathless groves, but nothing of the intense sense of place embodied in Hardy's *The Woodlanders*.

Pope pays his tribute to the smiling, prosperous Augustan world; he also shows appreciation of the Gothic mode, which was shortly to become so popular, and which his successor Walpole did much to cultivate. *Eloisa and Abelard* and *Elegy to the Memory of an Unfortunate Lady* have an impressive stock of moonlight shades, polished marbles, flower-strewn graves, beckoning ghosts, awful cells, grots and caverns, rugged rocks, and mouldering towers overgrown with pale ivy. Yet his real talent lay in other directions – in mockery, either affectionate or bitter. One of his finest landscapes, in the 'Epistle to Miss Blount, on her leaving the Town after the Coronation', is not a carefully composed landscape at all: it is an evocation of his friend Martha Blount's life at her neighbouring home, Mapledurham House, to which she is obliged to return from the excitements of town and the spectacle of the coronation of George I:

> She went to plain-work, and to purling brooks,
> Old-fashioned halls, dull aunts, and croaking rooks:
> She went from opera, park, assembly, play,
> To morning walks, and prayers three hours a day;
> To part her time 'twixt reading and bohea,
> To muse, and spill her solitary tea,
> Or o'er cold coffee trifle with the spoon,
> Count the slow clock, and dine exact at noon;
> Divert her eyes with pictures in the fire,
> Hum half a tune, tell stories to the 'squire;
> Up to her godly garret after seven,
> There starve and pray, for that's the way to Heaven.

In his *Epistle to Burlington, IV*, he writes directly of his interest in landscape gardening, expressing his philosophy in the famous lines beginning

> Consult the genius of the place in all:
> That tells the waters or to rise or fall;

Or helps the ambitious hill the heavens to scale,
Or scoops in circling theatres the vale;
Calls in the country, catches opening glades,
Joins willing woods, and varies shades from shades . . .

though one cannot fail to note that the helping hand being offered to nature must be a giant one. More successful as poetry rather than as theory is the derision poured on the son of Sabinus, for lopping his father's groves and turning his 'mournful family of yews' into ignoble broomsticks, and his description of Timon's villa mocks the geometric style with great verve:

The whole, a labour'd quarry above ground,
Two cupids squirt before: a lake behind
Improves the keenness of the northern wind.
His gardens next your admiration call,
On every side you look, behold the wall!
No pleasing intricacies intervene,
No artful wildness to perplex the scene:
Grove nods at grove, each alley has a brother,
And half the platform just reflects the other.
The suffering eye inverted Nature sees,
Trees cut to statues, statues thick as trees;
With here a fountain, never to be play'd;
And there a summer-house, that knows no shade:
Here Amphitrite sails through myrtle bowers;
There gladiators fight, or die in flowers;
Unwater'd see the drooping sea-horse mourn,
And swallows roost in Nilus' dusty urn.

Pope disliked Blenheim, Vanbrugh's great monument to the taste of the immediately preceding age, and described it in similar terms, as 'a great quarry of stones above ground'. He says, 'I never saw so great a thing with so much littleness in it . . . It is a house of entries and passages; among which there are three vistas through the whole, very uselessly handsome . . . In a word, the whole is a most expensive absurdity . . .'

Yet his own taste was hardly for nature unadorned, much as he warns us never to forget her. His famous garden at Twickenham, with its celebrated grotto, took years of planning, and he lured his friends thither with descriptions of 'enchanted bowers, silver streams, opening avenues, rising mounts and painted grottoes'. The grotto, herald of a new vogue, linked his house and his garden, passing under the main road; it sparkled with crystal, amethyst, angular pieces of looking-glass, Cornish diamonds and Brazilian pebbles, and opened in the garden on a view of a shell temple 'rough with shells, flints and iron-ore'. From the temple, Pope wrote, 'you look through a sloping arcade of trees, and see the sails on the river passing suddenly and vanishing, as through a perspective glass'. When the doors at the end of the grotto were closed, it became 'on the instant a camera obscura, on the walls of which all the objects of the river, hills, woods, and boats are forming a moving picture in their visible radiations'. It would be hard to imagine a more artful contrivance, and it is surely mere casuistry to argue that the shells and lumps of rock represented 'Nature's Primitive State', as described and advocated by Shaftesbury.

The debate on art and nature reached heights of comedy, as one of Pope's letters to his fellow gardening enthusiast Lord Bathurst displays. In a consultation about the designing of a princely garden, he writes (13 September 1739):

> Several Criticks were of several opinions: One declar'd he would not have too much Art in it; for my notion (said he) of gardening is, that it is only sweeping Nature: Another told them that gravel walks were not of a good taste, for all of the finest abroad were of a loose sand: A third advis'd peremptorily there should not be one Lyme-tree in the whole plantation; a fourth made the same exclusive clause extend to Horse-chestnuts, which he affirm'd not to be Trees, but Weeds; Dutch Elms were condemn'd by a fifth; and thus about half the trees were proscrib'd, contrary to the Paradise of God's own planting, which is expressly said to be planted with all trees. There were some who cou'd not bear Ever-greens, and call'd them Never-greens; some, who were angry at them only when cut into shapes, and gave the modern Gard'ners the name of Ever-green Taylors;

some who had no dislike to Cones and Cubes, but wou'd have 'em cut in Forest-trees; and some who were in a passion against anything in shape, even against clipt hedges, which they call'd green walls.

These disputes were to divert men of taste for the rest of the century, and to produce much harmless entertainment.

Pope himself, despite his leanings towards the Picturesque, was at heart on the side of daylight and common sense, even of utility: 'agreeable disorder', such as that produced by his neighbour Lord Burlington at Chiswick, was all very well, but it must not become true disorder, and Pope drew the line at preferring 'rocks and dirt to flowery meads and lovely Thames, and brimstone and fogs to roses and sunshine'. His attitude towards Bathurst's immense plans for Cirencester Park is characteristic: he teases Bathurst for his 'many Great and Noble works, worthy a large Mind and Fortune', such as 'enclosing a Province with Walls of Stone, Planting a whole Country with Clumps of Firs, digging Wells . . . erecting Palaces, raising Mounts, undermining Highways . . .', yet was full of admiration for Bathurst's mingling of art and utility in his vast programme of planting. Bathurst was enthusiastic about economically productive forestry, and followed the advice of Evelyn's *Sylva*, creating a great park with timber that is at its finest today: he planted for posterity, justifying Pope's claim that ''tis use alone that sanctifies expense'. In Pope's day, many of the glories of Cirencester were 'future and as yet visionary beauties'; but it still roused in him the most intense aesthetic appreciation: 'No words, nor painting, nor poetry can give the least image proportionate to the daily views of the noble scenes, openings and avenues of this immense design', he wrote to Lady Mary Wortley Montagu in September 1721. In this context, it is interesting and reassuring to note that most of the great parks were not in fact, as sometimes appeared, carved out of farmland, but located, as Hugh Prince points out, 'on poor, often excessively dry soils, on steep slopes or remote from existing settlements . . . The meagre results of the wartime plough-up campaign in the 1940s demonstrated the unsuitability of these lands for arable farming and indicated a probable reason why they were originally chosen for parks.' Art did not flourish wholly at the expense of food.

Pope's successor as arbiter of taste was Horace Walpole, whose theories of gardening and descriptions of parks and landscapes occupy a large place in any scholarly treatment of this subject. He had a strong feeling for the Gothic and the Picturesque; he made the Grand Tour with Thomas Gray in 1739, and responded enthusiastically to the Grande Chartreuse and the Alps, but on balance, unlike Gray, he seems to have shared Pope's preference for nature in a highly organized form. His is the famous sentence describing one of the most famous of all landscape gardeners – 'Kent first leaped the fence and saw all nature was a garden' – which in a sense is merely a variation of the old habit of comparing nature, favourably, to art: the Alps had naturally inspired him with thoughts of Salvator Rosa. Like Pope, he spent many happy years adorning his own home and garden; like Pope, he was interested in small playful pedantic points, and expresses his dislike of the temple at Pain's Hill in amusing terms: 'The whole is an unmeaning edifice. In all Gothic designs, they should be made something that was of that time, a part of a church, a castle, a convent or a mansion. The Goths never built summer-houses or temples in a garden.' Nor, one might point out, did the Goths build ruined chapels, or ruined castles such as the one built by Sanderson Miller at Hagley, which so enchanted Walpole.

Walpole's response to the great gardens and vistas of his age was, however, at times both broad and intense. His description of Hagley has already been quoted (p. 54), and even while he is complaining about the 'paltry Chinese buildings at Wroxton' he is able to enthuse about one of the adjacent views: 'This scene consists of a beautiful lake entirely shut in with wood: the head falls into a fine cascade, and that into a serpentine river, over which is a little Gothic seat like a round temple, lifted up by a shaggy mount' – a sentence containing in close proximity two of the key words of Picturesque vocabulary, 'serpentine' and 'shaggy'. He writes with rapture of the great gardens of Stourhead and Stowe and Rousham: Stourhead is 'one of the most picturesque scenes in the world', a view with Owhich our twentieth-century arbiter Nikolaus Pevsner seemed to agree: with unusual emotion, he wrote, 'In thinking back on the whole of the grounds of Stourhead, and especially the walk round the lake, the reader may agree with the writer that English picturesque landscaping of the

eighteenth century is the most beautiful form of gardening ever created...'
(*Wiltshire*, 1963).

Walpole's influence was, in his time, immense; his mixture of wit and sensibility capture the essence of his period, with its dilettante, aristocratic delight in a finely composed view. Luckily, some of the views that so delighted him remain, as living memorials to a time of intense interest in landscape as art, in garden architecture and landscape gardening. It was an age of taste, leisure and expense; although Victorian country houses were to dwarf many of their predecessors, principles and standards were largely lost in a confusion of eclecticism. The small circle of amateur connoisseurs was to lose its hold on the nation's imagination, and literary and artistic feeling for nature was to be utterly changed by the growing swell of the Romantic movement. Looking back at Pope, Walpole, Kent, Capability Brown, even Gray, one cannot help but be struck by their preference for the planned rather than the wild; what could be further from nature as Wordsworth was to see it than a view composed pictorially with the aid of a Claude glass, or a reflection of a river in a camera obscura in a grotto? This is nature not only arranged, but at second hand, through glass. Walpole summed up his own outlook in a letter written in old age to his cousin Thomas, in which he complains of a wet June:

> If I turn to the left, I see my hay yonder soaking under the rain; and on the right I have a good fire – 'tis pity we ever imported from the continent ideas of summer: nature gave us coal mines in lieu of it, and beautiful verdure, which is inconsistent with it, so that an observation I made forty years ago, is most true, that this country exhibits the most beautiful landscapes in the world when they are framed and glazed, that is, when you look at them through the window.

The emergence of the Romantic imagination from the Picturesque obsessions and formal language of the eighteenth century is one of the most fascinating topics in literary history. Are we to view Gray's poetry as the dawn of a new consciousness, or the fading twilight of an old? Was William Gilpin, Picturesque traveller, a precursor of Wordsworth and Coleridge, preparing minds and hearts and eyes, or did he represent attitudes that had to be ruthlessly swept away? Are the words 'Picturesque' and 'Romantic' synonyms, or do they represent a fundamental opposition?

Certainly an admiration for the sublimity of nature, so essential to the Romantic, was well in evidence before the birth of Wordsworth. Burke, in his essay 'On the Sublime and the Beautiful' published in 1756, newly defined the Sublime: the Sublime was obscure, vast, difficult, giving rise to feelings of 'delightful horror, a sort of tranquillity tinged with terror'. Stonehenge was sublime; so were mountains, vast cataracts, raging storms, night skies. Formal gardens were not sublime. Vastness was particularly significant, for 'hardly anything can strike the mind with its greatness which does not make some sort of approach towards infinity' (Wordsworth on the Alps was to echo this view). Order and precision were not sublime, for, says Burke rather boldly, 'A clear idea is another name for a little idea.' Walpole, writing in 1772 to George Selwyn, praises the sublimity of Castle Howard and its grounds in terms that recall Burke:

> Nobody had told me that I should at one view see a place, a town, a fortified city, temples on high places, woods worthy of being each a metropolis of the Druids, the noblest lawn in the world fenced by half the horizon, and a mausoleum that would tempt one to be buried alive; in short I have seen gigantic places before but never a sublime one.

If Castle Howard was an example of man-made sublimity, mountain scenery obviously qualified as the naturally sublime; a vogue for it set in during the mid-eighteenth century, and is still with us. Earlier travellers had regarded mountains as dangerous obstacles, aesthetically unpleasing: Defoe found the Lake District 'barren and frightful' compared with the pleasingly 'rich, populous and fruitful' Preston which he had just left, and Celia Fiennes, although favourably impressed by waterfalls, seems not to have known the word 'waterfall', that essential part of any descriptive writer's vocabulary. She writes, 'From these great fells there are several springs out of the rock that trickle down their sides, and as they meete with stones and rocks in the way when something obstructs their passage and so they come with more violence that gives a pleaseing sound and murmuring noise . . .' Elsewhere she uses the less euphonious word 'cataract'. Of Windermere and Ullswater she writes plainly, 'I observed the boundaries of all these great waters, which are a sort of deep lakes or kind of standing waters, are those sort of barren rocky hills which are so vastly high . . .' Not much poetic feeling to be detected here.

A similar lack of by then fashionable sensibility can be noted in Dr Johnson's *Journey to the Western Islands of Scotland.* He deplores the absence of 'vegetable decoration' (i.e. trees), and contents himself with describing the countryside round romantic Dunvegan Castle on Skye as 'rough and barren', observing that although the sea was rough, 'being broken by the multitude of islands, [it] does not roar with so much noise, nor beat the shore with such foamy violence as I have remarked on the coast of Sussex'. (Boswell admitted that the 'wild, hilly and craggy appearances, gave a rude magnificence to the scene', but even he contented himself with remarking that the castle was 'partly old and partly new' – Scott was to do better.) Of Loch Lomond he writes that, had it been in a happier climate,

> it would have been the boast of wealth and vanity to own one of the little spots which it encloses, and to have employed on it all the arts of embellishment. But as it is, the islets, which court the gazer at a distance, disgust him at his approach, when he finds, instead of soft lawns and shady thickets, nothing more than uncultivated ruggedness.

So much for nature in the raw, unadorned. When Boswell at Glenshiel described a mountain as immense, Johnson prosaically rejoined, 'No; it is no more than a considerable protuberance.'

Johnson himself summed up his attitude to landscape in his description of Glenshiel and its hills. He said:

> They exhibit very little variety; being almost wholly covered with dark heath, and even that seems to be checked in its growth. What is not heath is nakedness, a little diversified by now and then a stream

rushing down the steep. An eye accustomed to flowery pastures and waving harvests is astonished and repelled by this wide extent of hopeless sterility. The appearance is that of matter incapable of form or usefulness, dismissed by nature from her care and disinherited of her favours, left in its original elemental state, or quickened only with one sullen power of useless vegetation. It will very readily occur, that this uniformity of barrenness can afford very little amusement to the traveller; that it is easy to sit at home and conceive rocks and heath, and waterfalls; and that these journeys are useless labours, which neither impregnate the imagination, nor enlarge the understanding.

Nevertheless he goes on to refute this view, and his journey in itself refutes it. Indeed, it was in the next valley that he 'sat down on a bank, such as a writer of Romance might have delighted to feign' and planned to write his narration. His own imagination was impregnated, though he remarks that the thoughts 'excited by the view of an unknown and untravelled wilderness are not such as arise in the artificial solitude of parks and gardens . . . man is made unwillingly acquainted with his own weakness, and meditation shows him how little he can sustain, and how little he can perform'. If he had had more sense of the Picturesque, he would have studied the mountains for themselves: as it was, the barrenness of the high hills 'forced the mind to find entertainment for itself'. His pleasure lies in ascertaining the economy of the country, in talking to lords, old ladies, and fishermen; the Highland harvest song struck Wordsworth as 'a melancholy strain', but Johnson found it full of 'regularity and cheerfulness'. Ignoring the scenery, he comments with interest on the absence of hogs in the Hebrides, and of rats and mice in Skye – where, however, the weasel was so frequent 'that he is heard rattling behind chests or beds, as rats in England'.

Yet in a sense the whole expedition was deeply romantic. It was a brave enterprise for a man of sixty-three, in a country where roads and inns were poor or absent altogether. Johnson thought nothing of dossing down on a bundle of hay if nothing better offered, endured the rough crossings from island to island with fortitude, waded vigorously ashore to Iona and slept there in a barn with his clothes on. He earned the satisfaction with which he declared, as they sailed by moonlight between the black and gloomy rocks, 'If this be not *roving among the Hebrides*, nothing is.' One cannot help feeling that he must have been a pleasanter travelling companion than those who insisted on the delicacy of their own sensibility, and despised inferior manifestations of feeling when confronted by the beauties of nature. Mrs Thrale said he was 'an admirable companion on the road, as he picqued himself upon feeling no inconvenience, and on despising no accommodations'.

His attitude was certainly more robust than that of his contemporary, Thomas Gray. Gray was strongly attracted to mountain scenery; he wrote rapturously of the 'magnificent rudeness and steep precipices' of the Alps, which he saw on his Grand Tour in 1739; and after a tour of the Scottish Highlands in 1765 wrote to William Mason, 'A fig for your poets, painters, gardeners, and clergymen, that have not been among them: their imagination can be made up of nothing but bowling-greens, flowering shrubs, horse-ponds, Fleet ditches, shell grottoes, and Chinese rails.' His *Journal of the Lakes*, published in 1775, was widely read and admired, and much increased the influx of tourists into the area. Yet his descriptions reveal a sense of nervous apprehension which for him was perhaps part of the pleasure: it is not surprising to learn that contemporaries at Cambridge laughed at this timidity, his fastidiousness, his tea and apricot marmalade, his morbid fear of fire. His trembling before the wilder manifestations of nature beautifully bears out Burke's thesis that the Sublime is tinged with terror. After a description of a heavenly day in Borrowdale, and the magnificent heights of Wallow-crag, which he observed through his Claude glass, he passes by the waterfall of Lodore, 'foaming with fury', and thence to Gowdar-crag,

> a hill more formidable to the eye, and to the apprehension, than that
> of Lodore; the rocks at top deep-cloven perpendicularly by the rains,
> hanging loose and nodding forwards, seen just starting from their
> base in shivers. The whole way down, and the road on both sides is
> strewed with piles of the fragments, strangely thrown across each
> other, and of a dreadful bulk; the place reminds me of those passes

in the Alps, where the guides tell you to move with speed, and say nothing, lest the agitation of the air should loosen the snows above, and bring down a mass that would overwhelm a caravan. I took their counsel here, and hastened on in silence.

Gray seems to enjoy this sense of danger, unlike Cowper, who was even more morbid, and who disliked violent scenery because it disturbed him too much. Cowper wrote to the Rev. John Newton in 1792:

> The cultivated appearance of Weston (near Olney) suits my frame of mind far better than wild hills that aspire to be mountains, covered with vast unfrequented woods, and here and there affording a peep between their summits at the distant ocean. Within doors all was hospitality and kindness, but the scenery *would* have its effect; and though delightful in the extreme to those who had spirits to bear it, was too gloomy for me.

These wild hills, one might note, were in Sussex, not the Highlands of Scotland.

Gray's famous description of Gordale Scar at Malham in Yorkshire is perhaps one of the most complete illustrations of the literary concept of the Sublime. Gordale Scar is a famous beauty spot, and has been much painted by a succession of artists, from Smith of Derby in the mid-eighteenth century to Thomas Girtin, James Ward, Turner and John William Inchbold in the nineteenth, and John Piper in the twentieth. Sir George Beaumont, Wordsworth's friend and connoisseur of the Picturesque, thought the scene 'beyond the range of art', but this proved no deterrent: Gray writes:

> On the cliffs above hung a few goats: one of them danced and scratched an ear with its hind foot in a place where I would not have stood stockstill 'for all beneath the moon' and as I advanced the crags seemed to close in, but discovered a narrow entrance turning to the left between them. I followed my guide a few paces, and lo, the hills opened again into no large space, and then all

farther away is barred by a stream, that at a height of about fifty feet gushes from a hole in the rock, and spreading in large sheets over its black front dashes from steep to steep, and then rattles away in a torrent down the valley . . . it is to the right, under which you stand to see the fall, that forms the principal horror of the place . . . one black and solid mass . . . overshadows half the area below with its dreadful canopy . . . the drops which perpetually distil its brow, fell on my head . . . there are loose stones which hang in air, and threaten visibly . . . I stayed there (not without shuddering) a full quarter of an hour, and thought my trouble richly paid for the impression will last for life.

This passage, coupled with Ward's painting in the Tate Gallery, inspired me to visit Gordale, and the experience was interesting: the Scar is less frightening than Gray and Ward make it appear, but it is also more beautiful. Of course, Gray saw it on a 'gloomy uncomfortable day', and I have seen it only in good weather; nevertheless, it appeared at once less vast and savage, and more deserving of attention. It also struck me that any post-Freudian would of necessity see this landscape in terms of sexual imagery – the hollow cavern, the gushing water, the secrecy of the approach, the tufted trees – and would remark how notably this vocabulary is missing from Gray and Gilpin, though it is present enough in Milton, whose references to the womb of waters, to genial moisture, to heaving mountains, laps and entrails and bosoms, to shaggy hills and bushes with frizzled hair and hills with 'hairie sides', make the creation of the world sound a thoroughly sexual process: he sees the world as a living being, conceived, gestated, born, passing through unadorned childhood to the springing tender grass of puberty. This organic vision was lost for a century and a half after Milton: it was deeply inaccessible to Gray and his contemporaries. (I described the Scar in the most 'romantic' of my novels, *The Waterfall*, of 1969, where it has a deeply sexual connotation.)

Gray's poetry has elements both of the Picturesque and of the Sublime. His Pindaric ode, 'The Bard', certainly possessed the sublime quality of obscurity recommended by Burke: the poet condemned by Edward I stands on a rock overlooking Conway's foaming flood and prophesies disaster:

Cold is Cadwallo's tongue,
That hush'd the stormy main:
Brave Uriel sleeps upon his craggy bed:
Mountains, ye mourn in vain
Modred, whose magic song
Made huge Plinlimmon bow his cloud-top'd head.
On dreary Arvon's shore they lie,
Smear'd with gore, and ghastly pale:
Far, far aloof th'affrighted ravens fail;
The famish'd eagle screams, and passes by.
Dear lost companions of my tuneful art,
Dear, as the light that visits these sad eyes,
Dear, as the ruddy drops that warm my heart,
Ye died amidst your dying country's cries –
No more I weep. They do not sleep.
On yonder cliff, a griesly band,
I see them sit, they linger yet,
Avengers of their native land . . .

Gray had never seen the Welsh landscape he here invokes, but he knew the ingredients of sublimity, and in another ode, 'The Fatal Sisters', based on an eleventh-century Icelandic poem, he confirms the view that the Celtic outposts of Britain were more sublime than England itself. The famous 'Elegy', with its lowing herds winding slowly o'er the lea, its rugged elms and yew trees, and its nodding beech with old fantastic roots, is in contrast distinctly picturesque, and manifests in fully developed form the love of melancholy landscape and graveyards that so many poets were to imitate. It unites the picturesque elements more thoughtfully and gracefully than many writers were able to do; like the pastoral, the Picturesque became a five-finger exercise. There is something faintly ridiculous in Gilpin's pedantic definitions of what may or may not be admired in nature; his feeling for the ruins of Tintern is genuine enough, but who needs to be told that mountains 'rising in regular, mathematical lines, or in whimsical, grotesque shapes are displeasing', or that we should find the lines of Saddleback 'disagreeable'? Or that peasants are picturesque but not artisans?

Compared with Walpole and Pope, Gilpin's strictures are earnest and humourless, and it is not surprising that the vogue for the Picturesque, with its rules and demands on the sensibility, should produce a reaction in comedy and satire. Whether or not Gilpin and Gray, Knight and Uvedale Price contributed to the Romantic movement with their fiercely held theories, they certainly provided the background for many of Jane Austen's conflicts of feeling, and the juxtaposition of the words 'sense' and 'sensibility' suggests a central theme in her work.

By Jane Austen's day, the picturesque attitude to landscape had become so fashionable that it was impossible for a writer to avoid it. Austen was thoroughly familiar with its rules, and so were her heroines, but she herself, with her keen sense of the ridiculous, takes a characteristically detached and ironic view of the movement's excesses. Marianne, in *Sense and Sensibility*, is her most enthusiastic admirer of the Picturesque, and her impressionable nature leads her into much suffering: Austen criticizes the uncontrolled, self-willed nature of Marianne's feelings for both people and places, and even Marianne herself, who is ready to weep over a fallen avenue, is able to admit that 'the admiration of landscape scenery is become a mere jargon'. Edward Ferrars, discussing landscape with Marianne, tells her:

> You must not inquire too far, Marianne – remember, I have no knowledge of the picturesque, and I shall offend you with my ignorance and want of taste . . . I shall call hills steep, which ought to be bold; surfaces strange and uncouth, which ought to be irregular and rugged; and distant objects out of sight, which ought only to be indistinct through the soft medium of hazy atmosphere . . . You must be satisfied with such admiration as I can honestly give. I call it a very fine country – the hills are steep, the woods seem full of fine timber, and the valley looks comfortable and snug – with rich meadows and several neat farmhouses . . . It exactly answers my idea of a fine country, because it unites beauty with utility . . .

He goes on, in a manner that beautifully illustrates the mixed influences of Pope and Thomson, Walpole and Gilpin,

I like a fine prospect, but not on picturesque principles. I do not like crooked, twisted, blasted trees. I admire them much more if they are tall, straight and flourishing . . . I do not like ruined, tattered cottages. I am not fond of nettles, or thistles, or heath blossoms. I have more pleasure in a snug farmhouse than a watchtower – and a troop of tidy, happy villagers please me better than the finest banditti in the world.

Despite his disclaimers, Edward shows himself very much the master of picturesque theory. Jane Austen herself admired Gilpin, and in *Northanger Abbey* Henry Tilney, by no means a foolish character, is allowed to educate the innocent Catherine in terms that suggest she really has something to learn:

It seemed as if a good view were no longer to be taken from the top of an high hill, and that a clear blue sky was no longer proof of a fine day . . . He talked of foregrounds, distances and second distances; sidescreens and perspectives; lights and shades; and Catherine was so hopeful a scholar, that when they gained the top of Beechen Cliff, she voluntarily rejected the whole city of Bath, as unworthy to make part of a landscape.

Catherine may be rushing into Marianne's excesses here, but this does not imply that Tilney's views are exaggerated or uninteresting. Fanny, in *Mansfield Park*, is full of sensibility, moved by a starlit night, grieving over the improvements threatened to Mr Rushworth's estate of Sotherton, quoting Cowper's much-quoted lines, 'Ye fallen avenues, once more I mourn your fate unmerited.' Anne in *Persuasion* is a heroine permitted to unite sense and sensibility in equal parts, and while her conduct is always impeccably restrained, she can feel deeply for the beauties of nature. They are perhaps a poor substitute for human attention and love, but maybe Jane Austen herself might have concurred in these feelings, aroused by an autumn walk:

Anne's object was, not to be in the way of anybody . . . Her pleasure in the walk must arise from the exercise and the day, from the view of the last smiles of the year upon the tawny leaves and withered hedges, and from repeating to herself some few of the thousand poetical descriptions extant of autumn, that season of peculiar and inexhaustible influence on the mind of taste and tenderness, that season which has drawn from every poet, worthy of being read, some attempt at description, or some lines of feeling . . .

As the walk continues, the party passes on to agricultural land, and 'the sweets of poetical despondence' are counteracted by the sight of ploughs at work and fresh-made paths.

Jane Austen demonstrates here that she is as much aware as anybody of the emotional and literary attractions of landscape; also, that she was very much influenced by current attitudes. An admiration for autumn tints is part of the picturesque movement's permanent contribution to our way of seeing; it is now commonplace to express pleasure in the changing colours of trees and foliage, but in the early eighteenth century this was not so – Pope would go so far only as to say, 'The very dying leaves add a variety of colours that is not unpleasant', and Thomson in his 'Autumn', despite his love of colour, makes little use of it, referring to foliage as 'dusk and dun'. Gilpin, Price and Knight had changed all that, by Jane Austen's day; Price considered autumn the 'painter's season', and claimed that the colouring of the Venetian painters, particularly Giorgione and Titian, was founded principally on autumn tints. Sir George Beaumont considered that there should be one brown tree in every landscape; Kent had planted dead ones in Kensington Gardens; Gilpin in his *Remarks on Forest Scenery (Relating Chiefly to Picturesque Beauty)* of 1791 instructs the reader in appreciation of the blasted tree. While some still find a dead tree too bleak an object to arouse much pleasure, few dislike the reds and golds and browns of autumn. Marianne's sister recalls the former world when she says to Marianne, 'It is not everyone who has your passion for dead leaves': Anne belongs firmly to our own. Hopkins's famous autumn poem, 'Spring and Fall', unites the two: Margaret, as might Fanny and Marianne, grieves for the death of nature, but her grief overwhelms any sense of beauty in the event, and all that Hopkins can promise her is a different kind of sorrow.

Margaret, are you grieving
Over Goldengrove unleaving?
Leaves, like the things of man, you
With your fresh thoughts care for, can you?
Ah! as the heart grows older
It will come to such sights colder
By and by, nor spare a sigh
Though worlds of wanwood leafmeal lie;
And yet you will weep, and know why . . .

Such lines Anne Elliot might well have repeated to herself, could she have known them, to console herself for the lack of Captain Wentworth's conversation.

Elizabeth Bennet in *Pride and Prejudice* makes fun of the vogue for picturesque travel in her acceptance of her aunt's proposal to visit the Lakes. 'My dear, dear aunt,' she rapturously cried,

what delight, what felicity! You give me fresh life and vigour. Adieu to disappointment and spleen. What are men to rocks and mountains? Oh, what hours of transport we shall spend! And when we do return, it shall not be like other travellers, without being able to give one accurate idea of anything. We *will* know where we have gone — we *will* recollect what we have seen. Lakes, mountains, and rivers shall not be jumbled together in our imaginations; nor, when we attempt to describe any particular scene, will we begin quarrelling over its relative situation . . .

How well this evokes a previous generation's equivalent of family disputes accompanying the holiday slide show! In the event, Elizabeth went not to the Lakes but to Pemberley, where her sensitive appreciation shows her a worthy prospective mistress: 'She had never seen a place for which nature had done more, or where natural beauty had been so little counteracted by an awkward taste.' The description of the house and its prospects, of the ridge of high woody hills behind, the bridge, the river, the winding valley, the scattered trees, the hanging wood — all show how carefully author and heroine had read and absorbed their Gilpin. In fact, despite her mockery, Jane Austen proves herself the perfect student; her landscapes rarely stir the imagination, as do Wordsworth's or Emily Brontë's, but they are in a true sense picturesque – that is, they are composed as for a picture, with the appropriate ingredients, arranged in an appropriate order. In Chapter 11 of *Persuasion* she describes Lyme, its Cobb and its neighbourhood in considerable detail:

> as there is nothing to admire in the buildings themselves, the remarkable situation of the town, the principal street almost hurrying into the water, the walk to the Cobb, skirting round the pleasant little bay, which in the season is animated with bathing machines and company, the Cobb itself, its old wonders and new improvements, with the very beautiful line of cliffs stretching out to the east of the town, are what the stranger's eye will seek; and a very strange stranger it must be, who does not see charms in the immediate environs of Lyme, to make him wish to know it better. The scenes in its neighbourhood, Charmouth, with its high grounds and extensive sweeps of country, and still more its sweet retired bay, backed by dark cliffs, where fragments of low rock among the sands make it the happiest spot for watching the flow of the tide, for sitting in unwearied contemplation; – the woody varieties of the cheerful village of Up Lyme, and, above all, Pinny, with its green chasms between romantic rocks, where the scattered forest trees and orchards of luxuriant growth declare that many a generation must have passed away since the first partial falling of the cliff prepared the ground for such a state, where a scene so wonderful and so lovely is exhibited, as may more than equal any of the resembling scenes of the far-famed Isle of Wight: these places must be visited, and visited again, to make the worth of Lyme understood.

We have Lyme here, as in a series of engravings – yet it is not her descriptive powers that have drawn thousands of tourists to the spot where Louisa Musgrove fell. The setting, in Jane Austen, is merely the setting: it is the human drama that counts, and it is not surprising to find her writing a letter to her sister while writing *Mansfield Park*, enquiring, 'If you could discover whether Northamptonshire is a country of Hedgerows I should be glad again.' She wishes to be accurate, but her accuracy is somewhat technical: Mansfield Park could find itself in any number of counties without losing any of its significance, whereas George Eliot's Middlemarch, and Elizabeth Gaskell's Cranford, and Charlotte Brontë's Briarfield in *Shirley* are all precisely located in a known landscape, and are all influenced by a more Romantic and simultaneously more realistic conception of nature and place. In some curious way, the picturesque movement, with its emphasis on sensibility and emotional response, remained oddly academic and dry: nature is not art, and to describe it in terms of art is unsatisfactory, however satisfactory the paintings to which the writers refer may be. The double filter of paintings and words distorts the reality. It was the Romantic movement that taught writers to forget Claude, Poussin and Salvator Rosa when looking at an English valley or a Welsh mountain: Jane Austen, for all her disavowal of Rosa's banditti, was too well instructed to ignore them.

The habit of viewing landscape as art did not disappear with the popularity of the Picturesque movement. Certain landscapes, particularly man-made ones, are hard to see in any other way. Oxford, Bath, Brighton, Bristol – what are they but composite artefacts? And certain writers have a pronounced tendency to see landscape pictorially, to interpret it in terms of artistic associations. Even Hardy, who of all writers used his own eyes, cannot resist references to Correggio and Dürer, Ruysdael and Hobbema, Turner and Wouvermans. *Under the Greenwood Tree* was subtitled 'A Rural Painting of the Dutch School', and Hardy clearly took to heart early reviews of his first published novel, *Desperate Remedies*, which made favourable comparisons with the paintings of Wilkie and Teniers. But perhaps the most evocative of what one might call the neo-picturesque writers is Henry James, whose *English Hours* has proved an irresistible source of quotations, whose novels and stories show that keen perception of the essentially English nature of the English countryside and its towns and buildings which newcomers so often possess.

Like so many Americans, James came to England with his imagination already alight with artistic and literary allusions, and he spent his life checking the reality against the image. The result is one of the richest pictures of English life in the language. His characters are often, like himself, newcomers: the narrator in *A Passionate Pilgrim*, one of his own favourites amongst his early stories, responds with an aching awareness to Hampton Court, to the 'dark, rich flats of hedgy Worcestershire and the copse-checkered slopes of rolling Hereford, white with the blossom of apples', to the ineffable English light, to Oxford, 'one of the supreme gratifications of travel, the perfect prose of Gothic'. At Hampton Court, the visitor wanders round the multitudinous rooms of the palace, round the 'antique geometry' of the gardens, and, while strolling along the great avenue of horse-chestnuts, feels the

> rare emotion, familiar to every intelligent traveller, in which the mind, with a great passionate throb, achieves a magical synthesis of its impressions . . . Over against us, amid the deep-hued bloom of its ordered gardens, the dark-red palace, with its formal copings and its vacant windows, seemed to tell of a proud and splendid past; the little village nestling between park and palace, around a patch of turfy common, with its tavern of gentility, its ivy-towered church, its parsonage, retained to my modernized fancy the lurking semblance of a feudal hamlet. It was in this dark composite light that I had read all English prose; it was this mild moist air that had blown from the verses of English poets; beneath these broad acres of rain-deepened greenness a thousand honoured dead lay buried.

Who ever responded to the Picturesque with more feeling? It is difficult to limit one's quotations. The American pilgrims are stirred by Oxford to emotions 'too large and various to be compassed by words'. The town itself, with its arching portals, its sacred and sunless courts, its slender shaftings and misty towers, fills them with rapture, as does the surrounding countryside, so dear to Matthew Arnold – 'the sweetest, flattest, reediest streamside landscape that the heart need demand'. But it is in the garden of St John's College, appropriately landscaped by Capability Brown, that the narrator's dying companion chooses to make his last lament, to take his last farewell. The college gardens seemed to us the fairest things in England and the ripest and sweetest fruits of the English system. Locked in their antique verdure, guarded (as in the case of New College) by gentle battlements of silver-grey, outshouldering the matted leafage of centenary vines, filled with perfumes and privacy and memories, with students lying bookishly on the turf . . . they seem places to lie down on the grass in forever, in the happy faith that life is all a vast old English garden, and time an endless English afternoon.

Henry James is also the great poet of English country house life, that peculiar English art form: 'the great invention' of the English, as he described it. Isobel Archer, in *Portrait of a Lady*, is in a sense James himself, wooed by England, wooed by antiquity. When she first sees Lord Warburton's house, a

stout, grey pile, of the softest, deepest, most weather-fretted hue, rising from a broad, still moat, it seemed to Isobel like a castle in a fairy-tale. The day was cool and rather lustreless; the first note of autumn had been struck; and the watery sunshine rested on the walls in blurred and desultory gleams, washing them, as it were, in places tenderly chosen, where the ache of antiquity is keenest.

One of Isobel's problems, in fact, is that she cannot believe Lord Warburton and his offer of marriage to be real, to be part of real, everyday life: 'You think us picturesque', he objects to her at one point, with some pain. And so she does; when he proposes, she cannot get away from the picture in her own mind, of 'the park of an old English country house, with the foreground embellished by a local nobleman in the act of making love to a young lady'. So she refuses him, not wishing to have her life dominated by the Picturesque and by the past.

Like Trollope, James admires the inimitable, unpurchasable gleam of time, and he deepens and intensifies Trollope's vision: his description of Mr Longdon's home in *The Awkward Age* surely owes much to Trollope's literary perceptions. It is old, square, red-roofed, well assured of its right to the place it took up in the world, and it has everything mixed with it, in the form of old windows and doors, the tone of old red surfaces, the style of old white facings, the age of old high creepers, the long confirmation of time. Suggestive of panelled rooms, of precious mahogany, of portraits of women dead, of coloured china glimmering through glass doors, and delicate silver reflected on bared tables, the thing was one of those impressions of a particular period that it takes two centuries to produce.

And, says James,

> the final touch in all the picture before them was just the painter's ignorance. Mr Longdon had not made his house, he had simply lived it, and the 'taste' of the place . . . was nothing more than the beauty of his life. Everything, on every side, had dropped straight from heaven, with nowhere a bargaining thumb-mark, a single sign of the shop.

James himself, unlike Mr Longdon, is certainly not an ignorant painter, nor are all his characters as innocent in their creations as Mr Longdon. In *The Spoils of Poynton* he describes the dangers of discrimination. Mrs Gereth lives for her house and above all for her possessions, and Poynton, 'an exquisite old house itself, early Jacobean, supreme in every part', is 'a provocation, an inspiration, a matchless canvas for the picture'. Des-criptions of the contents of this house – Louis Quinze brasses, Venetian velvets, rare French furniture and Oriental china, not to mention the gem of the collection, the famous Maltese cross – give rise to the suspicion that her much lauded taste might have been not far removed from ordinary Victorian eclecticism: Poynton, perhaps, was a Mentmore in miniature. Certainly, we are not intended wholly to admire Mrs Gereth's collection, or her attitude to it – if the two are separable, a point on which James himself seems undecided. One of his major themes is the conflict between the moral and the aesthetic impulses, and it is not for nothing that his connoisseurs are often portrayed as heartless and selfish. Art is not life, and it is wrong to prefer art to life – this is the message, yet James is himself such an aesthete, his own responses so finely tuned, that the message becomes desperately intricate, feverishly ambiguous. How can the aesthete ever credit the artistically insensitive with a truly good heart? Is not the choice of a bad wallpaper a sin of moral obtuseness? Mrs Gereth and her protégée Fleda Vetch are tormented by the 'aesthetic misery' of the big Victorian house at which they find themselves guests in the first chapter of the novel. Mrs Gereth is convinced that 'the flowers at Waterbath would probably go wrong in colour and the nightingales sing out of tune', and as if to vindicate her view, the healthy, bouncing, bossy daughter of Waterbath proves as stubborn and acquisitive as her mother-in-law, although she entirely lacks her 'taste'. Those with good eyes may have bad hearts, but James finds it hard to imagine that those with bad eyes may have good hearts – they may be childishly innocent perhaps, but not truly good. Hence his satisfaction at the moral goodness of Mr Longdon's home. Mitchy's in the same novel is beautiful enough, with its peacocks and parapets, its scattered trees and green glades, its high walls of plums and nectarines – but it is tainted by the temporary newness of acquisition, by the machinations of his far from beautiful guests. One cannot purchase real beauty, as Mitchy, himself a discriminating man, admits.

James acquainted himself with country house life at the homes of various friends – with Charles Milnes Gaskell at Wenlock Abbey, with the Carters near Kenilworth, who offered him a fine prospect of Kenilworth Castle, with Lord Houghton at Fryston Hall, Yorkshire, with the Roseberys at Mentmore, with Lady Portsmouth at Eggesford Manor, which he found very dull. As a guest, his role was not unlike that of the poet James Thomson, repaying hospitality by discriminating appreciation and description. As a host, however, the boot was on the other foot – what should a visitor expect of so stringent a critic, in his own home? James seems to have taken an easy way out, in renting Lamb House at Rye, a readymade English treasure, with its high old brick wall, its paved courtyard, its ancient mulberry tree. Unlike his predecessors, Pope and Walpole, he did not try to create his own version of the Picturesque, and was so ignorant of gardening, landscape or otherwise, that he had to rely on a Miss Muir Mackenzie for advice about where to tell his gardener to plant crocuses, tobacco plants, fuchsias, geraniums. He seems to have lived modestly; he avoided the horrors of vulgar ostentation by an affectation of 'severe plainness', which he excused on the grounds of economy. Edith Wharton, a highly observant and discriminating visitor, said that he would apologize (unnecessarily, she adds) for the meagreness of his luncheons, and that he 'lived in terror of being thought rich, worldly or luxurious'. Self-appointed arbiters of taste cannot afford to let their standards lapse below those that they recommend for others, and Lamb House is certainly no disappointment – unlike Thomas Hardy's Max Gate, which is an almost perfect negation of the ideal country home, being ugly, uncomfortable, and in Hardy's day administered with a meanness and meagreness for which apologies were by some accounts all too necessary.

Like Henry James, Virginia Woolf was also deeply moved by the image and mystique of the great country house. When she fell in love with Vita Sackville-West, she fell in love with Knole, with all the Sackvilles, with a life style and a history, as she readily admits. In *Orlando* she indulges this passion, delighting in ancient literary associations, in the privilege of her friendship with Vita, in the beauty of the house and the park, which she describes thus in the second chapter:

> He opened his eyes, which had been wide open all the time, but had seen only thoughts, and saw, lying in the hollow beneath him, his house.
>
> There it lay in the early sunshine of spring. It looked a town rather than a house, but a town built, not hither and thither, as this man wished or that, but circumspectly, by a single architect with one idea in his head. Courts and buildings, grey, red, plum colour, lay orderly and symmetrical; the courts were some of them oblong and some square; in this was a fountain; in that a statue; the buildings were some of them low, some pointed; here was a chapel, there a belfry; spaces of the greenest grass lay in between and clumps of cedar trees and beds of bright flowers; all were clasped – yet so well set out was it that it seemed that every part had room to spread itself fittingly – by the roll of a massive wall; while smoke from innumerable chimneys circled perpetually into the air. This vast, yet ordered

building, which could house a thousand men and perhaps two thousand horses, was built, Orlando thought, by workmen whose names are unknown. Here have lived, for more centuries than I can count, the obscure generations of my own obscure family. Not one of these Richards, Johns, Annes, Elizabeths has left a token of himself behind him, yet all, working together with their spades and their needles, their love-making and their child-bearing, have left this.

Never had the house looked more noble and humane . . .

Why, then, had he wished to raise himself above them? For it seemed vain and arrogant in the extreme to try to better that anonymous work of creation; the labours of those vanished hands. Better was it to go unknown and leave behind you an arch, a potting shed, a wall where peaches ripen, than to burn like a meteor and leave no dust. For after all, he said, kindling as he looked at the great house on the greensward below, the unknown lords and ladies who lived there never forgot to set aside something for those who come after; for the roof that will leak; for the tree that will fall. There was always a warm corner for the old shepherd in the kitchen; always food for the hungry; always their goblets were polished, though they lay sick; and their windows were lit though they lay dying. Lords though they were, they were content to go down into obscurity with the mole-catcher and the stone-mason.

The terms of her praise take us, deliberately, back to Ben Jonson on Penshurst, to Carew on Saxham, to Marvell on Appleton – to the great days of patronage, to the days when riches spilled from the cornucopia to the poor shepherd and the poet alike. English history lived in Knole, for Virginia Woolf, and it is not surprising that she rejoiced in a first-hand sense of it. *Orlando* was published in 1928: six years earlier Vita Sackville-West had written *Knole and the Sackvilles*, at the beginning of which she makes the glorious and proud disclaimer, 'I have no erudition, I have only personal familiarity.' Like Woolf, she seizes on the Englishness of Knole:

From the top of a tower one looks down upon the acreage of roofs, and the effect is less that of a palace than of a jumbled village upon the hillside. It is not an incongruity like Blenheim or Chatsworth, foreign to the spirit of England. It is, rather, the greater relation of those small manor houses which hide themselves so innumerably away among the counties . . . The great Palladian houses of the eighteenth century are in England, they are not of England, as are these irregular roofs, this easy straying up the contours of the hill, these cool coloured walks, these calm gables, and dark windows mirroring the sun.

'*Irregular*' – how often that word, a key word of picturesque appreciation, has been echoed in these descriptions. Irregularity, to the English eye, seems to be a key, a touchstone, a mystic pledge of some indefinable authenticity, and an accumulation of architectural styles seems equally to represent, to Trollope, to James, to Virginia Woolf and Vita Sackville-West, the assimilating, slow, evolutionary, non-revolutionary genius of the English people.

Vita Sackville-West and her husband Harold Nicolson were in fact to create at Sissinghurst one of the most celebrated of contemporary English gardens: influenced by Lawrence Johnston's astonishingly beautiful masterpiece at Hidcote Bartrim, they restored a derelict wilderness to its present state, with its Tower Lawn, its Yew Walk, Rose Garden and Cottage Garden – and what could be more literary, more artistic than their conception of a White Garden, carefully planted with white flowers and silvery foliage?

The other house which featured largely in Virginia Woolf's life, and the life of many other writers of the time, was Garsington, where Ottoline Morrell held court and was abused for her generosity. Phillip and Ottoline Morrell bought the house in 1913, though they did not move into it until 1915, when it quickly became a refuge for conscientious objectors. Ottoline's account of the purchase is revealing; she had fallen in love with the house for the sake of its appearance, and bought it when its inhabitant, an old farmer of ninety, fell dead on his horse in the stable. She said that the fact that Phillip's father owned a good deal of property in the village made the choice seem not 'unreasonable', a curious but familiar kind of rationalization of such a purchase, when the reasons of ancient heritage are lacking.

She is eager not to appear an interloper, a destroyer of the old order. She clearly saw herself as a hostess of cultural significance, bringing together the writers, artists and thinkers of her day – Yeats, Bertrand Russell, Lytton Strachey, the Woolfs, T. S. Eliot, Aldous Huxley, D. H. Lawrence, amongst many others all accepted her hospitality. Uncreative herself, she saw her way of life as an art form, and Garsington was a perfect setting.

Its reflection in literature has been varied. Aldous Huxley was a regular visitor, and his portrait in *Crome Yellow* is mocking but friendly. D. H. Lawrence's portrayal of her as Hermione Roddice in *Women in Love* caused her great offence, not surprisingly, though the evocation of life at Breadalby with luncheon under the cedar tree is not without its attractions, and Ursula and Gudrun admit that the food is good, which is kind of them and their creator. Lawrence transfers Garsington to Derbyshire and turns it into a Georgian house with Corinthian pillars. Even he is irresistibly drawn towards the Picturesque when describing so English a scene in Chapter 8:

> The summer was just coming in when Ursula and Gudrun went to stay the second time with Hermione. Coming along in the car, after they entered the park, they looked across the dip, where the fish ponds lay in silence, at the pillared front of the house, sunny and small like an English drawing of the old school, on the brown of the green hill, against the trees. There were small figures on the green lawn, women in lavender and yellow moving to the shade of the enormous, beautifully balanced cedar tree.
> 'Isn't it complete!' said Gudrun. 'It is as final as an old aquatint.' She spoke with some resentment in her voice, as if she were captivated unwillingly, as if she must admire against her will.

Lawrence's fullest evocation of Garsington as itself, however, is in a long letter written to Ottoline on 1 December 1915. It is a strange kind of prose poem, containing passages like these, and many more:

> Shafted, looped windows, between the without and the within, the old house, the perfect old intervention of fitted stone, fitted perfectly about a silent soul . . . The wet lawn drizzled with brown

sodden leaves; the feathery heap of the ilex tree; the garden-seat all wet and reminiscent . . . the stone, old three-pointed house with its raised chimney stacks, the old manor lifting its fair, pure stone amid trees and foliage, rising from the lawn, we pass the pond where white ducks hastily launch upon the lustrous dark grey waters . . . It is the vision of a drowning man, the vision of all that I am, all I have become and ceased to be. It is me, generations and generations of me, every complex gleaming fibre of me. Every lucid pang of my coming into being . . .

Not perhaps the ideally docile guest, but not a wholly unappreciative one, either. Virginia Woolf's response was equally mixed. In letters to Ottoline, she describes Garsington as perfect, a work of art, but in letters to others she is less civil: Ottoline, she writes to Barbara Bagenal (24 June 1923), has 'a drawl and crawl and smell which might be harmless in the stir of normal sunlight. Only is the sun ever harmless at Garsington? No, I think even the sky is done up in pale yellow silk, and certainly the cabbages are scented . . .'

Turning landscape into art has been, as we have seen, largely an expensive and aristocratic occupation. Gardening on a more modest scale has left fewer lasting marks, fewer records, and we have little means of knowing what the cottage garden of earlier centuries looked like. Elizabeth Gaskell, in *Sylvia's Lovers*, says that in the late eighteenth century

Gardening was not a popular art in any part of England; in the north it is not yet. Noblemen and gentlemen may have beautiful gardens; but farmers and day-labourers care little for them north of the Trent, which is all I can answer for. A few 'berry' bushes, a blackcurrant tree or two (the leaves to be used in heightening the flavour of tea, the fruit as medicinal for colds and sore throats); a potato ground (and this was not so common at the close of the last century as it is now), a cabbage bed, a bush of sage, and balm, and thyme, and marjoram, with possibly a rose-tree and 'old man' growing in the midst; a little plot of small strong coarse onions, and perhaps some marigolds, the petals of which flavoured the salt-beef broth: such plants made up a well-furnished garden to a farm-house at the time and place to which my story belongs.

This a tantalizing glimpse into the past, but it is only a glimpse. The frequent references to flowers and their common names in Shakespeare would indicate that farmers and day-labourers were far from indifferent to gardening, and that the British love of possessing and cultivating their own little plots was deeply rooted. The garden city is a characteristically English dream: a plot of land is good for the soul.

There are some small gardens that have achieved lasting literary fame, and one of these is Mary Russell Mitford's at Three Mile Cross in Berkshire. Mitford was the daughter of a doctor who was both improvident and a quack, and she wrote to repay his debts and to earn her own living, producing a minor classic, *Our Village*, which is full of deliberately picturesque descriptions of village life and country scenery. She also gardened, with the help of a young man called Ben, and *Our Village* and her letters are full of her enthusiasm, an enthusiasm shared by many men and women living in modest circumstances today – for gardening remains one of the less expensive pastimes, as well as one of the most rewarding. Unlike the gardeners of the landscape school, she did not despise flowers as a source of aesthetic pleasure, and many a bloom was named after her, 'it being a pretty proof of the way in which gardeners estimate my love of flowers, that they are constantly calling plants after me, and sending me one of the first cuttings as presents. There is a dahlia now selling at ten guineas a root under my name . . .' (Perhaps not too inexpensive a pursuit, after all, for the purchaser, and in a later letter she boasts of selling one of her own seedlings for twenty pounds, again a dahlia – 'white, of the most exquisite shape and cleanness, tipped with puce colour'.)

In a letter to one of her most loved correspondents, Elizabeth Barrett Browning, she says that she is sending flowers, and exclaims,

> Oh, how I wish we could transport you to the garden where they grow! . . . On one side (it is nearly an acre of show flowers) a high hedge of hawthorn, with giant trees rising above it beyond the hedge, while all down within the garden are clumps of matchless

hollyhocks and splendid dahlias; the top of the garden being shut in by the old irregular cottage, with its dark brick-work covered with vines and roses, and its picturesque chimneys mingling with the bay tree, again rising into its bright and shining cone, and two old pear trees festooned with honeysuckle; the bottom of the garden and the remaining side consisting of lower hedgerows melting into wooded uplands, dotted with white cottages and patches of common. Nothing can well be imagined more beautiful than this little bit of ground is now. Huge masses of lupins (say fifty or sixty spiral spikes), some white, some lilac; immense clumps of the enamelled Siberian larkspur, glittering like some enormous Chinese jar; the white and azure blossoms of the variegated monkshood; flags of all colours; roses of every shade, some covering the house and stables and overtopping the roofs, others mingling with tall apple trees, others again (especially the beautiful double Scotch rose) low but broad, standing in bright relief to the blues and purples; and the oriental poppy, like an orange lamp (for it really seems to have light within it) shining amidst the deeper greens; above all the pyramid of geraniums, beautiful beyond all beauty, rising in front of our garden room, whilst each corner is filled with the same beautiful flower, and the whole air perfumed by the delicious honeysuckle . . .

This is what the English call a real garden: the classical vistas of Stourhead and Stowe are all very well, but most of the English still like flowers and 'a nice bit of colour', as that characteristically English institution the Chelsea Flower Show continues to demonstrate. Despite the efforts of modern landscapers to interest us in architectural planting, stone gardens and labour-saving decking, we still love herbaceous borders.

THE ROMANTICS

The eighteenth century on the whole preferred to view nature through a Claude glass or a drawing room window: to compose it, to organize it, and to avoid (except in verse) its more violent manifestations. In one decade, Wordsworth swept away the antiquarian aestheticism of the past, replacing it with a feeling of passionate urgency and deep involvement. The snowbound shepherds of Thomson's 'Winter' belong to a different order from those in Wordsworth's *Prelude*. Wordsworth's moments of revelation by the dark lake are different in kind from Gray's reflections in a country churchyard: his daffodils dancing by the lake at Grasmere have nothing to do with Thomas Warton's April vision of 'the vegetable blaze of Flora's brightest 'broidery'. Wordsworth forged a new relationship between man and the natural world: he lived in a new communion, and when he was young he found the language, in Shelley's phrase, like clay in his hands.

He was, as he himself many times declared, fortunate in his birth. His was an exceptionally lovely part of the country: his subject matter lay around him in his infancy. The river Derwent and the mountains of Cumberland were as mother and father to him. Despite travels and wanderings, some happy, some tormented, he knew that the Lake District was his home; like Constable, with whom as an artist he has much in common, he felt that his own landscapes had formed him, and he returned there to work as soon as he could find the means. Unlike Thomson, who moved to London when opportunity called, or Goldsmith, who wrote of deserted villages while frequenting taverns in Fleet Street, Wordsworth needed to live what he believed; he was no weekend enthusiast, but a man who saw the integrity of the life and of the work. His own life style, of 'plain living and high thinking' has become an image in itself.

As we have seen, the Lakes had already been 'discovered' as picturesque some time before Wordsworth's birth in 1770, and no doubt had
he never been born tourists would still flock to visit them, but it is
through his eyes that we see them, not through the calculating eyes of
Gilpin or the apprehensive ones of Gray. Wordsworth was not a tourist,
but a native of the region, and knew intimately the places he describes;
they were the images of his childhood, the associations of daily life. His
poetry had made each place he mentions a place of pilgrimage, and he
has probably added more names than any other writer to a literary map
of England: Grasmere, Esthwaite, Cockermouth, Derwentwater, Rydal
Mere, Patterdale, Hawkshead, Ullswater, Windermere, Helvellyn – the
list is endless. Yet he is in no sense a descriptive writer, content to cata-
logue outward appearances. Nor does he use natural description as an
excuse for moralizing on the state of the nation. For him, the landscape
is the message, and he himself is the landscape. It is not fanciful to see in
him and his work the qualities of the region that reared him, for he
himself was constantly seeking such affinities, seeking the animate in the
inanimate, with a persistence that goes far beyond traditional anthro-
pomorphism. Born into a grand setting, he had grand ambitions:
frequently he compared his own ambition to a star, a mountain peak.

Wordsworth's attitude to nature was not a fixed creed; it changed and
developed. As a small boy, he tells us, he enjoyed 'the animal pleasures' –
bathing naked in the Derwent, climbing crags for birds' nests, boating,
fishing, skating. But this idyllic freedom was clouded over from time
to time by darker portents, and he was troubled by 'grave and serious
thoughts'; in the famous episode of the stolen boat, in Book 1 of
The Prelude, he tells us that the sight of the huge cliff which reared up
from the lake and seemed to stride after him like a living thing disturbed
him deeply:

> . . . and after I had seen
> That spectacle, for many days, my brain
> Work'd with a dim and undetermin'd sense
> Of unknown modes of being; in my thoughts
> There was a darkness, call it solitude,

Or blank desertion, no familiar shapes
Of hourly objects, images of trees,
Of sea or sky, no colours of green fields;
But huge and mighty Forms that do not live
Like living men mov'd slowly through my mind
By day and were the trouble of my dreams.

As he grew older, he was drawn to the grander and darker aspects of nature – to Burke's 'Sublime' – and was later to reproach himself for the enthusiasm with which he had pursued them, almost as though reproaching himself for seeking too violent a stimulant, too powerful a drug. One of his many tributes to his sister Dorothy gives her the credit for curing him of this excess. In Book 13 of *The Prelude* he writes:

In nature and in life, still to the last

. . .

I too exclusively esteem'd that love,
And sought that beauty, which, as Milton sings,
Hath terror in it. Thou didst soften down
This over-sternness; but for thee, sweet Friend,
My soul, too reckless of mild grace, had been
Far longer what by Nature it was framed,
Longer retain'd its countenance severe,
A rock with torrents roaring, with the clouds
Familiar, and a favourite of the Stars:
But thou didst plant its crevices with flowers,
Hang it with shrubs that twinkle in the breeze,
And teach the little birds to build their nests
And warble in its chambers.

It is perhaps significant that this softening process took place largely in the milder region of the West Country Quantocks, in the first youth of the Wordsworths' friendship with Coleridge: significant, also, that he clings to his faith that nature herself had appointed him as the familiar of rocks and mountains. Dorothy, not nature, taught him to see the violet by the mossy stone, but she conceded his feeling for the Sublime, and named 'the lonesome peak' of Stone-Arthur, near Grasmere, after him:

> . . . 'Tis in truth
> The loneliest place we have among the clouds.
> And She who dwells with me, whom I have loved
> With such communion, that no place on earth
>
> Can ever be a solitude to me,
> Hath to this lonely Summit given my Name.

It is also interesting that Wordsworth managed to find the bleak aspects even in Somerset and Devon; while Coleridge was writing of jasmine and bean flowers, and Dorothy of glittering miles of grass, of green ferns in waterfalls, of springing wheat and turnips, Wordsworth wrote of hail storms and the stunted thorn that became the centre of one of his most austere ballads, *The Thorn*.

It is impossible, in this space, to do justice to the complexity and originality of Wordsworth's contribution to the literature of landscape. He painted place as it had never been painted before, and connected it in new ways with man's thought processes and moral being. Many of his descriptions are indeed severe and terrible: take this passage in *The Prelude*, where he describes the experience of losing his father. It is Christmas time, the holidays are about to begin, and Wordsworth impatiently climbs a crag to look for the horses that will carry him and his brother home:

> . . . 'Twas a day
> Stormy, and rough, and wild, and on the grass
> I sate, half-shelter'd by a naked wall;
> Upon my right hand was a single sheep,
> A whistling hawthorn on my left, and there,
> With those companions at my side, I watch'd,
> Straining my eyes intensely, as the mist
> Gave intermitting prospect of the wood

And plain beneath. Ere I to School return'd
That dreary time, ere I had been ten days
A dweller in my Father's House, he died

     . . .

And afterwards, the wind and sleety rain
And all the business of the elements,
The single sheep, and the one blasted tree,
And the bleak music of that old stone wall,
The noise of wood and water, and the mist
Which on the line of each of those two Roads
Advanced in such indisputable shapes,
All these were spectacles and sounds to which
I often would repair and thence would drink,
As at a fountain; and I do not doubt
That in this later time, when storm and rain
Beat on my roof at midnight, or by day
When I am in the woods, unknown to me
The workings of my spirit thence are brought.

This is a remarkable analysis of the interaction of place and emotion, of past and present, of reality and imagination. Never since Shakespeare has scenery been made to bear such a weight of significance.

Wordsworth lost both his parents while still a child: his mother died when he was seven, his father when he was eleven. His dual attitude to nature – seeing her both as stern mentor and consoling nurse – seems to be related to these two vanished figures: the grand, dark landscapes are associated with the admonishing father, the homely images of the sunny river and the beloved vale of Esthwaite and the green valley of the Wye with his mother and his sister.

Wordsworth not only saw the natural world as a vital formative influence on man; he was at least half persuaded that every living object, even plants and trees, could experience joy and sorrow. The world was a living symbol, but more than that, it lived in its own right. At times he seems to recognize that this pantheistic approach is half fantasy, half pathetic fallacy: he speaks of the poet who, 'pleased within his own passions and volitions is delighted to contemplate similar volitions and passions as manifested in the goings-on of the Universe, and *habitually impelled to create them where he does not find them*' (my italics). He was much mocked by more rational contemporaries in parodies like *The Simpliciad* for his 'breathing blossoms' and his 'twigs that pant with pleasure'. Yet what he says is tentative enough: it is his *faith*, he says, 'that every flower enjoys the air it breathes', and of the budding twigs he writes

> And I must think, do all I can,
> That there was pleasure there . . .

– the qualifying phrase 'do all I can' implying that he is trying to be rational, but, in the pull of so much spring happiness, failing. His outpouring is spontaneous, deeply felt, utterly different in quality from such poems as Cowper's 'The Yardley Oak', in which the poet appoints himself 'oracle' for the tree, and speaks through its imagined history.

Wordsworth and Coleridge felt in their bones a natural piety: it was a crime against the living universe to kill wild life. (Wordsworth regretted his boyhood birds-nesting, though he continued to fish.) Both wrote poems about the consequences of idle slaughter: the albatross in 'The Ancient Mariner' and the hart in 'Hart Leap Well' are memorable symbols, the more memorable in an age of hunting and shooting. Dorothy taught Wordsworth that it was a crime to kill a butterfly or uproot a strawberry plant. We hear more now of the possible feelings of small creatures and plants, but in their day such an approach was unusual: Gilbert White of Selborne, fondly though he observed the worm and the snake, felt no inhibition against killing them through scientific curiosity. It is true that many of Wordsworth's poetic predecessors had taken pleasure in personifying the vegetable kingdom: James Hurdis in *The Village Curate* celebrates the 'martial pea', 'the gay bean' and the 'soporific lettuce', and Erasmus Darwin in his *Loves of the Plants* was firmly committed to the idea that plants could feel, and for that reason preferred insectivorous, climbing and sensitive plants, such as *Mimosa*, which seemed 'almost human' to him. He particularly loved sundew, *Drosera*, as did his grandson Charles, who was to write to his friend Charles Lyall,

'I care more about *Drosera* than the origin of all the species in the world.'
'That wicked dear little Drosera' was very dear to the younger Darwin.
Yet Erasmus Darwin's playful ascribing of sexual passions to flowers and
vegetables is largely a literary device, a charming and novel way of con-
veying botanical information. Wordsworth half meant what he said.

I am beginning to think that one of the reasons why Wordsworth
called forth so deep a response is that he was drawing on deep sources of
collective feeling, on a primitive animistic view of the world, certainly
present in earlier times, but powerfully suppressed by the scientific seventeenth and eighteenth centuries. The child and peasant see inanimate
objects and natural forces as possessed of a life of their own.
Wordsworth was able, like Freud in later days, to restore an essential
contact with the primitive, to divine its workings, and to restore an earlier
vision. Man, cut off from nature by centuries of rationalism, was restored
to her bosom. Yet Wordsworth makes no grand claims. When he writes
of his sister,

> . . . Her the birds
> And every flower she met with, could they but
> Have known her, would have lov'd . . .

he is not claiming that birds and flowers can possess human knowledge;
they would, if they could. Flowers and birds no longer speak, as they did
in fairy tales and legends: something of paradise is lost. Yet we can still
make contact with the mighty Being that animates the universe:
Wordsworth, sitting under the sycamore in the valley of the Wye above
Tintern, looking at the 'wild green landscape' and the little farms and
hedgerows, can declare in 'Tintern Abbey':

> . . . And I have felt
> A presence that disturbs me with the joy
> Of elevated thoughts; a sense sublime
> Of something far more deeply interfused,
> Whose dwelling is the light of setting suns,
> And the round ocean and the living air,

And the blue sky, and in the mind of man;
A motion and a spirit, that impels
All thinking things, all objects of all thought,
And rolls through all things.

Similarly, on his ascent of Snowdon, he seems almost to see and hear 'The Soul, the Imagination of the whole':

> . . . I looked about, and lo!
> The Moon stood naked in the Heavens, at height
> Immense above my head, and on the shore
> I found myself of a huge sea of mist,
> Which, meek and silent, rested at my feet:
> A hundred hills their dusky backs upheaved
> All over this still Ocean, and beyond,
> Far, far beyond, the vapours shot themselves,
> In headlands, tongues and promontory shapes,
> Into the Sea, the real Sea, that seem'd
> To dwindle, and give up its majesty,
> Usurp'd upon as far as sight could reach.

This is the kind of landscape that had not appeared in English since Milton, and, after it, it was difficult to look upon nature as a prettily arranged prospect, subject to man's domination.

As we have seen, it has been since Roman times a commonplace to claim that the shepherd's life is better than the courtier's, the country purer than the town. Wordsworth seriously believed this. He saw the city as a contaminating force, an imprisonment; many times he pities Coleridge for his deprived childhood, 'in city pent'. Wordsworth was one of the few who knew shepherds in real life, and had observed their domestic and working lives. Critics have complained that he reads his own feelings into them, and thus elevates them unnaturally, but Wordsworth make it clear that he knows he is tempted to do precisely this: he tends to see them in superhuman terms, he says, because this is how they presented themselves to him as a child:

Seeking the raven's nest, and suddenly
Surpriz'd with vapours, or on rainy days
When I have angled up the lonely brooks
Mine eyes have glanced upon him, few steps off,
In size a giant, stalking through the fog,
His Sheep like Greenland Bears; at other times
When round some shady promontory turning,
His Form hath flash'd upon me, glorified
By the deep radiance of the setting sun:
Or him have I descried in distant sky,
A solitary object and sublime,
Above all height! . . . Thus was Man
Ennobled outwardly before mine eyes . . .

A far cry this, in setting and sentiment, from the oaten stops, pastoral songs and garlanded nymphs of Arcadia. Similarly, in 'Michael, A Pastoral Poem', he admits that he first loved shepherds

> . . . not verily
For their own sakes, but for the fields and hills
Where was their occupation and abode.

Not much pretence here; nor in a cancelled draft of the same poem, where he says of the old shepherd:

No doubt if you in terms direct had ask'd
Whether he lov'd the mountains, true it is
That with blunt repetition of your words
He might have stared at you, and said that they
Were frightful to behold, but had you then
Discours'd with him in some particular sort
Of his own business, and the goings on
Of earth and sky, then truly had you seen
That in his thoughts there were obscurities,
Wonders and admirations, things that wrought
Not less than a religion in his heart.

This is great poetry, and profound knowledge. Wordsworth was so rich in both that he could afford to discard such lines.

I see that my own bias has combined with Wordsworth's and that, inevitably, I have stressed the Sublime rather than the homely in his nature and his work. Wonderfully though he conveyed the huge panorama and the grand view from the mountain top of effort, he was equally good at the precise observation, at the 'little unpretending rill', the withered celandine, the bird's nest. Indeed, there was something in him that seemed increasingly to fear the loneliness and exposure of the lofty summits of his own fame, that sought as he grew older the steady lake, the moss-grown garden, the kettle whispering its faint undersong by the half-kitchen half-parlour fire. It was Dorothy who encouraged these milder, safer pleasures, and his debt to his sister is fully revealed in her *Journals*, which have a rare, and in her day new, delicacy of natural observation. How many thousands of nineteenth-century country ladies followed in her footsteps, making notes, sketching, recording their own lonely and incommunicable feelings, and the year's changes. Dorothy was bad at drawing, unlike many well-educated girls of her time, but her descriptions are sensitive to every change of mood and weather, reflecting a delicate inner balance between the two.

Like her brother, she had strong views on the naturalness of nature, and the folly of interfering with it. In 1798 she records a visit to a garden in the neighbourhood of Alfoxden, where they were then living, in these terms:

> April 15th. Walked about the squire's grounds. Quaint waterfalls about, about which Nature was very successfully striving to make beautiful what art had deformed – ruins, hermitages, etc, etc. In spite of all these things, the dell romantic and beautiful, though everywhere planted with unnaturalised trees. Happily we cannot shape the huge hills, or carve out the valleys according to our fancy.

She was equally censorious a few years later on a visit to Windermere, on 8 June 1802:

> Ellen and I rode to Windermere. We had a fine sunny day, neither hot nor cold. I mounted the horse at the quarry. We had no

difficulties or delays but at the gates. From the High Ray the view is very delightful, rich and festive, water and wood, houses, groves, hedgerows, green fields and mountains; white houses, large and small. We passed 2 or 3 nice-looking statesmen's houses. Mr Curwen's shrubberies looked pitiful enough under the native trees. We put up our horses, ate our dinner by the water-side, and walked up to the Station. Then we walked to the Island, walked round it, and crossed the lake with our horses in the Ferry. The shrubs have been cut away in some parts of the Island. I observed to the boatman that I did not think it improved. He replied, 'We think it is, for one could hardly see the house before.' It seems to me, however, no better than it was. They made no natural glades; it is merely a lawn with a few miserable young trees, standing as if they were half-starved. There are no sheep, no cattle upon these lawns. It is neither one thing or another – neither natural nor wholly cultivated and artificial, which it was before. And that great house! Mercy upon us, if it could be concealed, it would be well for all who are not pained to see the pleasantest of earthly spots deformed by man.

She felt much more at home in her own valley, by her own lake of Grasmere, and her *Journal* is full of descriptions of her walks – for, like her brother, she was a great walker, and was reprimanded in childhood for her unladylike fondness for rambling alone. The lake seems at times a mirror to her soul: on parting with her dear brother, 'The lake looked to me, I knew not why, dull and melancholy, and the weltering on the shores seemed a heavy sound . . .' (14 May 1800). In happier mood (with William) she reports, 'The lights were very grand upon the woody Rydale hills. Those behind dark and topped with clouds. The two lakes were divinely beautiful. Grasmere excessively solemn and the whole lake was calm, and dappled with soft grey ripples' (20 October 1800). With William again, on 15 April 1802 she saw the immortal daffodils:

When we were in the woods beyond Gowbarrow Park we saw a few daffodils close to the water-side. We fancied that the lake had floated the seeds ashore, and that the little colony had so sprung up.

But as we went along, there were more and yet more; and at last, under the boughs of the trees, we saw that there was a long belt of them along the shore, about the breadth of a country turnpike road. I never saw daffodils so beautiful. They grew among the mossy stones about and about them; some rested their heads upon the stones as on a pillow for weariness; and the rest tossed and reeled and danced, and seemed as if they verily laughed with the wind . . .

Her height of happiness is achieved in the company of her two loved ones, William and Coleridge, on a walk on a hot day in May:

We almost melted before we were at the top of the hill. We saw Coleridge on the side of the water; he crossed the Beck to us . . . William and I ate a luncheon, then went on towards the waterfall. It is a glorious wild solitude under that lofty purple crag. It stood upright by itself. Its own self, and its shadow below, one mass – all else was sunshine. We went on further. A Bird at the top of the crags was flying round and round, and looked in thinness and transparency, shape and motion like a moth. We climbed the hill, but looked in vain for a shade, except at the foot of the great waterfall, and there we did not like to stay on account of the loose stones above our heads. We came down, and rested upon a moss-covered rock, rising out of the bed of the river. There we lay, ate our dinner, and stayed there until about 4 o'clock or later. William and C. repeated and read verses. I drank a little Brandy and water and was in Heaven.

Significantly, a more sombre, quiet peace possesses her, soon after William's marriage to Mary Hutchinson; the wild days are over, for better or worse, and from now on she will have to share William, or steal him away:

October 30th, 1802. William is gone to Keswick. Mary went with him to the top of the Rays. She is returned, and is now sitting near me by the fire. It is a breathless, grey day, that leaves the golden woods of autumn quiet in their own tranquility, stately and beautiful in their decaying; the lake is a perfect mirror.

And a perfect mirror of more than the woods and skies.

The Wordsworths led a deliberately retired life, moving by only a margin of miles as their family and income expanded, returning home from their excursions with delight; they died where they had lived. Not so their friend Coleridge, who saw himself as a restless wanderer, too soon transplanted, 'a tree with leaf of feeble stem'. He too was born in a small country town, Ottery St Mary in Devon, but unlike Wordsworth never felt rooted in security – partly, he maintains, because he was sent to school in London after his father's death when he was only ten years old. While the orphaned Wordsworth was happily lodged with a motherly dame in Hawkshead, enjoying such boyish pursuits as riding, skating, fishing and playing cards by the peat fire of the cottage, Coleridge was precociously frequenting London taverns, coffee-houses and bookshops, far from the 'beauteous forms or grand' that enlarged his friend's sympathies. Wordsworth says, with reason, that he was himself

> Much favoured in my birthplace, and no less
> In that beloved Vale, to which, ere long
> I was transplanted.

Coleridge's transplant was less happy, and throughout his life he was perplexed by a sense of rootlessness, blaming himself and his early years for the ease with which he was deceived by 'false and fair-foliaged tempters', for the rashness with which he chased 'chance-started friendships'.

Coleridge's fame as a poet does not rest on his landscapes, though it is perhaps significant that his finest descriptive work is of his native West Country, in such poems as 'This Lime Tree Bower my Prison', 'The Nightingale', and 'Frost at Midnight'. These, written at Nether Stowey between 1797 and 1799, in the early years of friendship with Wordsworth, show him at his most happily responsive to the natural world, and appear more deeply felt than later effusions on Skiddaw and Saddleback.

The landscapes of childhood remain nearest the heart. Like Wordsworth, he believed in the power of the environment and early association, though he was much more given to expounding his faith in terms of philosophic theory, quoting Locke, Hume, Berkeley, Godwin and David Hartley in his support. In some of his poems we see him putting this faith into practice. In 'The Nightingale' he tells us that his infant son Hartley (named after the philosopher) 'knows well the evening star', and that he once soothed the baby's crying by taking him out to the orchard to show him the moon. He has a touching faith that Hartley will grow up more happily than he did, and writes, in 'Frost at Midnight':

> My babe so beautiful! it thrills my heart
> With tender gladness, thus to look at thee,
> And think that thou shall learn far other lore,
> And in far other scenes! For I was reared
> In the great city, pent 'mid cloisters dim,
> And saw nought lovely but the sky and stars.
> But *thou,* my babe! shalt wander like a breeze
> By lakes and sandy shores, beneath the crags
> Of ancient mountain, and beneath the clouds . . .
> Therefore all seasons shall be sweet to thee,
> Whether the summer clothe the general earth
> With greenness, or the redbreast sit and sing
> Betwixt the tufts of snow on the bare branch
> Of mossy apple-tree, while the nigh thatch
> Smokes in the sun-thaw; whether the eave-drops fall
> Heard only in the trances of the blast,
> Or if the secret ministry of frost
> Shall hang them up in silent icicles,
> Quietly shining to the quiet Moon.

This hope, alas, was not to be fulfilled: the idyll of thatched cottage with roses peeping through the window and jasmines twining round the porch was not to last. (The cottage, in fact, was plagued with mice, because Coleridge, true to his principles, thought it cruel to set traps.) Coleridge's marriage was unhappy, and he found family life increasingly difficult. Eventually he followed Wordsworth up to the Lakes, and settled his wife at Keswick, where she was shortly joined by the Southeys, but he himself remained a wanderer, tempted by other scenes – by London, and the dreaming opium towers and palaces of Xanadu. There is much pathos in his optimistic letter to his friend Godwin, before the departure for Greta Hall:

> if I cannot procure a suitable house at Stowey I return to Cumberland and settle at Keswick, in a house of such prospect, that if, according to you and Hume, impressions and ideas *constitute* our being, I shall have a tendency to become a god, so sublime and beautiful will be the series of my visual existence . . .

When established there in 1800 he wrote proudly, 'I question if there be a room in England which commands a view of mountains, and lakes, and woods and vales superior to that in which I am now sitting.' But it was too late for the mountains and lakes to gain ascendancy over Coleridge's established mental habits; the greatest poem he wrote in the Lake District was fittingly called 'Dejection', and it was in part an analysis of his own self-destructive tendencies. His response to the district described in his *Tour in the Lake Country, 1802*, is enthusiastic enough – indeed, perhaps too enthusiastic. There is little of the settled quiet of his friend's response or of his own West Country days; it is all exclamation marks, wonder, dizziness. Writing on the top of Scafell he notes: 'O! what a look down just under my feet! The frightfullest Cove that might ever be seen, huge perpendicular Precipices, and one Sheep upon its only Ledge . . .' And the language in which he writes of the waterfall of Moss Force on Buttermere is as turbulent as its subject:

> The third and highest (of the waterfalls) is a mighty one indeed. It is twice the height of both the others added together, nearly as high as Scale Force, but it rushes down an inclined Plane, and does not fall, like Scale Force; however, if the Plane had been smooth, it is so near a Perpendicular, that it would have appeared to fall, but it is indeed

so fearfully savage, and black, and jagged, that it tears the flood to pieces . . . What a sight it is to look down on such a Cataract! The wheels, that circumvolve it, the leaping up and plunging forward of that infinity of Pearls and Glass Bulbs, the continual change of the Matter, the perpetual Sameness of the Form – it is an awful Image and Shadow of God and the World.

Coleridge's most impressive landscapes are not English at all: they are the lurid imaginary seascapes of *The Ancient Mariner*, the deep romantic chasms and cedarn covers of an ambiguously Oriental Xanadu. Similarly, the finest descriptive writing of two second generation Romantics, Byron and Shelley, describes not their native land, but their chosen land of exile, Italy. Shelley spent his boyhood in the countryside of West Sussex, and lived in England for more than twenty of his thirty years, but his skylark sang near Leghorn, and his 'Ode to the West Wind' was composed near Florence. The place names that he added to our literature are grand and Romantic enough – Mont Blanc, the Apennines, the Euganean Hills, Naples, Hellas – but they are foreign. Most of his English poems are political, and savage. Leafing through his *Collected Works*, I hoped I had discovered an exception, when I came across 'A Summer Evening Churchyard, Lechlade, Gloucestershire'. This seemed a precise enough location, and was written when he, Peacock, Mary Godwin and Charles Clairmont were on a boating trip in 1815. Alas, the poem is just another disembodied dirge, full of abstract personifications and Gothic horrors – the dusky braids of evening, the mouldering dead in their sepulchres, the awful hush of darkness – and there is nothing to differentiate Lechlade church from any other, apart from one phrase – 'the dry church-tower grass' – which sounds as though it were drawn from observation. One poem, 'The Question', written in 1820, seems to evoke (although in dream) a memory of England:

> And nearer to the river's trembling edge
> There grew broad flag-flowers, purple pranked with white,
> And starry river-buds among the sedge,
> And floating water-lilies, broad and bright,

Which lit the oak that overhung the hedge
With moonlit beams of their own watery light;
And bulrushes, and reeds of such deep green
As soothed the dazzled eye with sober sheen . . .

But these, as he says, are 'visionary flowers'. The absence of English beauty in his poetry is not accidental: writing, again in 1820, his 'Letter to Maria Gisborne', he describes 'the chaos of green leaves and fruit', the unsickled corn and fireflies of Italy, contrasting them with the London he has left:

But what see you beside? – a shabby stand
Of Hackney coaches – a brick house or wall
Fencing some lonely court, white with the scrawl
Of our unhappy politics . . .

He did not leave England for nothing.

Byron was equally neglectful of home-grown charms, in his poetry at least. Not many Romantic poets are lucky enough to have a converted twelfth-century Augustinian priory for an ancestral home, and its decaying Gothic splendours must have affected his imagination: however, apart from a passage in *Don Juan*, and a few lines of farewell to Newstead Abbey's windy battlements and 'once smiling garden', now choked with hemlock and thistle, he seems for the most part to have cried with his wandering Childe Harold:

Welcome, ye deserts and ye caves,
My native land, Good Night!

Athens, Rome, Venice, Seville, the Isles of Greece – he sang of anywhere but home. He made an exception of Scotland, familiar from his childhood years in Aberdeen, writing with nostalgia of the days when his cap was the bonnet, his cloak was the plaid: five stanzas celebrate Lochnagar, 'one of the most most sublime and picturesque amongst our Caledonian Alps', but he manages to turn his praise for its foaming cataracts and pine-covered glades into an attack on the England that had treated him, he felt, so badly:

> Years have rolled on, Loch na Garr, since I left you,
> Years must elapse ere I tread you again:
> Nature of verdure and flowers has bereft you
> Yet still are you dearer than Albion's plain.
> England! thy beauties are tame and domestic
> To one who has roved o'er the mountains afar;
> Oh! for the crags that are wild and majestic!
> The steep frowning glories of dark Loch na Garr.

But Byron only played at being a Scottish patriot, donning the theatrical costume and remembering his Scottish ancestry when it suited him. It was Sir Walter Scott who made familiar the Romantic glories of Scottish scenery and Scottish history.

Walter Scott was born in 1771, the year after Wordsworth. His novels and poems now gather dust in second-hand bookshops, and are reprinted largely for the benefit of Scottish universities, but his legend and some of his stories live on (with a strange after-life in Hollywood film and television plots as well as in folklore) and in his day he was far more popular than Wordsworth: Dorothy wrote in 1807 of her brother's new work *The White Doe of Rylstone*, 'I can never expect that poem, or any which he may write, to be immediately popular, like the *Lay of the Last Minstrel . . .*' His novels, which appeared at first anonymously, earned him many admiring titles: he was the Wizard of the North, the Great Unknown, the Scottish Prospero. The French idolized him, and he had an immense influence on the work of Balzac. John Hayden, in his introduction to *Scott's Critical Heritage*, states boldly, 'No writer before had been so well received by his contemporaries – *ever.*' His influence was incalculable, and amongst other achievements, he did for Scotland what Wordsworth had done for the Lakes: he praised her beauties, created a new vision, and encouraged the tourist trade. He also restored his country's history and dignity. As we have seen, Dr Johnson considered Scotland quaint and barbaric, its landscapes monotonous, its people and its scenery in decline.

Burns, whose grave was already a place of pilgrimage by the time the Wordsworths toured the country in 1803, had provided some excuse for those who wished to see the Scots nation as a nation of picturesque but feckless drunkards: his poetry has been admired but his cult deplored by most patriots. Scott set himself the task of recovering his nation's faith in itself, of rewriting and rediscovering her past. His diligence, his intellectual energy and his success were enormous.

Like Wordsworth, he was fortunate in the scenery of his childhood, and faithful to it. He was brought up in the Border country, and was to celebrate Tweed and Teviot, Kelso and Liddesdale, the Eildons and the Lammermuirs, Ettrick Forest and St Mary's Loch, in many a rhyme and story. He was familiar with the countryside from his earliest years: as a little boy at his grandfather's farm at Sandy Knowe he would spend days on the hills with the shepherd, watching the flock, the kestrels and the curlews. One day, according to Carole Oman's biography, when a storm came on he was left on the hillside, forgotten, and 'his auntie came running to fetch him home. She found him lying on his back amongst the knolls, clapping his hands at the lightning and crying at every fresh flash, "Bonny! Bonny!"' Such enthusiasm for the wilder aspects of nature remained with him, and infected many a Victorian armchair traveller.

His first major literary work was a collection of carefully restored border ballads, *Minstrelsy of the Scottish Border*. It proved an instant success; so did the *Lay of the Last Minstrel*, in 1805, which drew admiration from both Pitt and Fox, as well as from the Wordsworths, who were treated to a pre-publication reading on their first meeting. Its fame was such that Constable offered him £1,000 for his next work, *Marmion*, without seeing a word of it. This appeared in 1808, to widespread acclaim, both for its romantic and patriotic tale and for its fine landscapes, which included Bamburgh, Whitby, Lindisfarne, Flodden and Loch Skene, amongst many others.

The Lady of the Lake was an even more sensational success, and caused a rush of tourists to Loch Katrine and the Trossachs; a hotel had to be built at Callander for visitors to Ellen's Isle. George Gilfillan, the diligent Victorian editor, wrote in his *Memoir* in 1857,

1810 was one of Scott's brightest years. The Lady of the Lake appeared in May, and was received with boundless enthusiasm. Critics vied with each other in eulogiums. On all the roads leading to the Trossachs was suddenly heard the rushing of many chariots and horsemen. Inns were crowded to suffocation. Post-hire permanently rose. Every corner of that fine gorge was explored, and every foot of that beautiful loch was traversed by travellers carrying copies of the book in their hands, or, as they sailed round Ellen's Isle, or climbed the gray scalp of Ben An, or sate in the shady hollow of Coirnanuriskin, or leaned over the still waters of Loch Achray, repeating passages from it with unfeigned rapture. He had hit the public between wind and water. It was as if a ray from heaven had fallen on and revealed a nook of matchless loveliness, and all rejoiced in the gleam and in its revelation.

The days when Dr Johnson could complain that the roads of Scotland afford 'little diversion to the traveller, who seldom sees himself either encountered or overtaken' were over: the age of Bed and Breakfast and crowded caravan sites was on its way.

Scott's novels followed the poems, and added a vast array of ruined abbeys, castles, lochs, mountains and views to the common literary store. He covered the country from coast to coast, including Orkney and the Hebrides, venturing over the border to include Rokeby and Kenilworth, Ditchley, Warwick and York, and a score of other historic sites, on which his comments are quoted in most modern guide books. Like the poems, the novels were read with passionate enthusiasm, and the heroines of later novels pay their debt to their originator. George Eliot's Mary Garth and Maggie Tulliver are both addicts, like George Eliot herself, who did the Scott tour in 1846, visiting Loch Katrine, Melrose and Abbotsford. The Brontës admired and imitated; Emily chose Sir Walter and his protégé James Hogg, the Ettrick Shepherd, as Chief Men for her imaginary childhood games, and Charlotte's happiness when she visited Edinburgh in 1850 is clearly Scott-inspired, as she wrote in a letter to W. S. Williams:

My dear Sir, do not think I blaspheme when I tell you that your great London town, as compared to Dun-Edin (mine own romantic town), is as prose compared to poetry . . . You have nothing like Scott's monument or if you had that and all the glories of architecture, assembled together, you have nothing like Arthur's Seat, and above all you have not the Scotch national character . . .

In another letter, she writes 'Melrose and Abbotsford, the very names possess music and magic'.

Thomas Love Peacock, Jane Austen, Dickens, Wellington, Thomas Hardy, Tennyson, Gladstone – the diverse list of admirers is endless. Victoria and Albert both read him, and knew his verses by heart; on their first visit to Scotland in 1842 we find Albert writing, 'There is . . . no country where historical traditions are preserved with such fidelity . . . Every spot is connected with some interesting historical facts, and with most of those Sir Walter Scott's accurate descriptions have made us familiar.' Sixty years earlier, Dr Johnson had found the Scots lacking, precisely, in historical tradition and written history: Scott had achieved a one-man revolution of attitude. Victoria fell in love with Scotland at first sight, enthused over Edinburgh, quoted *The Lady of the Lake* in her *Journal* when recording her visit to Loch Muich in 1850, and carried the poem with her as a guidebook when she did her tour of the Trossachs and Rob Roy country in 1869. In 1867, when she toured the Borders, she endorsed Scott's advice:

If thou would'st view fair Melrose aright,
Go visit it by pale moonlight.

The purchase of Balmoral set the seal of royal approval on Scottish scenery, but Victoria and Albert were looking at the country partly through Scott's eyes: it was he that taught them to praise the beauty of the heather, to prefer the purple hillsides to the Swiss Alps, to find 'solitude, romance and wild loveliness' in what they considered the 'proudest, finest scenery in the world'.

Such descriptive talents were and still are admired: pilgrims still flock to the sites, even though they may not read the novels. But was Scott, in the final judgment, any more than a glorified literary guidebook, a 'picturesque tourist', as Coleridge unkindly called him? Wordsworth, who admired him as a man, was in a sense right to complain (in a letter to R. P. Gillies, 28 April 1815, on *Guy Mannering*) of the 'laborious manner in which everything is placed before your eyes for the production of picturesque effect. When (pictures) are placed upon an easel for the express purpose of being admired, the judicious are apt to take offence.' Many of the set pieces, precise in their roll-call of place names, are dim in outline, as in this extract from *The Lady of the Lake*:

> The noble stag was pausing now,
> Upon the mountain's southern brow,
> Where broad extended, far beneath,
> The varied realms of fair Menteith.
> With anxious eye he wandered o'er
> Mountain and meadow, moss and moor,
> And pondered refuge from his toil
> By far Lochard or Aberfoyle.
> But nearer was the copse-wood gray,
> That waved and wept on Loch-Achray,
> And mingled with the pine-trees blue,
> On the bold cliffs of Ben-venue.

This is incantatory stuff, but as Coleridge wrote to Wordsworth, all you need for this kind of verse is 'a vast string of patronymics, and names of Mountains, Rivers etc.' The novels are much more accurate in their sense of place, but even here, the scenes and set pieces are stage-managed.

Scott's success heralded the golden age of the nineteenth-century novel. He was followed by scores of imitators, many now forgotten, some more distinguished than their model. His painting of everyday country life inspired George Eliot and Elizabeth Gaskell; his sense of place and romantic atmosphere influenced the Brontës, Thomas Hardy and a host of lesser writers. He confirmed that it was unnecessary to look abroad, as the 'Radcliffe school' of Romantic novelists had done: there were stores of undiscovered riches nearer home. Italy and Spain were forgotten, as

Cornwall and Cumberland, Yorkshire and Dorset, Devon and Shropshire found their chroniclers.

The Brontë sisters have always been rightly identified with their Yorkshire home. Their genius flourished in isolation. Their lonely childhood at Haworth parsonage and their rambles on the surrounding moors formed their characters and their work. For Emily in particular, place was more important than people. There was nothing of the tourist in her: she left home rarely and reluctantly, and when away she fell ill pining for the heather and harebells and familiar sights of Haworth. Her landscapes are among the finest in the language, and all of them are drawn from her own immediate and narrow experience. Unlike Scott's, they are never posed, never picturesque, never held up for admiration. They are an integral part of the book. The characters of *Wuthering Heights* grow out of its scenery as naturally as the trees and rocks themselves. Emily constantly sees and describes people in terms of landscape: in her famous outburst to Nelly Dean, Catherine exclaims, 'My love for Linton is like the foliage in the woods. Time will change it, I'm well aware, as winter changes the trees. My love for Heathcliff resembles the eternal rocks beneath – a source of little visible delight, but necessary.' After her death, Heathcliff says, 'I cannot look down to this floor, but her features are shaped on the flags! In every cloud, in every tree – filling the air at night, and caught by glimpses in every object, by day I am surrounded with her image!' Nelly describes her daughter's face as being 'just like the landscape – shadows and sunshine flitting over it, in rapid succession . . .' This insistence is more than a literary device: it shows a sense of the affinity of man and nature so profound that many have described Emily as a mystic.

Yet there is hardly a set description in the whole novel. The overpowering physical reality of its world is built up from a hundred small natural touches, each revealing some character trait or making some dramatic point, or providing a turning point in the action. The exposed situation of the Heights is part of Emily's plot: in the second chapter the narrator Lockwood looks out of the window 'to examine the weather. A sorrowful sight I saw: dark night coming down prematurely, and sky and hill mingled in one whirl of suffocating snow.' Only a few phrases, and we see the snowstorm through Lockwood's apprehensive eyes: it is this storm that imprisons him for the night at the Heights, and provides the pretext for the whole story.

Slowly, with unobtrusive details, Emily Brontë builds up the contrast between the old farmhouse with its stunted firs, gaunt thorns and rough-spoken inhabitants, and Thrushcross Grange, with its pleasant park, its sheltering fences and plantations, its summer murmur of foliage, its orchard of apples; a contrast which, again, *is* the plot, for Catherine has to choose between the two representatives of these places, and is doomed for choosing wrongly. The book has a fine variety: although we tend to think of the tempestuous and gloomy scenes first, the mood is by no means always dark, nor is the tone indulgently romantic. The gloom is balanced by the tone of Nelly Dean, perceptive yet matter-of-fact, a country woman who knows the goings-on of earth and sky. Nelly's comments are always both accurate and evocative: 'It was a close, sultry day: devoid of sunshine, but with a sky too dappled and hazy to threaten rain . . .' There are more enthusiastic raptures about the beauties of nature in Jane Austen than in Emily Brontë, the only possible exception being the dreams of young Catherine and Linton, in Chapter 24:

> He said the pleasantest manner of spending a hot July day was lying from morning till evening on a bank of heath in the middle of the moors with the bees humming dreamily about among the bloom, and the larks singing high up over head . . . mine was rocking in a rustling green tree, with a west wind blowing, and bright, white clouds flitting rapidly above; and not only larks, but throstles, and blackbirds, and linnets, and cuckoos pouring out music on every side, and the moors seen at a distance, broken into cool, dusky dells; but close by great swells of long grass undulating in waves to the breeze; and woods and sounding water, and the whole world awake and wild with joy. He wanted all to lie in an ecstasy of peace: I wanted all to sparkle and dance in a glorious jubilee.

But Catherine and Linton are still children: they soon learn better.

Visitors to Haworth will not be surprised to find that Emily, whose home overlooks the graveyard, writes with an easy familiarity of death and gravestones. Perhaps she played among them, as did Catherine and Heathcliff. There is no element of Gothic extravagance in her use of graves and burials: even Heathcliff's embracing of Catherine's corpse seems in a different tradition from its literary predecessors. It is a real world that she draws, with its changing seasons, a world where the bleak winds and bitter northern skies give way to summer, as Lockwood finds on his return after nearly a year's absence (Chapter 32):

> The grey churchyard looked greyer, and the lonely churchyard lonelier. I distinguished a moor sheep cropping turf on the graves. It was sweet, warm weather – too warm for travelling; but the heat did not hinder me from enjoying the delightful scenery above and below: had I seen it nearer August, I'm sure it would have tempted me to waste a month among its solitudes. In winter nothing more dreary, in summer nothing more divine, than those glens shut in by hills, and those bluff, bold swells of heath.

Emily's poetry is similarly imbued with her feeling for purple heather bells, storm-worn walls, skyscapes, storms, and warm summer afternoons. To her, Haworth was no prison, for, as she writes in 'Often Rebuked, yet always back Returning', the path to the moors that leads away from the parsonage leads to freedom unlimited:

> I'll walk where my own nature would be leading:
> It vexes me to choose another guide:
> Where the grey flocks in ferny glades are feeding;
> Where the wild wind blows on the mountain side.

> What have those lonely mountains worth revealing?
> More glory and more grief than I can tell:
> The earth that wakes *one* human heart to feeling
> Can centre both the worlds of Heaven and Hell.

Her sisters, Charlotte and Anne, were not so content with their solitary lives; Charlotte in particular yearned to travel, and her descriptions of Brussels show a more heightened excitement than her Yorkshire novel, *Shirley*. On the first page, she claims *Shirley* will be as 'unromantic as Monday morning', and makes visible efforts to check and counterbalance her own poetic impulses, reminding us, as Emily does not, that Yorkshire was already a county of flourishing industry, and that if one walked in the other direction from Haworth one reached not the moors but the mills of Keighley, and its Mechanics' Institute Library. Yet there is something Romantic in her appreciation of the industrial landscape. The unpoetic curate Malone, 'not given to close observation of Nature', fails to notice the drama of the sky – 'a muffled, streaming vault, all black, save where, towards the east, the furnaces of Stillbro' ironworks threw a tremulous lurid shimmer on the horizon' – but Charlotte is highly responsive. Charlotte mocks Shirley's suitor, Sir Philip, for his 'literary turn', which expresses itself in moonlight walks, reading long ballads, and seeking sequestered rustic seats, and tries hard to reconcile herself to a more practical vision of man's relation to landscape: in the last chapter, 'The Winding-Up', we find industrialist Robert Moore telling the romantic Caroline of the changes he plans in these terms:

'. . . I can double the value of their mill-property: I can line yon barren Hollow with lines of cottages, and rows of cottage-gardens –'

'Robert? And root up the copse?'

'The copse shall be firewood ere five years elapse: the beautiful wild ravine shall be a smooth descent; the green natural terrace shall be a paved street: there shall be cottages in the dark ravine, and cottages on the lonely slopes: the rough pebbled track shall be an even, firm, broad, black, sooty road, bedded with cinders from my mill: and my mill, Caroline – my mill shall fill its present yard.'

'Horrible! You will change our blue hill-country air into the Stillboro' smoke atmosphere.'

'I will pour the waters of Pactolus through the valley of Briarfield.'

'I like the beck a thousand times better.'

'I will get an act for enclosing Nunnely Common, and parcelling it out into farms.'

'Stillboro' Moor, however, defies you, thank Heaven! What can you grow in Bilberry Moss? What will flourish on Rushedge?'

Here Charlotte accurately foretells the future of the landscape, and the days, not too far distant, when only the wildest and most resistant regions would defy man. Moore clearly suspects that the National Parks and 'areas of outstanding natural beauty' that the future would learn to protect would simply prove to be areas that were not worth exploiting. He is on the side of Jane Austen's sensible heroes, preferring the useful to the Picturesque – yet with how much more sinister a warning than Jane Austen could deliver, a warning of pollution and spreading industrial estates, instead of a dream of neat and prosperous farming.

Charlotte sees both sides: her heart is with Caroline, but she is ashamed to appear in the already conventional role of the soft-hearted, soft-headed, girlish 'nature lover'. More self-conscious, and therefore more self-critical than Emily, she is more aware of the traps of romance and romantic fiction. Yet she too could respond at times with a violence that made her speechless. There is something deeply moving in the account of her first sight of the sea, at Bridlington, in 1839. She went with her prosaic friend Ellen Nussey, who later wrote that Charlotte was so overpowered by the scene that 'she could not speak till she had shed some tears'. She signalled to Ellen to move on, to leave her to experience the fulfillment of her intense anticipation alone. When Ellen returned, 'her eyes were red and swollen, she was still trembling', and for the rest of the day she remained subdued and exhausted. Years later, this scene was repeated, when she visited Ireland with her husband Mr Nicholls: he too had to withdraw tactfully as she admired the wild foam of the Atlantic and its rocky 'iron-bound' coast at Kilkee.

Anne too loved the sea, which she first saw at Scarborough, a few miles north of Bridlington; she was working as a governess at the time, and suffering from deep depression. The sea revived her, and she conveyed her gratitude in both her novels. Her heroine Agnes Grey chooses Scarborough as the location for her little school, in the novel's poignantly happy ending:

There was a feeling of freshness and vigour in the very streets, and when I got free of the town, when my foot was on the sands and my face towards the broad, bright bay, no language can describe the effect of the deep, clear azure of the sky and ocean, the bright morning sunshine on the semi-circular barrier of craggy cliffs sur-mounted by green swelling hills, and on the smooth, wide sands, and the low rocks out at sea – looking, with their clothing of weeds and moss, like little grass-grown islands – and above all, on the brilliant, sparkling waves. And then the unspeakable purity and freshness of the air!

Anne herself was less fortunate: she went to die there at the age of twenty-nine, in Charlotte's words 'where she would be happiest', and passed away at two o'clock on a cloudless afternoon, sitting in an arm-chair, gazing at the view she loved so well. The distressed doctor wondered at 'her fixed tranquillity of spirit.' Nature proved kind to Anne, but little else in her life did.

The Brontë lives and landscapes inspired many tributes, from Matthew Arnold's moving elegy, 'Haworth Churchyard', written after Charlotte's death in 1855, to Sylvia Plath's 'Wuthering Heights', published in 1971. Arnold's Haworth is mournfully accurate, catching both the industrial and romantic aspects of the region:

> Where, behind Keighley, the road,
> Up to the heart of the moors
> Between heath-clad showery hills
> Runs, and colliers' carts
> Poach the deep ways coming down,
> And a rough, grimed race have their homes –
> There on its slope is built
> The moorland town. But the church
> Stands on the crest of the hill,
> Lonely and bleak; – at its side
> The parsonage-house and the graves.

Elizabeth Gaskell's famous life of Charlotte has some finely evocative descriptions of the district, and on her first visit she wrote to a friend, 'The wind goes piping and wailing and sobbing round the square, unsheltered house in a very strange, unearthly way', revealing herself as an impressionable visitor, like Lockwood at the Heights. Plath too paid tribute to the tragedy in the countryside; she writes of the sheep, the pale skies, the tilted horizons, the pouring wind that flattens everything. One tragic poet writing of another, she says:

> If I pay the roots of the heather
> Too close attention, they will invite me
> To whiten my bones among them.

As the nineteenth century progressed, other regions found their poets and their novelists. It was inevitable, perhaps, that Exmoor would produce its *Lorna Doone*, *Westward Ho!* its Westward Ho! (an inverse relationship, this, for the place was named after Kingsley's novel) – Tintagel its Tennyson and Swinburne, Dorset its Hardy, Cornwall its *Rebecca*, Shropshire its Housman and Mary Webb. The taste for the Romantic became, more generally, a taste for the unspoiled and wild, for the kind of scenery that could resist the growing population and industry of the busy Victorian age. Writers began to sense that wildness might disappear, and appreciated it the more. Far from fearing it, they started up the refrain that Hopkins voiced when he wrote:

> What would the world be, once bereft
> Of wet and of wildness? Let them be left –
> Let them be left. O, wildness and wet;
> Long live the weeds and the wilderness yet.

Some regions have become hackneyed shrines of literary pilgrimage; others would seem at first sight to have had less than their share of romantic appreciation. Wales, which is romantic enough, with its wild mountains, its fierce history, its ruined castles and Arthurian legends, produced no Walter Scott, and there are few Welsh novelists of the nineteenth century, though the eighteenth-century artist Richard Wilson, born in the Vale of the Dyfi, declared that 'everything the landscape painter could want was to be found in North Wales'. This apparent lack is probably a tribute to the comparative strength of the indigenous Welsh culture and literature, which remains inaccessible to the ordinary English reader, and which needed no imported enthusiasts. Tourists in their thousands now flock there every year, but they understand little beyond what meets their eyes (though that is certainly worth seeing). George Borrow's classic account, *Wild Wales*, was coldly received when it appeared in 1862, and illustrates the difficulties encountered by the traveller. Borrow, though English born and bred, could speak and read Welsh, and his pilgrimage took him to shrines little visited, some unmarked on any map: as he told one of his many chance acquaintances who asked him why he would not take the railroad, 'I am fond of the beauties of nature; now it is impossible to see much of the beauties of nature unless you walk. I am likewise fond of poetry, and take special delight in inspecting the birth-places and haunts of poets.' His interest aroused astonishment in the Welsh, unaccustomed to such visitors. Borrow included in his pilgrimage the poets Huw Morris and Goronwy Owen, the patriot Owen Glendower and his bard, Iolo Goch, quoting from them in appropriate moments – on Snowdon and at Glendower's home at Sycharth, where he dismissed his guide to contemplate the lost past in solitude, and reduced himself, Charlotte Brontë-like, to tears – 'covering my face with my hands, I wept like a child'. Snowdon was to him the Parnassus of Europe, and he describes the view with rapture: from the top he saw 'a scene inexpressibly grand . . . Peaks, pinnacles and huge moels stood up here and there, about us and below us, partly in glorious light, partly in deep shade . . .'; below them lay 'numerous lakes and lagoons, which, like sheets of ice or polished silver, lay reflecting the rays of the sun in the deep valleys at his feet'. Yet, oddly, one of his most descriptive phrases is one of his least poetic: of the cele-brated waterfall of Pistyll Rhaeadr in Denbighshire he wrote that seen from a distance it looked like 'a strip of gray linen hanging over a crag'.

The greatest twentieth-century novelist of Welsh landscape, John Cowper Powys, had a complex relationship with his national identity. Born in Derbyshire, and brought up in the South West of England (about which he wrote great topographical novels, including *A Glastonbury Romance* (1932) and *Weymouth Sands* (1934), he was also deeply conscious of and proud of his ancient Welsh lineage, and of the bardic tradition. He spent the last three decades of his long and intensely creative life in Wales, first in Corwen and then in Blaenau Ffestiniog, in a countryside which inspired two magnificent historical novels, *Owen Glendower* (1940) and *Porius* (1951). His evocations of the sublimity of Snowdon and Cader Idris and Lake Bala have a Miltonic grandeur, but he also had the keenest eye for the smallest botanical detail, for 'the slippery knots of the exposed roots of heather, the burnished stalks of bracken, the dead blackness of crowberries, the scaly surface of yellow-green lichens, the orange-pink clumps of stone-crop'. His modest home in Blaenau, not the most con-ventionally attractive of Welsh towns, became a site of literary pilgrimage for admiring younger writers, who would visit him and his life's compan-ion, Phyllis Plater, and wonder why they had chosen to live so remotely amongst the slate quarries.

Other more obviously romantic sites were more accessible to visitor and writer. Tintagel, acclaimed by Malory and Geoffrey of Monmouth as the birthplace of King Arthur, would have found its poets had the Arthurian legend never settled on it, though, no doubt, the legend helped. The picturesque ruins appear, in fact, to be built on the remains of an earlier Celtic monastery rather than on an Arthurian stronghold, but fact has little to do with it. Malory spares it hardly a descriptive phrase, but this lack the Victorians made good. The Reverend R. S. Hawker, vicar of Mor-wenstow, claimed the distinction of having introduced Tennyson and Kingsley to the charms of the region, and his own tales of smugglers, ship-wrecks and storms, as described in Charles Tennyson's *Life of Tennyson*, show a Byronic pleasure in the grandeur of the elements, as well as a Chris-tian compassion for the victims: 'So cruel is that shore that after a wreck he would send a man with a basket to collect the gobbets of flesh cut from the bodies of the poor sailors by the sharp rocks against which the waves bat-tered them. These . . . he would bury with all reverence.' Baring-Gould, in his popular life of Hawker (1876), writes dramatically, 'The coast from Tintagel to Hartland is almost unrivalled for grandeur. The restless Atlantic is ever thundering on this iron-walled coast. The roar can be heard ten miles inland; flakes of foam are picked up after a storm at Holsworthy . . . The swell comes unbroken from Labrador to hurl itself against this coast, and to be shivered into foam on its iron cuirass.'

Appreciation of the grandeurs and beauties of the sea was largely a Romantic innovation. In earlier times, not surprisingly, men had tended to associate the sea with peril rather than with beauty. Fear was more powerful than the romance of travel. Houses were built safely inland, and those near the coast were built with their backs to the coast, avoiding a sea view – Seaton Delaval, in Northumberland, is an often-quoted example of this attitude. By the beginning of the nineteenth century, this aversion was beginning to abate, and resorts were developed as holiday-makers learned of the newly proclaimed health-giving properties of sea bathing. Jane Austen in her unfinished *Sanditon* (1817) describes the turning point of the story: the book marks, precisely, the shift from the old eighteenth-century view towards the new Romantic conception of the coast. Mr Parker, who has built a new house by the sea, sings the praises of the grandeur of storms, and presents being rocked in bed by them as a positive pleasure. Sensible Charlotte sees the advantages of his former home, a sheltered snug-looking inland place rich in orchards, meadows and fields. Yet even Charlotte's spirits rise at the prospect of the sea from her bedroom window, dancing and sparkling in sunshine and freshness. The age was on the side of Mr Parker, and resorts were developed all round Britain, inevitably ruining some of the beauty that visitors came to seek, yet creating at the same time some of our more elegant Regency architecture – Brighton, Weymouth, Eastbourne are all products of the new passion. And despite *Sanditon* 's bias, one of Jane Austen's most celebrated moments takes place by the sea: all Austen readers know the scene in *Persuasion* where Louisa Musgrove falls from the Cobb. When Tennyson visited Lyme in 1867, he went at once to call on his friend Palgrave (of *Palgrave's Golden Treasury*) and said 'Now take me to the Cobb and show me where Louisa Musgrove fell.' More recently, John Fowles, who lived for years at Lyme, set some of the most dramatic moments of his popular novel *The French Lieutenant's Woman* in the same location. One might fancy the spirit of the place drew writers to it. The spirit of the place, the spirit of Jane Austen – the two are now intermingled, for any visitor.

The Romantic poets also paid their tribute to the sea. Byron cried in *Childe Harold's Pilgrimage*:

> Roll on, thou deep and dark blue Ocean – roll!
> Ten thousand fleets sweep over thee in vain;
> Man marks the earth with ruin – his control
> Stops with the shore . . .

and succeeding generations were to praise the merciless waves, the violence of the elements, in a way that the more sensible eighteenth century would have found ridiculous. Arthur Hugh Clough's stanza,

> On stormy nights when wild north-westers rave,
> How proud a thing to fight with wind and wave!
> The dripping sailor on the reeling mast
> Exults to bear, and scorns to wish it past . . .

cannot have found many sympathetic echoes from real mariners. Tennyson has some fine seascapes, some from early recollections of Mablethorpe on the Lincolnshire coast, some from his years at Freshwater on the Isle of Wight, some from his ramblings in Cornwall in pursuit of King Arthur, where his companion Palgrave would infuriate him by running after him calling 'Tennyson! Tennyson!' whenever he strayed too near the edge of a cliff or rock. Yet Tennyson's most famous sea poem,

> Break, break, break
> On thy cold gray stones, O Sea –

was written as he walked along a Lincolnshire lane, many miles inland.

Swinburne also visited Tintagel, and was attracted by the violence of the coast. *Tristram of Lyonesse* is full of descriptions of the sea, of foam-flowers and sea-roses, of the wild wrath of the Cornish foam, of 'wind-hollowed heights and gusty bays'. In a letter to Mary Gordon, 2 September 1864, he writes enthusiastically of Boscastle:

You can imagine how the sea swings to and fro between the cliffs, foams, swells, beats and baffles itself against the steep faces of the rock. I should guess it must be unique in England. Seen from above and on horseback it was very queer, dark grey swollen water, caught as it were in a trap, and heaving with rage against both sides at once, edged with long panting lines of incessant foam that swung and lapped along the deep steep cliffs without breaking, and had not room to roll at ease.

(Not surprisingly, he was so taken by the wild North Sea when staying at Wallington, Newcastle, that he wrote to his friend Richard Monckton Milnes in discreet French expressing his regret that the 'cher et digne' Marquis de Sade had never imagined 'des supplices de mer'.)

More peaceably, though more tragically, Keats composed his last sonnet, 'Bright Star!', on board ship off the coast of Dorset, after a day exploring the caves and rock pools at Lulworth: he was on his way to Rome, his last resting place, and his vision of

> The moving waters at their priestlike task
> Of pure ablution round earth's human shores

was his last sight of England.

Mathew Arnold's 'Forsaken Merman' is a fine example of a newly popular genre, the subaqueous landscape. More importantly, 'Dover Beach' is one of the most impressive and moving of Victorian seascapes:

> The sea is calm tonight.
> The tide is full, the moon lies fair
> Upon the straits; – on the French coast the light
> Gleams and is gone; the cliffs of England stand,
> Glimmering and vast, out in the tranquil bay.
> Come to the window, sweet is the night air!
> Only, from the long line of spray
> Where the sea meets the moon-blanch'd land,
> Listen! you hear the grating roar

Of pebbles which the waves draw back, and fling,
At their return, up the high strand,
Begin, and cease, and then again begin,
With tremulous cadence slow, and bring
The eternal note of sadness in . . .

Place, sound, mood and thought intermingle marvellously in this poem; Arnold's stoic melancholy as he contemplates the 'long, withdrawing roar' of the Sea of Faith rises with the utmost grace and inevitability from the scene itself. The sea has always provided man with a store of images: much could be written of its changing symbolic significance in the imagination. Coventry Patmore, almost an exact contemporary of Arnold's, was to become a Catholic, finding the faith that Arnold could not intellectually approve. He too uses the sea as an image, in an extremely interesting little poem, '*Magna est Veritas*', as characteristically Victorian as 'Dover Beach':

Here, in this little bay,
Full of tumultuous life and great repose,
Where, twice a day,
The purposeless, glad ocean comes and goes,
Under high cliffs, and far from the huge town,
I sit me down.
For want of me the world's course will not fail:
When all its work is done, the lie shall rot;
The truth is great, and shall prevail,
When none cares whether it prevail or not.

No earlier poem, surely, could so have combined religious faith with an awareness of the insignificance of man and of mankind: the purposeless glad ocean of truth needs no recognition, it was and will be. Man's insignificance is itself insignificant.

Wordsworth, Scott, Byron and the Brontës were romantic but bracing: there is nothing enervating about their landscapes. This was not true of a later generation of poets, over whom crept a mood of listlessness that somehow turned the most turbulent dramas into lotus-eating swoons. While most of this languor can be traced to the increasing irrelevance of 'poesy' in an age when the novel was tackling the more interesting (and picturesque) problems, perhaps a little can be laid at Tennyson's door, and, more specifically, at the door of his birthplace. The effect of Somersby and the Lincolnshire landscape on Tennyson was profound, and through him, on mid- and late Victorian literature as a whole.

Lincolnshire is a varied county, and Somersby lies in one of its more varied regions. The poet's grandson Charles Tennyson describes it thus:

> Somersby is a tiny hamlet tucked remotely away in a corner of the Lincolnshire wolds, a range of hills reaching here and there a height of five hundred feet. One line of these (then a complete wilderness, untilled and overrun by rabbits) stretches north and south, between the village and the sea, and from it another range goes north-westwards towards Market Rasen and Caister. The old Rectory lies in the angle of the two, about 150 feet above sea level, in a pleasant valley, down which flows the brook that formed the basis of so many of Alfred's similes and descriptions. The slopes of wold and valley are dotted with copses and noble trees, amongst which lie tiny villages and square-towered churches . . . Beyond the eastern range of hills lies the marsh, a flat strip of rich pasture land about five to eight miles wide, divided up into fields by broad ditches, which are filled in summer with tall, feathery reeds. Beyond this is the North Sea, peculiar for the long rise and fall of the tide over the flat sandy shore and fringed by a line of high sand dunes on which Alfred loved to wander, feeling as though he were standing 'on the spine bone of the world'.

Through this landscape the poet would wander, as a boy and a young man, sometimes walking all night long, and his poetry is full of impressions of his surroundings. He was very short-sighted, which one might guess from the writing alone, for it is marked by extremely precise, close descriptions – of black ash buds, of flecks of sea foam, of pebbles, of caterpillars – and by huge, vague, misty horizons. The prevailing mood is one of melancholy and heaviness, even in the early poems, before the death of Tennyson's loved friend Arthur Hallam, the inspiration of *In Memoriam*: the characteristically Tennysonian world is one of dying swans, decaying flowers, dark rooks in elm trees, dark wolds, desolate creeks, dim meres, and dew-drenched wood walks. His heroines are the Sleeping Beauty, the Lady of Shalott who can observe the real world only through a mirror, Mariana waiting wearily in her moated grange. The languid atmosphere that breathes from the poems is overwhelming, and it captured the Victorian imagination – partly, perhaps, because it was new, newly formulated, utterly unlike the rugged mountainous scenery of Tennyson's poetic predecessors, and partly because it suited the Victorian mood so well – and, by suiting it, helped to create it.

Many of the poems are set in a specifically Lincolnshire setting, with the sound of the bells of Lincoln Cathedral ringing in the distance, the willows stooping over the river Witham or the lush vegetation of wood and garden in the foreground. *In Memoriam* in particular is a portrait of a much-loved landscape, combining minute detail – the rosy plumelets of the larch, the tulips dashed with fiery dew, the violets blowing in the roots of the ash tree, the daggers of ice on the eaves – with larger, dimmer prospects. Tennyson recalls the days when he and Hallam used to walk and talk together:

> Till now the doubtful dusk reveal'd
> The knolls once more where, couch'd at ease,
> The white kine glimmer'd, and the trees
> Laid their dark arms about the field:
>
> And suck'd from out the distant gloom
> A breeze began to tremble o'er
> The large leaves of the sycamore,
> And fluctuate all the still perfume,
>
> And gathering freshlier overhead,
> Rock'd the full-foliaged elms, and swung
> The heavy-folded rose, and flung
> The lilies to and fro, and said

'The dawn, the dawn,' and died away;
And East and West, without a breath,
Mixt their dim lights, like life and death,
To broaden into boundless day.

The landscape is made more dear by memories of Hallam:

I climb the hill: from end to end
Of all the landscape underneath,
I find no place that does not breathe
Some gracious memory of my friend;

No gray old grange, or lonely fold,
Or low morass and whispering reed,
Or simple stile from mead to mead,
Or sheep-walk up the windy wold;

No hoary knoll of ash and haw
That hears the latest linnet trill,
Nor quarry trench'd along the hill
And haunted by the wrangling daw;

No runlet tinkling from the rock;
Nor pastoral rivulet that swerves
To left and right thro' meadowy curves,
That feeds the mothers of the flock;

But each has pleased a kindred eye . . .

The poet's mood colours the landscape so powerfully that it is hard to imagine anyone writing of these scenes in a more energetic tone: even his descriptions of the beauties of spring and renewal are softened by alliteration into a dreamy melancholy – the birds 'build and brood', the violets 'bud and blossom', the poet sees 'the light-blue lane of early dawn'. Tennyson can write in lively metre: 'The Brook' babbles along cheerfully enough in between its banks of blank verse, and 'The Charge of the Light Brigade' and 'The Revenge' could hardly be accused of languor. But the prevailing atmosphere is infectious: Lincolnshire pervades even Lyonesse and Camelot. Wherever historic Camelot may have been located, it is easy to see whence he drew these lines:

> In the stormy east-wind straining,
> The pale yellow woods were waning,
> The broad stream in his banks complaining,
> Heavily the low sky raining
> Over tower'd Camelot;
> Down she came and found a boat
> Beneath a willow left afloat
> And round about the prow she wrote
> '*The Lady of Shalott*'.

Similarly, in the *Morte d'Arthur* the noise of battle may roll among the mountains by the wintry sea, but the landscape in its details is pure flat Lincolnshire: the many-knotted water flags 'that whistle stiff and dry about the marge' of the level lake, the incantatory music of the last lines –

> Long stood Sir Bedivere
> Revolving many memories, till the hull
> Look'd one black dot against the verge of dawn,
> And on the mere the wailing died away.

These are the sights and sounds of Lincolnshire, not of Lyonesse. The long, liquid, even Tennysonian line of iambic pentameter is the long, liquid, even line of the contours of the landscape: the master of onomatopoeia responds like an electrocardiograph to the heart's terrain.

Other writers describing Lincolnshire are full of Tennysonian echoes, inevitably. Dickens, the least enervating of writers, seems subdued by the scenery, and produces in *Bleak House* a dreariness that rivals the master's. Here is the opening description of Sir Leicester Dedlock's country house, Chesney Wold, in Chapter 2:

The waters are out in Lincolnshire. The arch of the bridge in the park has been sapped and sopped away. The adjacent low-lying ground, for half a mile in breadth, is a stagnant river, with melancholy trees for islands in it, and a surface punctured all over, all day long, with falling rain . . . The weather, for many a day and night, has been so wet that the trees seem wet through, and the soft loppings and prunings of the woodman's axe can make no crash or crackle as they fall. The deer, looking soaked, leave quagmires as they pass . . . On Sundays, the little church in the park is mouldy; the oaken pulpit breaks out into a cold sweat; and there is a general smell and taste as of the ancient Dedlocks in their graves.

An acquired taste, perhaps, this kind of atmosphere – but Tennyson acquired it early, and passed it on to others. On leaving Somersby for Epping in 1837 he wrote to a friend, 'A known landskip is to me an old friend that continually talks to me of my own youth and half-forgotten things, and indeed does more for me than many an old friend that I know.' He is well aware of the complex intermingling of the real, the ideal and the imagined, and would probably not have been surprised to learn that without his guidance, many readers would find it hard to see the country-side as he saw it: his landscapes, despite their precision of detail, are highly personal, much more so than those of Wordsworth, whose grasp of the outer world was stronger, whose Lake District is there for all to see. The imagination is a powerful force, welding together the most unlikely components: for Tennyson (and, subsequently, for a generation of Victorian poets) even the bright, heroic, southern world of Homer could become imbued with the damp colours of the North Sea: in 'Mablethorpe' he writes on revisiting the town as a man,

> How often, when a child I lay reclined,
> I took delight in this locality!
> Here stood the infant Ilion of the mind,
> And here the Grecian ships did seem to be.
> And here again I come and only find
> The drain-cut levels of the marshy Lea –

Gray sand banks and pale sunsets – dreary wind,
Dim shores, dense rains, and heavy-clouded sea!

Matthew Arnold also saw English landscape through a classical filter, filling his poems with allusions to Arcady, commemorating his friend Clough under the name of Thyrsis. Unlike Tennyson, he was not country born: he was reared at Rugby, Winchester and Oxford. He celebrated both Rugby and Oxford in characteristically elegiac cadences, Rugby in the gloom of an autumn evening; Oxford, 'that sweet city with her dreaming spires', in these famous lines from *Essays in Criticism* (1865):

> Beautiful city! So venerable, so lovely, so unravaged by the fierce intellectual life of our century, so serene! . . . steeped in sentiment as she lies, spreading her gardens to the moonlight, and whispering from her towers the last enchantments of the Middle Age . . . Adorable dreamer, whose heart has been so romantic! who has given thyself so prodigally, given thyself to sides and heroes not mine, only never to Philistines! home of lost causes, and forsaken beliefs, and unpopular names, and impossible loyalties!

Yet he also had a deep love of the countryside round Oxford, and in *The Scholar Gipsy* and 'Thyrsis the Sicilian' shepherds vie with English girls dancing round the Fyfield elm, and 'boys who in lone wheatfields scare the rooks'. Ilsley Down, Cumnor Hill, Bagley woods and Childsworth Farm hold their own with Thessaly and Enna, and the flora of the youthful Thames has never been so beautifully sung. Cowslips, bluebells, 'woods with anemones in flower till May', primroses, the spikes of purple orchises, the white flowering nettles, the pale pink convolvulus – it is almost too good to be true, too lush, too lovely, a landscape on the point of vanishing, a memory of a golden age. And so Arnold saw it: his poems are full of a sense of impending loss, a vague lament for passing glory, as well as a more precise lament for lost friends, lost youth.

Yet Arnold's sense of loss is very different from Wordsworth's. When Wordsworth wrote in the 'Ode on Intimations of Immortality',

> But there's a tree, of many, one
> A single field which I have looked upon,
> Both of them speak of something that is gone,

he is speaking of his own loss, not the world's: for him, nature endured, but man failed. Arnold's fears are larger, his faith less. We note in his verse the tone of hard-worked, weary modern man, seeking refreshment on weekend rambles, trying to find respite from 'this iron time / Of doubts, disputes, distractions, fears' ('Memorial Verses, to Wordsworth'). Arnold had the prosaic job of Inspector of Schools, and the prosaic public spirit and conscience of a Victorian public man. For him the country was not a way of life, as it was for Wordsworth, or a home, as it was for Tennyson – it was an evasion of the real business of existence, a consolation for the weekly grind, for the harsh statistics, the Blue Books on education, the ever-increasing speed and uncertainty he felt around him. Poetry was a refuge from this unpleasant world, and so was nature: she was 'the cool flowery lap of earth' where we had lain at birth, the womb to which man longed to return.

He longed, of course, in vain. Both Tennyson and Arnold turned to nature, the great comforter, on the death of loved friends; both sought a religious consolation in loved and familiar landscapes, endeared by the loved one. Yet nature did not truly console. The power of conviction that had sustained Wordsworth was slowly ebbing. Nature was not a god, nor was she even kindly: she did betray the hearts that loved her. Darwin revealed that she was red in tooth and claw. Tennyson cried,

> Are God and Nature then at strife,
> That Nature lends such evil dreams?

The God of Christianity and the Wordsworthian Great Being faded under the relentless questioning of science. Both Tennyson and Arnold were men of the new enlightenment, keenly interested in scientific discovery and progressive thought: they could not reject the new and alarming revelations of the nineteenth century, and Arnold at least could not fly 'the strange disease of modern life'. He was committed to waging war on modern ugliness and Philistinism, on the brick terraces of Margate – and, thus committed, he had no choice but to keep them in view. The conclusion of 'Thyrsis' sums it up: he has been forced to abandon the hopes youth, the landscapes glimmer only in ghostly italics from beyond the grave:

> Too rare, too rare, grow now my visits here!
>   'Mid city-noise, not, as with thee of yore,
>   Thyrsis! in reach of sheep-bells is my home.
> –Then through the great town's harsh, heart-wearying roar,
>   Let in thy voice a whisper often come,
>   To chase fatigue and fear:
> *Why faintest thou? I wander'd till I died.*
>   *Roam on! The light we sought is shining still.*
>   *Dost thou ask proof? Our tree yet crowns the hill,*
> *Our Scholar travels yet the loved hill-side.*

THE INDUSTRIAL SCENE

The industrial scene has always had its admirers. Even today, when it is more common to hear complaints about pollution and destruction of our national heritage, there are many who gain aesthetic pleasure from the sight of cooling towers, factory chimneys, pylons, radar stations, even from Birmingham's Spaghetti Junction. We admire Lowry, we read Lawrence and Sillitoe. But we do not go for our holidays to Wigan or Smethwick or Merthyr Tydfil, and an American friend of mine on a Bennett pilgrimage to the Potteries found the local inhabitants surprised to find her there; her Woolf pilgrimage to Cornwall had caused no such stir. Our admiration has an element of the self-conscious and the perverse. Industry is too much with us: even those who enthuse over its dramatic transformations of the landscape feel a fear for the future.

At the beginning of the Industrial Revolution, this fear did not yet exist, and it was considered proper to admire industrial architecture, feats of engineering, the glories of man's triumphs over nature. The early mill owners, far from retreating out of sight of their mills, proudly overlooked them from their homes, and commissioned paintings to commemorate them; Erasmus Darwin thought Arkwright's cotton mill at Cromford, 'where Derwent guides his dusky floods / Through vaulted mountains and a night of woods' a perfectly suitable subject for poetry – partly because the mill is situated in the most picturesque location, only a few miles from the famous beauty spot of Matlock Bath, and partly because Arkwright's machinery for spinning cotton by water-powered rollers inspired him with enthusiasm. The factory, a fine building, was restored in the 1980s and is open to the public, a link with the earliest days of the Industrial Revolution. It still stands in beautiful and largely unspoiled countryside, an eloquent reminder of a world when science had not yet reached an inhuman scale, and in the early eighteenth century had not yet divorced itself from the community it served.

Mills, canals, bridges, aqueducts, viaducts, the early railways – they were all signs of wealth and progress, evidence of Britain's booming economy. Reporters like Defoe rejoiced in industry, preferring stirring, populous districts to barren regions of what is now considered scenic beauty. In his day there was too much barrenness, and venturing through it was dangerous rather than romantic. Arthur Young, touring England half a century later than Defoe, was stirred by such sights as the Barton aqueduct which carried the Bridgewater canal over the river Irwell, and wrote in *A Six Months' Tour through the North of England* (1770), 'The effect of coming at once on to Barton Bridge, and looking *down* upon a large river, with barges of great burthen towing along it; and *up* to another river hung in the air, with barges sailing upon it, form altogether a scenery somewhat like enchantment...' Elsewhere, he compares James Brindley's plans for the canal to the noble undertakings of the Romans: such comparisons, from those favouring industry and progress, were to become commonplace in the Victorian Age. Shelley was inspired by William Alexander Madocks's project of building an embankment across the mouth of Traeth Mawr, the estuary of the river Glaslyn at what is now Tremadoc. Tremadoc itself was a complete new town built on land reclaimed by an earlier project of Madocks.

Such enterprises could be seen as poetic and heroic because they in no way threatened the entire landscape; in the eyes of most, they merely added to its interest. An uninhabited waste was not then considered in itself a relief to the eye and the spirit, as it now is: Thomas Pennant in *Tours in Wales* (1778–83) considered Plinlimmon 'an uninteresting object: the base most extensive, the top boggy, and the view from it over a dreary and almost uninhabited country...' One remembers Dr Johnson's similar complaints about Scotland. To such travellers, the sight of men and men's activities was welcome. Of course, not all industrial scenes were as clean and graceful as Arkwright's mill or Brindley's bridges, but Burke's theory of the Sublime managed for many to excuse a good deal of the dirt, noise and scenic violence of quarries, pits and furnaces. Burns and his friend Mr Nicol on their tour of Scotland in 1787 seem to have made a special effort to see the 'celebrated iron works' at Carron, and Burns's biographer Lockhart reports in his *Life of Burns* (1828),

I have heard that, riding one dark night near Carron, his companion teased him with noisy exclamations of delight and wonder whenever an opening in the wood permitted them to see the magnificent glare of the furnaces: 'Look, Burns! Good Heaven! Look, look! What a glorious sight!' 'Sir', said Burns, 'I would not look look at your bidding if it were the mouth of hell!'

Milton's Hell and Pandemonium are sources of many of Burke's examples of the sublime; furnaces came naturally enough into the same category. One of the places that inspired many visitors with a sense of the mingled Sublime and Picturesque was Coalbrookdale in Shropshire, described by Francis D. Klingender in his excellent *Art and the Industrial Revolution* (1947) as 'one of the growing points of the Industrial Revolution' which 'exercised an almost irresistible attraction over the artists of the English school of landscape drawing from its first beginnings to its culmination'. It was here that Abraham Darby discovered the process of smelting iron ore with coke, and Coalbrookdale combined in one place industry and the natural products it required – coal and ironstone – both in a most picturesque setting in the Severn Valley. No wonder the scene impressed its visitors: Arthur Young in 1776 found it 'horribly sublime', and clearly found Burke's theories a useful way of coming to terms with his own conflicting feelings. In *Annals of Agriculture, and other Useful Arts* he writes:

Coalbrook Dale itself is a very romantic spot, it is a winding glen between two immense hills which break into various forms, and all thickly covered with wood, forming the most beautiful sheets of hanging wood. Indeed too beautiful to be much in unison with that variety of horrors art has spread at the bottom: the noise of the forges, mills and with all their vast machinery, the flames bursting from the furnaces with the burning of the coal and the smoak of the lime kilns, are altogether sublime, and would unite well with craggy and bare rocks, like St Vincent's at Bristol.

A similar combination of emotions can be found in George Borrow's much later description of Neath and Merthyr Tydfil, in *Wild Wales*. By this time, in the mid-nineteenth century, the Romantic movement had taught travellers to seek and to admire solitudes and wildernesses, and on the whole Borrow, though an insatiable conversationalist, obeyed the Romantic spirit. But something in this vision impresses him despite himself, as here in Chapter 52:

I had surmounted a hill, and had nearly descended on that side of it which looked towards the east, having on my left, that is to the north, a wooded height, when an extraordinary scene presented itself to my eyes. Somewhat to the south rose immense stacks of chimneys surrounded by grimy diabolical-looking buildings, in the neighbourhood of which were huge heaps of cinders and black rubbish. From the chimneys, notwithstanding it was Sunday, smoke was proceeding in volumes, choking the atmosphere all around. From this pandemonium, at the distance of about a quarter of a mile to the south-west, upon a green meadow, stood, looking darkly grey, a ruin of vast size with window holes, towers, spires, and arches. Between it and the accursed pandemonium, lay a horrid filthy place, part of which was swamp and part pool: the pool black as soot, and the swamp of a disgusting leaden colour. Across this place of filth stretched a tramway leading seemingly from the abominable mansions to the ruin. So strange a scene I had never beheld in nature. Had it been on canvas, with the addition of a number of diabolical figures, proceeding along the tramway, it might have stood for Sabbath in Hell – devils proceeding to after-noon worship, and would have formed a picture worthy of the powerful but insane painter, Jerome Bos.

After standing for a considerable time staring at the strange spectacle I proceeded. Presently meeting a lad, I asked him what was the name of the ruin.

'The Abbey,' he replied.

'Neath Abbey?' said I.

'Yes!'

Having often heard of this abbey, which in its day was one of the most famous in Wales, I determined to go and inspect it. It was with some difficulty that I found my way to it. It stood, as I have already observed, in a meadow, and was almost every side surrounded by majestic hills. To give any clear description of this ruined pile would be impossible, the dilapidation is so great, dilapidation evidently less the effect of time than of awful violence, perhaps that of gunpowder.

This is much closer to our modern industrial landscapes of waste than those glimpsed by Burns and Young, yet Borrow nevertheless lends it a Miltonic grandeur; in the next chapter, he sees a glowing mountain of dross from the iron forges at Merthyr, which he describes as both 'wonderful' and 'terrible', and the industrial architecture there strikes him as remarkable, 'though of a gloomy horrid Satanic character'. One of the edifices, he says, of reddish brick with a slate roof, in front of four black towers and two white chimneys, would have served for a palace of Satan.

From the twenty-first century, it is not easy to look back to the eighteenth and to feel its confidence in the indestructibility of the landscape, in the beneficence of machinery and trade. Yet this optimism was powerful enough, and a poem such as John Dyer's *The Fleece* (1757) bears touching witness to a Golden Age of hope. Dyer holds an honourable place in the history of the poetry of landscape for his *Grongar Hill*, but *The Fleece* is in many ways a more interesting and curious performance, opening a window on a past when the man of sensibility had not yet learned to scorn the notion of manufacture. The more extensive and the uglier that industry became, the greater the rift between its bosses and its men and the worse the resulting mess in the landscape: mill and mine owners did not want to live within sight of the ruin they had themselves created, so they retreated further into the unspoiled countryside, building for their workers the terraces that are still so familiar a feature of the North of England, or leaving their workers to fend for themselves, to overcrowd existing city centres, creating new and appalling slums. Dyer lived before this process of separation took place, and although one must, as ever, beware of finding a Golden Age in any specific period of history, one cannot surely but be touched by the innocent confidence with which Dyer begins his work, in praise of the British wool industry:

> The care of sheep, the labours of the loom,
> And arts of trade, I sing. Ye rural nymphs,
> Ye swains, and princely merchants, aid the verse . . .

He goes on to describe in detail the different kinds of land which favour different breeds of sheep, from the wilds near Dover to the clovered lawns of Rutland, from the spacious plain of Sarum 'where solitary Stonehenge, gray with moss, ruin of ages, nods', to the tempestuous regions of Derbyshire, Snowdon and Cader Idris, with their goat-horned flocks with long and nimble shanks. He offers advice on sheep rot and infectious scabs, and sings the virtues of tar water; he describes combing and dyeing, weaving and spinning, and makes the noisy fulling-mill 'near some clear sliding river, Aire or Stroud', sound an attractive as well as an industrious spot. Attractive, too, is his account of trade and industry's improvements at Leeds:

> . . . Wide around
> Hillock and valley, farm and village, smile:
> And ruddy roofs and chimney-tops appear,
> Of busy Leeds, up-wafting to the clouds
> The incense of thanksgiving: all is joy;
> And trade and business guide the living scene,
> Roll the full cars, adown the winding Aire
> Load the slow-sailing barges, pile the pack
> On the long tinkling train of slow paced steeds
>
> . . .
>
> Thus all is here in motion, all is life;
> The creaking wain brings copious store of corn:
> The grazier's sleeky kine obstruct the roads;
> The neat-dressed housewives, for the festal board
> Crowned with full baskets, in the field-way paths
> Come tripping on; the echoing hills repeat
> The stroke of axe and hammer; scaffolds rise,
> And growing edifices; heaps of stone,
> Beneath the chisel, beauteous shapes assume

Of frieze and column. Some, with even line,
New streets are marking in the neighbouring fields,
And sacred domes of worship. Industry,
Which dignifies the artist, lifts the swain,
And the straw cottage to a palace turns,
Over the work presides. Such was the scene
Of hurrying Carthage, when the Trojan chief
First viewed her growing turrets. So appear
The increasing walls of busy Manchester,
Sheffield, and Birmingham, whose reddening fields
Rise and enlarge their suburbs . . .

There is no fear of the future here, no talk of preserving green belts, no sense that the suburbs might engulf the fields altogether; few hints, either, of the appalling conditions in the textile industry that were to arouse such bitter battles for factory reform. There is perhaps some hint of darker knowledge in Dyer's comparison of the work force to 'sedulous ants', and the lavish praise he heaps on a new workhouse in the valley of the Calder near Halifax, where the workers gain virtue and wealth,

While on their useful works
From day to day intent, in their full minds
Evil no place can find . . .

On the whole, however, the mood is buoyant, and Dyer's belief that 'cheerful are the labours of the loom' does not ring too hollow. Wordsworth was to admire this poem immensely (many of Dyer's contemporaries found it ridiculous), and in a note to his own *Excursion* remarks tellingly, 'He wrote at a time when machinery was first beginning to be introduced, and his benevolent heart prompted him to augur from it nothing but good.'

Dyer's auguries, alas, were not fulfilled, and Leeds did not turn into the Carthage or Athens that he foresees. The North of England and Wales were ravaged by industrial development, and as the nineteenth century wore on, it became increasingly common for writers to share

Wordsworth's condemnation of the industrial labourer's unceasing toil, of the dizzy wheels of the machinery and the unremitting fires of the furnaces, of the harsh summons of the factory bell, of the slavery of child labour. It must be remembered that Wordsworth's protests against the machine age were not inspired merely by a spirit of conservation, an unwillingness to see his own landscape ruined (the Lake District to this day has remained for obvious reasons free from industrial development, though one can be fairly sure Wordsworth would not have thought much of Windscale and its successor Sellafield). Wordsworth was moved by humanitarian passion, a pity for the inhuman work conditions and unremitting labour that the new machines and their greedy owners demanded. He was quick to see the way that things were going, and the warnings that he issued were timely, but the revolution was under way, and there was no stopping it.

Not all radicals or humanitarians were anti-machine or against industrial development: then as now, there were those who argued that economic growth was the only hope of bettering the lot of the working man. Harriet Martineau hailed the advent of the railways to the Lake District, predicting that they would bring improved markets for rural products, as well as a welcome 'infusion of the intelligence and varied interests of the townspeople'. Her view of country people is less respectful than Wordsworth's, and she writes in *A Complete Guide to the English Lakes* (1885),

> We have no fear of injury, moral or economical, from the great recent change, the introduction of railways. The morals of rural districts are usually such as cannot well be made worse by any change. Drinking and kindred vices abound wherever, in our day, intellectual resources are absent: and nowhere is drunkenness a more prevalent and desperate curse than in the Lake District . . .

(Wordsworth, as we have seen, deplored the railways: as he grew older his views became increasingly conservative.) Charlotte Brontë in *Shirley* attacks the Luddite bigotry of the machine-breakers, and tries to portray in Robert Moore a hero who believes in industrial progress.

Brontë herself was far from radical in her political views, but she is always interesting on the subject of industry, the workers and the environment. The presence of the radical businessman Joshua Taylor, father of her enterprising friend Mary Taylor, broods over her work, giving us some sense of issues that must have been eagerly discussed in the Taylor household. In *North and South*, Elizabeth Gaskell makes a heroic attempt to love the grim landscapes of the North, and to foresee a future for them: unlike Wordsworth, she lived late enough in the century to see that there was no return to a pastoral Britain, there was only a way forward.

The works of Ebenezer Elliott, the 'corn-law rhymer' of Sheffield, provide a neat illustration of radical attitudes to the industrial landscape in the nineteenth century. In the preface to one of his poems, *The Village Patriarch*, he writes: 'If my composition smell of the workshop and the dingy warehouse, I cannot help it; soot is soot; and he who lives in a chimney will do well to take the air when he can, and ruralize now and then, even in imagination.' He follows his own advice, and ruralizes, writing flower poems, poems about Fountains Abbey, the yews at Maltby, Bolton Abbey, Brimham Rocks, Kinder Scout, Win Hill, Stanage Edge – urging the young mechanic and the artisan to rise and worship the god of nature, to fill his thoughts with 'the greenwood's melody'. Yet he knows that nature is an escape, and the soot is real: even the soot is an irrelevance compared with the bread tax. And he cannot dismiss the works of man: in 'Verses on the Opening of the Sheffield and Rotherham Railway' he greets the train in heroic terms, as a force for progress:

> For Mind shall conquer time and space;
> Bid East and West shake hands!
> Bring, over Ocean, face to face,
> Earth's ocean-sever'd strands;
> And, on his path of iron, bear
> Words that shall wither, in despair,
> The tyrants of all lands.

Similarly, in a poem called 'Steam at Sheffield', he hymns trade as a force for progress:

Trade makes thee sage; lo! thou read'st Locke and Scott
While the poor rustic, beast-like, lives and dies . . .

and claims that the city's smoke was found beautiful by Milton and the artist John Martin. True, the countryside is lovely, but so is the noise of the hammer, and city landscapes are sublime:

Oh, there is glorious harmony in this
Tempestuous music of the giant, Steam,
Commingling growl, and roar, and stamp, and hiss,
With flame and darkness! Like a Cyclops' dream,
It stuns our wandering souls, that start and scream
With joy and terror . . .
It is beneficent thunder, though at times
Like heaven's red bolt, it lightens fatally . . .

The metal god

. . . shall chase
The tyrant idols of remotest lands,
Preach science to the desert . . .

Elliott's faith in progress and science renders even their workings beautiful, and it is gratifying to report that science and progress have removed the smoke that until 1956 made Sheffield one of the dirtiest cities in Britain: since the Clean Air Act the citizens of Sheffield no longer see 'unnumber'd chimneys o'er, / From chimneys tall the smoky cloud aspire', and modern Sheffield has become one of our more handsome cities, its impressive contours revealed and glittering in the smokeless air.

Views such as those of Ebenezer Elliott became increasingly rare as the nineteenth century drew on. A loud wail of outrage rose from radicals and romantics, conservationists and conservatives alike, as they saw mines and quarries and railway cuttings gouged into the landscape, as over-populated cities overflowed with sewage and cholera and paupers. Those profiting from the muck kept quiet, then as now, but the wail did not go unheeded: gradually from the 1840s onwards Parliament passed Nuisance Removal Acts (1846, 1855, 1860, 1863, 1866 – the numerous new Acts and amendments indicate the growth of the problem), Housing Acts, Public Health Acts, Sanitary Acts, Smoke Abatement Acts: in 1863 H.M. Inspectorate of Alkali was set up, to control industrial waste.

But by the time these acts were passed, it was too late for the country-side to recover; some of the scars are permanent. Defoe's and Dyer's enthusiasm for busy, prosperous, expanding towns turned into the bitter rage of Friedrich Engels, Elizabeth Gaskell, Dickens, D. H. Lawrence, George Orwell – some of whom saw touches of the Sublime or Pictur-esque in the industrial landscape, but none of whom would defend the human misery it represented.

Not all aspects of industrialization caused equal indignation. Railways have always been something of a special case, and loyalty to the romance of the railways has been continuous. The building of them was of course strongly and indeed violently opposed by some, principally by those who had reason to fear loss of income from the decreasing use of canals, and many disinterested witnesses feared their impact on traditional ways of life. Far more, however, appear to have welcomed their advent, and not wholly for commercial reasons; like Elliott and Harriet Martineau they welcomed the spread of culture and information, the linking of peoples, and they were also filled with admiration for the magnificence of the engineering feats that made the railways possible. Fanny Kemble, describ-ing a journey from Liverpool with the great George Stephenson himself in 1830 in her *Record of a Girlhood* (1878), writes with affection of the engine, 'a snorting little animal, which I felt rather inclined to pat', and with awe of the grandeur of Stephenson's imagination and enterprise:

> We had now come fifteen miles, and stopped where the road tra-versed a wide and deep valley. Stephenson made me alight and led me down to the bottom of this ravine, over which, in order to keep his road level, he has thrown a magnificent viaduct of nine arches, the middle one of which is seventy feet high, through which we saw the whole of this beautiful little valley. It was lovely and wonderful beyond words. He here told me many curious things respecting this

ravine: how he believed the Mersey had once rolled through it; how the soil had proved so unfavourable for the foundation of his bridge that it was built upon piles . . . His way of explaining himself is peculiar, but very striking, and I understood, without difficulty, all that he said to me.

She goes on to declare herself 'most horribly in love' with 'the master of all these marvels', who was then in his fifties: he was to her a new hero of a new age.

F. S. Williams, in *Our Iron Roads* (1852), writes with equal admiration of the High Level Bridge at Newcastle, designed by Robert Stephenson:

> It is scarcely possible to imagine a more interesting and beautiful sight than it presents, with the huge span of arches diminishing in perspective, and the opening at the furthest end of the bridge showing only like a bright spot in the distance . . . The pillars, which carry the bridge, add greatly to the picturesque effect . . . such a combination of beautiful lines is seldom seen . . .

Williams is eager to emphasize that the railways do not detract from nature, and praises the Britannia tubular bridge over the Menai Straits in these terms:

> Could the reader stand upon the shores of the Isle of Anglesea, and view the entire spectacle, though but for a few moments, on some fine spring evening, he would retire with impressions of its magnificence which neither pen nor pencil can create . . . Science and nature are mingled in harmonious contrast, and receive the grateful homage of 'every rightly-constituted heart'.

His account of Stephenson's speech at a dinner in Newcastle in 1850 recalls Pope's account of Bathurst's landscape gardening and planting projects:

> Hills had been cut down, and valleys had been filled up; and where this simple expedient was inapplicable, high and magnificent

viaducts had been erected; and where mountains intervened, tunnels of unexampled magnitude had been unhesitatingly undertaken. Works had been scattered over the face of our country, bearing testimony to the indomitable enterprise of the nation, and the unrivalled skill of its artists . . .

Artists, not engineers: no wonder the railways continue to compel our affection and admiration. Williams devotes the same kind of thought to the proper way of landscaping tunnels as Pope did to his grotto: tunnel entrances should combine plainness with boldness, massiveness without heaviness; they should aim to give an impression of 'gloom, solidity and strength'. Burke's categories linger on – and one might at this stage recall that Burke admitted into the category of the Sublime (though with evident hesitation) foul, sulphurous and smoky smells, as well as very loud noises. The steam engines of one's childhood, as well as the tracks on which they ran, were surely examples of the Sublime.

Not all nineteenth-century witnesses were as easily impressed by the railway romance, however. Trollope, in *The Way We Live Now*, attacked the greed, fraud and speculation that had surrounded their construction, and Dickens in *Dombey and Son* finds the construction itself appalling. He describes the digging of the Camden Town cutting as a great earthquake which

rent the whole neighbourhood to its centre. Traces of its course were visible on every side. Houses were knocked down; streets broken through and stopped; deep pits and trenches dug in the ground; enormous heaps of earth and clay thrown up; buildings that were undermined and shaking, propped by great beams of wood. Here, a chaos of carts, overthrown and jumbled together, lay topsy-turvy at the bottom of a steep unnatural hill; there, confused treasures of iron soaked and rusted in something that had accidentally become a pond. Everywhere were bridges that led nowhere; thoroughfares that were wholly impassable; Babel towers of chimneys, wanting half their height; temporary wooden houses and enclosures, in the most unlikely situations; carcasses of ragged tenements, and fragments of unfinished walls and arches, and piles of scaffolding, and wildernesses of bricks, and giant forms of cranes, and tripods straddling above nothing. There were a hundred thousand shapes and substances of incompleteness, wildly mingled out of their places, upside down, burrowing in the earth, aspiring in the air, mouldering in the water, and unintelligible as any dream . . .

There is no praise in this wonderfully evocative passage for the mighty conquering mind of man, for science and progress: Dickens sees nothing but confusion and chaos, a mighty disorder rather than a ruthless mechanical order.

Yet Dickens's response to the squalor of the industrial landscape and the grimy intricacies of Victorian London is full of ambiguity. He denounces, but he loves: the confusion itself has an irresistible appeal for him, and he prides himself on his intimacy with backways and byways, attics and cellars, warehouses and wharves, courtyards and towpaths. His attacks on materialism are genuine and impassioned: his description of Coketown in *Hard Times* (the only novel he set in the industrial North) could serve as a companion piece to A. W. N. Pugin's similar attack on the meanness of industrial architecture in his pioneering proclamation of the new Gothic, *Contrasts*, first published in 1836. Pugin draws a grim picture of the new modern town, with its jail, its gasworks, its lunatic asylum, its Socialist Hall of Science and its ugly proliferation of nonconformist chapels. Dickens writes in Chapter 5 ('The Key-Note'):

It was a town of red brick, that would have been red if the smoke and ashes had allowed it; but, as matters stood it was a town of unnatural red and black like the painted face of a savage. It was a town of machinery and tall chimneys, out of which interminable serpents of smoke trailed themselves for ever and ever, and never got uncoiled. It had a black canal in it, and a river that ran purple with ill-smelling dye, and vast piles of building full of windows where there was a rattling and a trembling all day long, and where the piston of the steam-engine worked monotonously up and down, like the head of an elephant in a state of melancholy madness. It contained several large streets all very like one another, and many small streets still more like one another, inhabited by people equally like one another, who all went in and out at the same hours, with the same sound upon the same pavements, to do the same work, and to whom every day was the same as yesterday and tomorrow, and every year the counterpart of the last and the next . . .

You saw nothing in Coketown but what was severely workful. If the members of a religious persuasion built a chapel there – as the members of eighteen religious persuasions had done – they made it a pious warehouse of red brick, with sometimes (but this only in highly ornamented examples) a bell in a bird-cage on the top of it.

The North of England shocked and appalled him in a way that familiar London, however full of crime and horror, did not: in *The Old Curiosity Shop* (Chapter 45) Nell and her grandfather in their flight pass through an industrial district which, although left deliberately vague in its location in the text, Dickens admitted in a letter was based on his own experience of a journey between Birmingham and Wolverhampton. The outskirts are bad enough:

A long suburb of red brick houses, – some with patches of garden-ground, where coal-dust and factory smoke darkened the shrinking leaves, and coarse rank flowers; and where the struggling vegetation sickened and sank under the hot breath of kiln and furnace, making them by its presence seem yet more blighting and unwholesome than in the town itself, – a long, flat, straggling suburb passed, they came by slow degrees upon a cheerless region, where not a blade of grass was seen to grow; where not a bud put forth its promise in the spring; where nothing green could live but on the surface of the stagnant pools, which here and there lay idly sweltering by the black roadside.

The inner heart of this desolate district is like a vision of Hell, painted, as Borrow might have said, by a Bosch or a Rogier van der Weyden:

On mounds of ashes by the wayside, sheltered only by a few rough boards, or rotten pent-house roofs, strange engines spun and writhed like tortured creatures; clanking their iron chains, shrieking in their rapid whirl from time to time as though in torment unendurable, and making the ground tremble with their agonies. Dismantled houses here and there appeared, tottering to the earth, propped up by fragments of others that had fallen down, unroofed, windowless, blackened, desolate, but yet inhabited. Men, women, children, wan in their looks and ragged in attire, tended the engines, fed their tributary fires, begged upon the road, or scowled half-naked from the doorless houses. Then came more of the wrathful monsters, whose like they almost seemed to be in their wildness and their untamed air, screeching and turning round and round again; and still, before, behind, and to the right and left, was the same interminable perspective of brick towers, never ceasing in their black vomit, blasting all things living or inanimate, shutting out the face of day, and closing in on all these horrors with a dense dark cloud.

But night-time in this dreadful spot! – night, when the smoke was changed to fire; when every chimney spirted up its flame; and places, that had been dark vaults all day, now shone red-hot, with figures moving to and fro within their blazing jaws, and calling to one another with hoarse cries – night, when the noise of every strange machine was aggravated by the darkness; when the people near them looked wilder and more savage; when bands of unemployed labourers paraded in the roads, or clustered by torchlight round their leaders, who told them in stern language of their wrongs, and urged them on to frightful cries and threats . . .

Yet even in this waste of desolation Dickens finds goodness: the blackened workman who shelters Nell and her grandfather by his furnace has a heart of gold. And the nearer to London Dickens gets, the more his love struggles with his disgust. The river Thames, which flows through his books, may be dangerous, dirty, corpse-laden, rat-infested and criminal-infested, stinking with drainage from graveyards and waste from slaughterhouses and gasworks, but it is also exciting, powerful, intensely alive. *Our Mutual Friend* from its opening pages chooses the Thames for its linking image, but how different a Thames from the upstream one which Pope and Walpole loved, from the sweet Thames apostrophized by Spenser, from the Thames which John Denham addresses in his famous lines,

> O, could I flow like thee, and make thy stream
> My great example . . .

Dickens's Thames is far from calm and clear: it is laden with blackened barges, old hulks, dead cats and dead men, and at times seems so full of menace that it appears intent on drowning all its cargo, as in Chapter 14:

> Not a ship's hull, with its rusty iron links of cable run out of hawse-holes long discoloured with the iron's rusty tears, but seemed to be there with a fell intention. Not a figure-head but had the menacing look of bursting forward to run them down. Not a sluice gate, or a painted scale upon a post or wall, showing the depth of water, but seemed to hint, like the dreadfully facetious Wolf in bed in Grandmamma's cottage, 'That's to drown you in, my dearest!' Not a lumbering black barge, with its cracked and blistered side impending over them, but seemed to suck at the river with a thirst for sucking them under. And everything so vaunted the spoiling influences of water – discoloured copper, rotten wood, honey-combed stone, green dank deposit – that the after-consequences of being crushed, sucked under and drawn down, looked as ugly to the imagination as the main event.

This hardly sounds like the same river as Pope's Old Father Thames with his reverend head, dew-dropped tresses and golden horns, but it is a hundred times more interesting, and a hundred times more closely observed.

Dickens is the great poet of pollution, reminding us of what London fog was like before the Smoke Abatement Acts of the nineteenth century and the Clean Air Acts of the twentieth century. His London is dirty, but it is also wonderfully mysterious and dramatic. The first chapter of *Bleak House* gives us London in November, with an amazing mixture of horror and relish:

London. Michaelmas Term lately over, and the Lord Chancellor sitting in Lincoln's Inn Hall. Implacable November weather. As much mud in the streets, as if the waters had but newly retired from the face of the earth, and it would not be wonderful to meet a Megalosaurus, forty feet long or so, waddling like an elephantine lizard up Holborn Hill. Smoke lowering down from chimney-pots, making a soft black drizzle, with flakes of soot in it as big as full-grown snow-flakes – gone into mourning, one might imagine, for the death of the sun. Dogs, undistinguishable in mire. Horses, scarcely better; splashed to their very blinkers. Foot passengers, jostling one another's umbrellas, in a general infection of ill-temper, and losing their foot-hold at street-corners, where tens of thousands of other foot passengers have been slipping and sliding since the day broke (if this day ever broke), adding new deposits to the crust upon crust of mud, sticking at those points tenaciously to the pavement, and accumulating at compound interest.

Fog everywhere. Fog up the river, where it flows among green aits and meadows; fog down the river, where it rolls defiled among the tiers of shipping, and the waterside pollutions of a great (and dirty) city. Fog on the Essex marshes, fog on the Kentish heights. Fog creeping onto the cabooses of collier-brigs; fog lying out on the yards, and hovering in the rigging of great ships; fog drooping on the gunwales of barges and small boats. Fog in the eyes and throats of ancient Greenwich pensioners, wheezing by the firesides of their wards; fog in the stem and bowl of the afternoon pipe of the wrathful skipper, down in his close cabin; fog cruelly pinching the toes and fingers of his shivering little 'prentice boy on deck . . .

The raw afternoon is rawest, and the dense fog is densest, and the muddy streets are muddiest, near that leaden-headed old obstruction, appropriate ornament for the threshold of a leaden-headed old corporation: Temple Bar. And hard by Temple Bar, in Lincoln's Inn Hall, at the very heart of the fog, sits the Lord High Chancellor in his High Court of Chancery.

It is odd to reflect that this kind of smog-bound townscape, so common and yet so striking in the nineteenth and early twentieth centuries, has now almost vanished from memory: when Arnold Bennett's *The Card* was filmed in 1951 with Alec Guinness in the lead, the absence of real nineteenth-century smoke in the Potteries presented a technical problem.

Many other features of Dickens's London have also disappeared forever. There are still places for the diligent tourist to visit: the George in Borough High Street stands as a reminder of the galleried inns in *Pickwick Papers*; St Saviour's and St Magnus still loom over London Bridge, and although it is a different bridge from the one where Nancy hid, the steps are still known as Nancy's Steps; Lincoln's Inn is still there, with Mr Tulkinghorn's house; so are Chancery Lane, Clifford's Inn and Took's Court where Mr Snogsby lived. But many other landmarks have vanished – the Marshalsea Prison, the King's Bench Prison, the extraordinary and infamous area known as Jacob's Island, vividly described by Mayhew as well as Dickens. One can hardly regret the passing of such places, yet Dickens writes with such colour, such energy, such enthusiasm, that one feels more than disgust or even social indignation, as here in Chapter 50 of *Oliver Twist*. Jacob's Island lay to the east of the present site of Tower Bridge:

> To reach this place, the visitor has to penetrate through a maze of close, narrow and muddy streets, thronged by the roughest and poorest of water-side people . . . beyond Dockhead, in the Borough of Southwark, stands Jacob's Island, surrounded by a muddy ditch, six or eight feet deep, and fifteen or twenty wide when the tide is in, once called Mill Pond, but known in these days as Folly Ditch. It is a creek or inlet from the Thames, and can always be filled at high water by opening the sluices at the Lead Mills from which it took its old name. At such times, a stranger, looking from one of the old wooden bridges thrown across it at Mill Lane, will see the

inhabitants of the houses on either side lowering, from their back doors and windows, buckets, pails, domestic utensils of all kinds, in which to haul water up; and when his eye is turned from these operations to the houses themselves, his utmost astonishment will be excited by the scene before him. Crazy wooden galleries come on to the back of half-a-dozen houses, with holes from which to look upon the slime beneath; windows, broken and patched, with poles thrust out, on which to dry the linen that is never there; rooms so small, so filthy, so confined that the air would seem too tainted even for the dirt and squalor which they shelter; wooden chambers thrusting themselves out above the mud and threatening to fall into it – as some have done; dirt-besmeared walls and decaying foundations; every repulsive lineament of poverty, every loathsome indication of filth, rot and garbage: all these ornament the banks of Folly Ditch.

In Jacob's Island the warehouses are roofless and empty; the walls are crumbling down; the windows are windows no more; the doors are falling into the streets; the chimneys are blackened, but they yield no smoke . . .

Dickens was clearly fascinated by districts such as these; like Blanchard Jerrold and Gustave Doré in their book *London: A Pilgrimage*, published in 1872, he found the squalor horrible but picturesque. Something in him preferred disorder to order, and much as he deplored dirt and smoke, he had no sympathy with Blue Books and would-be town planners either. The confusion of the Camden Town cutting was too extreme even for him, but he gloried in the do-it-yourself attitude of Wemmick in *Great Expectations*, who was able to build himself a tiny Gothic castle, complete with moat, flagstaff and cannon, in the district of 'back lanes, ditches and little gardens' which Walworth then was. His poorest characters keep birds in cages and grow plants in pots on window sills. They prefer the ramshackle crazy makeshift world of London's overcrowded cellars to the institution of the workhouse, of which Dyer had written so warmly a century earlier. Dickens's novels give the reader an overwhelmingly powerful impression of a London that did not exist in

Dyer's day – a London swarming with crime and commerce, busy, crowded, half its life submerged literally underground, full of the most extraordinary contrasts and eccentricities, a city utterly different from the ordered vision planned by architects at the beginning of the nineteenth century – a free-style hotchpotch of a place, where both buildings and people were crazily varied in size, dwarves and angels, monsters and matrons, miniature castles and dank hovels and *nouveau-riche* mansions, all jumbled up together, all interlocking and juxtaposed in real life as they were in Dickens's crazily constructed plots. The city, in Dickens, is in a state of flux and ferment – vast already, it was growing daily vaster, and in his novels we catch sight of an age when shabby Pentonville was still a region of shady groves and Finchley a village, when one could look back at the dome of St Paul's from the quiet countryside after an hour or two of walking. The overall impression, despite the sordid detail and the social rage, is of intense exhilaration, of wonder at life's infinite variety, and at the infinite variety of the London scene.

Elizabeth Gaskell is a more composed and reflective novelist, and she was more deeply interested than Dickens in the causes and long-term effects of the Industrial Revolution. London offered a wide variety of distractions, whereas the great manufacturing cities of the North obliged the writer to concentrate more specifically on industrial change. Dickens was in many ways a zealous reformer, and his novels certainly provided ammunition for politicians and philanthropists: his portrait of the Thames is a vivid illustration of the abuses condemned by those heroes of reform and sanitation, Edwin Chadwick, George Godwin, Dr John Snow and Dr John Simon. Yet he was not interested in or capable of grasping the real nature of the new industrial problem of labour relations: in *Hard Times* and in the passage just quoted from *The Old Curiosity Shop* he shows little understanding of the unions, and paints the proletariat as a frightening, menacing and undifferentiated mob.

Gaskell, who spent most of her adult life in Manchester, was more realistic and more sympathetic to the worker's cause. As we have seen, she was brought up in a small country town, and loved country life and landscape. Unlike Dickens, she did not find the cobbled alleys and cellars of the city exciting. But as a conscientious minister's wife she was familiar with them: her descriptions of little paved courts with open gutters and lines full of washing are closely observed. She notices the little contrivances whereby women make themselves comfortable in the most unpromising surroundings – the table made from an old board across two candle-boxes, the pots of geraniums, the Japan tea-caddy. She also notices the hopelessness of those who have given up, who have been reduced to pawning their last possessions. *Mary Barton* is a novel from the same city, the same years and the same spirit as Engels' *The Condition of the Working Class in England*: this is the Manchester of her day (Chapter 6):

It [Berry Street] was unpaved; and down the middle a gutter forced its way, every now and then forming pools in the holes with which the street abounded. Never was the Old Edinburgh cry of 'Gardez l'eau' more necessary than in this street. As they passed, women from their doors tossed household slops of every description into the gutter; they ran into the next pool, which overflowed and stagnated. Heaps of ashes were the stepping-stones, on which the passer-by, who cared in the least for cleanliness, took care not to put his foot. Our friends were not dainty, but even they picked their way till they got to some steps leading down into a small area . . . You went down one step even from the foul area into the cellar in which a family of human beings lived. It was very dark inside. The window-panes were many of them broken and stuffed with rags, which was reason enough for the dusky light that pervaded the place even at mid-day. After the account I have given of the state of the street, no one can be surprised that on going into the cellar inhabited by Davenport, the smell was so foetid as almost to knock the two men down. Quickly recovering themselves, as those inured to such things do, they began to penetrate the thick darkness of the place, and to see three or four little children rolling on the damp, nay wet, brick floor, through which the stagnant, filthy moisture of the street oozed up . . .

There is no hint here of the visual excitement of Jacob's Island: Gaskell sees the streets and cellars through the eyes of those obliged to live in them, and she shares their disgust. She had good cause to: drainage was so bad in those days that even the larger houses in good districts were at risk, and in 1865 her comfortable home, Plymouth Grove, had to be evacuated while the drains were cleared out and repaired. Nobody in Manchester could escape the effects of the environment: the cholera epidemics claimed more of the poor than of the rich, but the rich were far from immune.

In *North and South* Gaskell gives a telling account of the impact of the North upon a girl brought up in the gentle South. Margaret Hale is removed from a pretty rural vicarage in Hampshire to the Northern manufacturing town of Milton, where she suffers severely from culture shock, and is obliged to abandon her prejudices against trade and the manufacturing classes. At first everything surprises and offends – the people are busier and more 'purpose-like', their clothes are greyer: 'There were no smock-frocks, even among the country-folk; they retarded motion, and were apt to catch on machinery, so the habit of wearing them had died out.' Even their carts have more of iron and less of wood. Milton itself is covered with a deep leaden cloud, and it has 'long, straight, hopeless streets of regularly-built houses, all small and of brick': it is full of great loaded lorries. She is appalled even by the wallpaper of the house that she and her parents manage to rent. But gradually she learns her way about, makes friends, adjusts her expectations. At first she is surprised that Mr Thornton the mill-owner should choose to live so near his mill, for his house is handsome enough, and he is wealthy: it is blackened with smoke, she notes in Chapter 15 ('Masters and Men'),

> but with paint, windows and steps kept scrupulously clean. It was evidently a house which had been built some fifty or sixty years. The stone facings – the long, narrow windows and the number of them – the flights of steps up to the front door, ascending from either side, and guarded by railing – all witnessed to its age. Margaret only wondered why people who could afford to live in so good a house, and keep it in such perfect order, did not prefer a much smaller dwelling in the country, or even some suburb; not in the continual whirl and din of the factory . . . The yard, too, with the great doors

in the dead wall as a boundary, was but a dismal look-out for the sitting rooms of the house . . .

But by the end of the novel she has come to accept that Mr Thornton, far from being ashamed of his trade, is proud of it. The growth of their mutual respect, and her softening influence upon his attitude to his workers, is clearly intended to offer a suggestion of hope, a hint of the healing that could take place if employers stopped exploiting their men and talked to them, if the South stopped despising and exploiting the resources and landscapes of the North. Margaret learns that the prettiness of Hampshire depends indirectly on the smoke of Milton. In Gaskell's day, these reflections were relatively new, commonplace though they may be now.

Social protest became a dominant theme in the novel from the 1840s onwards. Frances Trollope, Disraeli, Charles Kingsley, Charles Reade reflected in their novels the concern and anger that Engels documents in *The Condition of the Working Class in England in 1844*. The despoliation of the landscape was inevitably an associated theme, though most of these writers viewed the subject not from an aesthetic, but from a humanitarian standpoint. Frances Trollope's novel, *The Life and Adventures of Michael Armstrong, The Factory Boy*, published in 1840, draws a vivid picture of a Lancashire manufacturing town, with its smoking chimneys and dirty alleys, its overcrowded houses and yards where half-starved cats, pigs, dogs and crawling infants root together amongst the garbage. Her hero Michael is lucky enough to escape from the dark valley to the clean hills of Westmoreland, where he becomes a shepherd. This idyllic pastoral conclusion was not widely available in real life. The portrait of Manchester drawn by Engels confirms the accounts of Gaskell and Frances Trollope: he too comments on

the multitude of pigs walking about in all the alleys, rooting into the offal heaps, or kept imprisoned in small pens . . . In almost every court one or several such pens may be found, into which the inhabitants of the court throw all refuse and offal, whence the swine grow fat; and the atmosphere, confined on all four sides, is utterly corrupted by putrefying animal and vegetable substances . . . Such is the Old Town of Manchester, and on re-reading my description, I am forced to admit that instead of being exaggerated, it is far from black enough to convey a true impression of the filth, ruin, and uninhabitableness, the defiance of all considerations of cleanliness, ventilation, and health which characterize the construction of this single district, containing at least twenty to thirty thousand inhabitants. And such a district exists in the heart of the second city of England, the first manufacturing city of the world.

Engels does not exaggerate: statistics support his observations. The *Report on the State of Large Towns and Populous Districts* of 1845 demonstrated that one privy was shared by an average of 212 people. No wonder the people were dirty and cholera triumphant: 'How', asks Engels, 'can people wash when they have only the dirty Irk water at hand?'

Yet Engels does not paint a picture of unremitting gloom: he is sensitive to landscape, to differences within the industrial landscape. The woollen district of the West Riding of Yorkshire is, he says, 'a charming region, a beautiful green hill country . . . The houses of rough grey stone look so neat and clean in comparison with the blackened brick buildings of Lancashire, that it is a pleasure to look at them.' Huddersfield he claims as 'the handsomest by far of all the factory towns of Yorkshire and Lancashire, by reason of its charming situation and modern architecture' – though it too, of course, had its bad quarter. Lancashire was once beautiful, and some of it remained so; he writes of 'the charming green valleys of the Ribble, the Irwell, the Mersey, and their tributaries . . .' It was only gradually that the nation awoke to the extent of the ruin that was spreading through green valleys, eating up arable land, depositing its heaps of waste with random indifference. Manufacturers were forced to accept some curbs on their activities: in Gaskell's *North and South* there is a long discussion about the rights and wrongs of the government's imposition of smoke control on factory owners. But the problem of derelict land was so vast that nobody tackled it; indeed, it has not been adequately confronted in our own day, as the tragedy of Aberfan in 1966 bore witness. People accepted slag heaps and waste land as necessary evils: nobody was held responsible.

This is not to say that nobody noticed. Dickens noticed, as we have seen. Queen Victoria, visiting Manchester in 1852, was displeased by the dirt, and wrote in her diary, 'As far as the eye can reach, one sees nothing but chimneys, blazing furnaces, many deserted but not pulled down, with wretched cottages around them . . .' James Nasmyth, himself the inventor of some of the beautiful functional objects of the Industrial Revolution, was appalled by what had happened to the Black Country, and writes:

> Amidst these flaming, smoky clanging works, I beheld the remains of what had once been happy farmhouses, now ruined and deserted. The ground beneath them had sunk by the working out of the coal, and they were falling to pieces. They had in former times been surrounded by clumps of trees; but only the skeletons of them remained, dilapidated, black, and lifeless. The grass had been parched and killed by the vapours of sulphurous acid thrown out by the chimneys; and every herbaceous object was of a ghastly gray – the emblem of vegetable death in its saddest aspect. Vulcan had driven out Ceres.

Regions that suffered severely from this attitude were those where industry was small-scale and scattered. The potteries of Staffordshire and the mining districts of Nottinghamshire are remarkable for the curious intermingling of countryside, housing and industrial development, for the apparently haphazard distribution of pitheads, pot banks, factories. Arnold Bennett and D. H. Lawrence, both products of such landscapes, describe the farms that linger on amidst the grime, the close interconnections of rural and industrial life. Both give a strong impression of men working in a man-made landscape, of the effect that the landscape has had upon those who have toiled to create it. The two men reacted differently to the grim surroundings of their childhood – Lawrence with an impassioned love of nature at its most exotic and most foreign, Bennett with indifference to nature but a deep love of unprovincial, sophisticated cosmopolitan life. Both turned their backs on the districts that nourished them, yet both commemorate them in novels inspired by a mingled love and hatred.

Bennett grew up in the Potteries, which he considered for years to be too ugly and uninteresting for fiction; his early stories are set in the realistic gloom of a poor clerk's London, or in the unreal glamour of luxury hotels. He did not find his true voice until he wrote his first Staffordshire novel, *Anna of the Five Towns*, in which he created the scene of his finest works. Interestingly, he credits George Moore with having opened his eyes to the fictional possibilities of the Potteries: he read and admired his *Mummer's Wife*, set in Hanley and based on a few weeks' research, and decided that he with his long and intimate experience could do even better. The love-hate is evident from the first chapter. Bursley (his version of Burslem) lies, he says,

> in an extensive valley, which must have been one of the fairest spots in Alfred's England, but which is now defaced by the activities of a quarter of a million people. Five contiguous towns – Turnhill, Bursley, Hanbridge, Knype, and Longshaw – united by a single winding thoroughfare some eight miles in length, have inundated the valley like a succession of great lakes . . . They are mean and forbidding of aspect – sombre, hard-featured, uncouth; and the vaporous poison of their ovens and chimneys has soiled and shrivelled the surrounding country till there is no village lane within a league but what offers a gaunt and ludicrous travesty of rural charms. Nothing could be more prosaic than the huddled, redbrown streets; nothing more seemingly remote from romance. Yet be it said that romance is even here – the romance which, for those who have an eye to perceive it, ever dwells amid the seats of industrial manufacture, softening the coarseness, transfiguring the squalor, of these mighty alchemic operations . . . Here, indeed, is nature repaid for some of her notorious cruelties. She imperiously bids man sustain and reproduce himself, and this is one of the places where in the very act of obedience he wounds and maltreats her. Out beyond the municipal confines, where the subsidiary industries of coal and iron prosper amid a wreck of verdure, the

struggle is grim, appalling, heroic – so ruthless is his havoc of her, so indomitable her ceaseless recuperation . . . The grass grows; though it is not green, it grows. In the very heart of the valley, hedged about with furnaces, a farm still stands, and at harvest-time the sooty sheaves are gathered in . . .

We hear an attitude very different from that of Elizabeth Gaskell, Dickens, and Engels. Bennett accepts the industrial landscape, he takes it for granted, his family for generations had known nothing else. Despite the lingering farm, the memory of unspoiled rural beauty has vanished into a past as mythical as Alfred's England. The scientific optimism of Dyer and Erasmus Darwin had passed through despair and disgust into a kind of acceptance, a realization that one must look for beauty even amidst the dirt, a recognition that millions of men were going to have to make the best of living with the reality of industry. Bennett and the characters in his books find their pleasure where they can, on canal banks, in churchyards and back streets, in municipal parks. He does not romanticize the squalor, but he finds it intensely interesting: he 'reads' it, in much the way that W. G. Hoskins and his successors learned to read landscape, looking for causes, changes, historical meanings, odd accidental aesthetic satisfactions.

The opening chapters of Bennett's two greatest novels, *The Old Wives' Tale* and *Clayhanger*, both give panoramic views of the whole region, using a technique not dissimilar to that employed by Dickens at the beginning of *Bleak House*: the wider setting narrows to the perceptions of one or two largely imperceptive people living within it, unaware of the forces that created their world. Yet Bennett is much more interested than Dickens in causes. Dickens evokes the fog, but does not add a lecture on air pollution. Bennett tells us everything – the influence of canals and railways, the quarrels that preceded their construction, the nature of the trade that made the Potteries wealthy, the dependence of the rest of the country on this trade. 'England can show nothing more beautiful and nothing uglier than the works of nature and the works of man to be seen within the limits of the county', he tells us – and elaborates, describing the river Trent, 'the calm and characteristic stream of middle England', 'the narrow boats passing in a leisure majestic and infinite over the surface of the stolid canals', and the muddle of ovens and chimneys, the slippery streets 'where the housewife must change white window-curtains at least once a fortnight if she wishes to remain respectable'. His evocation is tinged with a characteristic Northern contempt for those who use the products of such a place without even knowing where they came from; the shame at a despoiled landscape is mingled with defiant pride.

Bennett looks through the nineteenth-century nightmare to the brighter, cleaner age that went before. He finds a relic of the past, in a fine pot-work, 'a long two-storey building, purest Georgian, of red brick with very elaborate stone facings which contrasted admirably with the austere simplicity of the walls'. The canals in particular provided a fitting object for admiration, for they recalled the great days of grand hopes, the eighteenth century when the Potteries came to life, through the discovery of the Chinese process for firing porcelain, and through the vision and enterprise of the early manufacturers – above all of Josiah Wedgwood, who combined business sense, artistic flair and philanthropy. Wedgwood was a friend of Erasmus Darwin, and shared many of his enthusiasms. In the 1760s Wedgwood promoted the building of the Trent-and-Mersey canal, which was designed by the engineer James Brindley. Significantly, Bennett liked to claim a family connection with this colourful local hero, and said that the Bennetts were 'descended illegitimately . . . from Schemer Brindley the engineer'. The canals, then as now, provided an interesting world of their own, cutting their way past houses and factories, their towpaths providing a refuge for anglers, small boys, lovers and old men with dogs. *Clayhanger* opens with a description of young Edwin and his friend leaning on the stone parapet of a bridge watching the slow progress of a horse-drawn canal-boat roofed with tarpaulins.

The dignified union of art and industry which Wedgwood foresaw when he named one of his manufacturing suburbs Etruria did not of course come to pass; the canals bear witness to his lofty aspirations, but the wastes of spoiled land and slag-heaps present industry's other face. In this century, the Potteries were notorious for having more waste ground within their boundaries than any other boroughs in the country. Yet Bennett finds even the mess of interest. Like Edwin Clayhanger, he walked through it every day to school, and at least in retrospect saw beauty in it, writing in the opening chapter:

> To the south of them, a mile and a half off, in the wreathing mist of the Cauldon Bar Ironworks, there was a yellow gleam that even the capricious sunlight could not kill, and then two rivers of fire sprang from the gleam and ran in a thousand delicate and lovely hues down the side of a mountain of refuse. They were emptying a few tons of molten slag at the Cauldon Bar Ironworks. The two rivers hung slowly dying in the mists of smoke. They reddened and faded, and you thought they had vanished, and you could see them yet, and then they escaped the baffled eye, unless a cloud aided them for a moment against the sun; and their ephemeral but enchanting beauty had expired for ever.

These were not the beauties amongst which Bennett as a successful author chose to live: in later years he said that he could not even pass through the district by train without shuddering. He was sympathetic to the apparently hopeless efforts of those who tried to introduce improvements, and several times defends its parks, which, though unlovely, 'symbolized the first faint renascence of the longing for beauty in a district long given up to unredeemed ugliness'. In *Helen with the High Hand* he writes of Bursley's pride in its park:

> You may tell me that the terra-cotta constructions within it carry ugliness beyond a joke; you may tell me that in spite of the park's vaunted situation nothing can be seen from it save the chimneys and kilns of earthenware manufacturies, the scaffoldings of pitheads, the ample dome of the rate-collector's offices, the railways, minarets of nonconformity, sundry undulating square miles of monotonous house-roofs, the long scarves of black smoke which add such interest to the sky of the Five Towns – and, of course, the gold angel. But I tell you that before the days of the

park, lovers had no place to walk in but the cemetery; not the ancient church-yard of St Lukes (the rector would like to catch them at it!) – the borough cemetery! One generation was forced to make love over the tombs of another – and such tombs! – before the days of the park.

Bennett shows himself here as a man belonging to a world conscious of the need for town planning, garden cities, green belts. He would surely have sympathized with the heroic efforts of reclamation made by Stoke in the 1960s and '70s. He writes of the 'romance of machinery and manufacture', but never forgets the ordinary daily lives of women washing curtains and scrubbing steps, of children and lovers with nowhere to go. His response foreshadows that of those twentieth-century poets of suburban and provincial life, Larkin and Betjeman. On a return visit to the Potteries in 1907, after years away in Paris, he writes in his *Journal* with mingled horror and affection, in phrases that summon up a landscape and a life style with lovely economy:

> Sunday, 22 December, 1907: We came down to the Potteries yesterday afternoon. Seemed to have better ideas as to the scientific causes of provincialism.
> I went for a walk this morning up Sneyd Green. Untidiness; things left at a loose end. Broken walls, deserted entrances to what had been spacious gardens. Everything very misty . . . Men in bright neckties sallying forth, rather suspicious, defiant, meanly-shrewd look. Mean stunted boy crouching along smoking a pipe which he hid in his hand while holding it in his mouth. Complete waste of Sunday: deserted goal posts in gloomy mist. Mild wind. Cold, chilling, clammy . . .

What escaped provincial has not shuddered like him, at the sight of those gloomy goal posts?

D. H. Lawrence came from a similar social background, though his family, unlike Bennett's, had not clambered laboriously up into the middle classes: his writing is more impassioned, less scientific. Indeed, he blamed

Bennett for his acceptance, declaring that the novel should be 'a great kick at misery'. He shows the same recoil from overcrowding, from ugly housing and ugly lives. In 'Nottingham and the Mining Country', a piece written towards the end of his life, in 1929, he blames the ugliness squarely on the employers:

> The great crime which the moneyed classes and promoters of industry committed in the palmy Victorian days was the condemning of the workers to ugliness, ugliness, ugliness: meanness and formless and ugly surroundings, ugly ideals, ugly religion, ugly hope, ugly love, ugly furniture, ugly houses, ugly relationship between workers and employers. The human soul needs actual beauty even more than bread . . . If the company, instead of building those sordid and hideous Squares, then, when they had that lovely site to play with, there on the hill top: if they had put a tall column in the middle of the small market-place, and run three parts of a circle of arcade round the pleasant space, where people could stroll or sit, and with the handsome houses behind! If they had made big, substantial houses, in apartments of five or six rooms . . . You may say the working man would not have accepted such a form of life: the Englishman's home is his castle, etc., etc., – 'my own little house'. But if you can hear every word the next-door-people say, there's not much castle. And if you can see everybody in the square if they go to the wc! And if your one desire is to get out of the 'castle' and 'your own little home'! – well, there's not much to be said for it . . . There's nothing to be said for the 'little home' any more: a great scrabble of ugly pettiness over the face of the land.

Yet Lawrence found more than ugliness in the landscapes of his childhood, and as Alan Sillitoe points out in his essay 'Lawrence and District' (1972), his preoccupation with its ugliness grew with absence: his early works show a powerful though painful love, an appreciation of the harsh industrial hillsides, a keen sense of the pleasures of ordinary working people – outings, bicycle rides, walks by the Trent, visits to nearby beauty spots – Matlock, the Hemlock Stone, Wingfield Manor, Lincoln Cathedral. As Arnold Bennett could see the picturesque charm of Bruges in the canals and pony-drawn crate-floats of Burslem, so Paul Morel in *Sons and Lovers*, as he and his mother hang over the canal parapet in Nottingham: "'It's just like Venice", he said, seeing the sunshine on the water that lay between high factory walls.' This pleasure gradually dissolves, as Sillitoe says, into the 'final maniac rantings of Mellors the gamekeeper in *Lady Chatterley's Lover* who scorns the young colliers who go off to dances in Mansfield on their motorbikes', but in his youth it was real enough, and as late as 1926 he wrote to Ralph Gardner from Florence, of the region round Eastwood, 'That's the country of my heart' – a warmer tribute than Bennett ever bestowed on the Potteries.

And the district of which he wrote did contain more beauties than Bennett's, though as much ugliness. The mines which disfigure it are small, though not as small as the 'gin-pits' of the days of Charles II, described in the first paragraph of *Sons and Lovers*. The financiers had taken over in the nineteenth century, building the housing Lawrence condemns so fiercely, themselves living apart in the luxury of houses like the Crich mansion in *Women in Love*. But much of the countryside remained rural, and to this day the pit at Eastwood is surrounded by cornfields. The strange intermingling of farms and pits is reflected directly in the imagery of Lawrence's novels: the idyllic descriptions of Haggs Farm in *Sons and Lovers* and of Marsh Farm in *The Rainbow* are not so much contrasted as inextricably interwoven with descriptions of the views of the twinkling lights of distant collieries, of children playing street games beneath lamp posts, of railways and canal embankments and allotments. Indeed, Lawrence seems to make a point of combining pit and cornfields, Ceres and Vulcan, in one reference.

Lawrence's feelings for the landscape are as mixed as the landscape itself: like his feelings for people, they pulse and throb and shift from love to hatred in a restless flux and swirl of emotion. At times his characters are overwhelmed by the beauty of a summer night, an orchard, a lake: at other times they are repelled even by what they love. In *Sons and Lovers* there are moments of calm, when his characters inhabit their streets and houses with an ordinary pleasure, and the setting of their lives is evoked without turmoil or indignation; Scargill Street, in Chapter 4 (the street in Eastwood on the corner of which the Lawrences lived when David was born), was ordinary enough, yet its children, playing in the dark without their overcoats,

> felt quite select . . . The entry was very dark, and at the end the whole great night opened out, in a hollow, with a little tangle of lights below where Minton pit lay, and another far away opposite for Selby. The farthest tiny lights seemed to stretch out the darkness forever . . . There was only this one lamp-post. Behind was the great scoop of darkness, as if all the night were there. In front, another wide, dark way opened over the hill brow . . . They all loved Scargill Street for its openness, for the great scallop of the world it had in view. On summer evenings, the women would stand against the field fence, gossiping, facing the west, watching the sunsets flare quickly out, till the Derbyshire hills ridged across the crimson far away, like the black crest of a newt.

Paul Morel, travelling by train home from work, felt 'rich in life' and happy as he watched the lights of the town 'like myriad petals shaken to the ground from the shed stars; and beyond was the red glare of the furnaces, playing like hot breath on the clouds'. But these feelings can quickly turn to hatred: Clara and Paul, leaning on the wall above the cliff at Nottingham Castle in Chapter 10, look down at dwellings like

> black, poisonous herbage, in thick rows and crowded beds, stretching right away, broken now and then by taller plants, right to where the river glistened in a hieroglyph across the country. The steep scarp cliffs across the river looked puny. Great stretches of country darkened with trees and faintly brightened with corn-land, spread towards the haze, where the hills rose blue beyond grey.
>
> 'It is comforting', said Mrs Dawes, 'to think the town goes no farther. It is only a little sore upon the country yet.'
>
> 'A little scab', Paul said.
>
> She shivered. She loathed the town.

In later novels, Lawrence's loathing becomes hysterical: even his pleasure has an element of the perverse. In *Women in Love* Gudrun's response as she walks through the town with her sister is charged with sexuality; she runs the gauntlet of the miners' attentions, enjoying but hating their louche comments. The unfinished, town-and-country muddle of landscape is brilliantly suggested in Chapter 9:

> On the left, as the girls walked silently, the coal-mine lifted its great mounds and its patterned head-stocks, the black railway with the trucks at rest looked like a harbour just below, a large bay railroad with anchored wagons.
>
> Near the second level-crossing, that went over many bright rails, was a farm belonging to the collieries, and a great round globe of iron, a disused boiler, huge and rusty and perfectly round, stood silently in a paddock by the road. The hens were pecking round it, some chickens were balanced on the drinking trough, wagtails flew away in among trucks, from the water.

In this 'hot world silted with coal dust', with its dusty corn, Gudrun like the young Edwin Clayhanger perceives a certain beauty:

> The girls descended between the houses with slate roofs and blackish brick walls. The heavy gold glamour of approaching sunset lay over all the colliery district, and the ugliness overlaid with beauty was like a narcotic to the senses. On the roads silted with black dust, the rich light fell more warmly, more heavily, over all the amorphous squalor a kind of magic was cast, from the glowing close of day.
>
> 'It has a foul kind of beauty, this place', said Gudrun evidently suffering from fascination. 'Can't you feel in some way, a thick, hot attraction in it? I can. It quite stupefies me.'

The industrial landscape for her is charged with 'a glamorous thickness of labour and maleness', which threatens and attracts her, as it clearly did Lawrence. No wonder his reactions, endowing as they did the landscape itself with human characteristics, were so violent and so ambivalent.

In *The Lost Girl,* he sums up this ambivalence himself in a striking phrase. His heroine, Alvina, is smitten with 'the nostalgia of the repulsive, heavy-footed Midlands'. Alvina, like Gudrun and Ursula, is allowed to escape, as Lawrence did himself, to wilder, more violent and grandiose scenery – in her case the mountains of Italy – but most of the book is devoted to the Midlands, and Alvina like Gudrun feels their sinister charm. In the fourth chapter, she is taken down a mine by her father, and on emerging from the underground darkness into the daylight she sees her home town with new eyes:

> When she was up on the earth again she blinked and peered at the world in amazement. What a pretty, luminous place it was, carved in substantial luminosity. What a strange and lovely place, bubbling iridescent-golden on the surface of the underworld. Iridescent-golden – could anything be more fascinating! Like a lovely glancing surface on fluid pitch. But a velvet surface. A velvet surface of golden light, velvet-pile of gold and pale luminosity, and strange beautiful elevations of houses and trees, and depressions of fields and roads, all golden and floating like atmospheric majolica. Never had the common ugliness of Woodhouse seemed so entrancing. She thought she had never seen such beauty – a lovely luminous majolica, living and palpitating, the glossy, svelte world-surface, the exquisite face of all the darkness. It was like a vision. Perhaps gnomes and subterranean workers, enslaved in the era of light, see with such eyes. Perhaps that is why they are absolutely blind to conventional ugliness. For truly nothing could be more hideous than Woodhouse, as the miners had built it and disposed it, and yet, the very cabbage-stumps and rotten fences of the gardens, the very back-yards were instinct with magic, molten as they seemed with the bubbling-up of the under-darkness, bubbling up of majolica weight and luminosity, quite ignorant of the sky, heavy and satisfying.

In his poetry, Lawrence fulminates again and again against the dominion of the machine, and the new slavery of mankind – a rhetoric in a strong and respectable tradition, linking him with Wordsworth, Carlyle, Matthew Arnold, with all the great Victorians who protested against the ugliness of materialism. While the twentieth century, like the nineteenth, produced its champions of machinery, amongst them the Vorticists, who proclaimed the aesthetic beauty of the machine, and saw themselves as the poets and artists of the future, this movement had few adherents: more pervasive was the attitude of left-wing writers of the 1920s and '30s, torn between a desire to show respect for the working man by describing his habitat, taking his life seriously, and an equally high-principled desire to denounce that habitat as uninhabitable. A new kind of urban poetry appears in Stephen Spender's and W. H. Auden's laconic, unromantic verse, liberally sprinkled with references to gas-works, sour canals, pylons, motor bicycles and factory girls; Auden prays for 'new styles of architecture, a change of heart'. The poetry is at once a cry of protest and an act of homage.

This ambivalence runs through much of the literature of the period; films and novels which intend to denounce the modern age of machinery often end up perversely celebrating it. H. G. Wells, Aldous Huxley and Evelyn Waugh in different ways show a similar conflict: they condemn or question the advance of science, but at the same time they are enthralled by it, and cannot resist their admiration for a Brave New World of skyscrapers, aluminium furniture, glittering glass walls, aeroplanes and motorcars. A strange new beauty was growing out of the muddle, new forms, new aesthetic concepts, a new man-made paradise. Artists and architects responded more enthusiastically to this vision than writers, for obvious reasons, but writers could not fail to reflect a glimmer of it.

A world of pure form, however, remains an unrealizable dream: the reality is still muddle, some of it so extreme that it has its own purity. There are architects, planners and writers who defend the beauty of dereliction. The lunar landscape of the china-clay district of Cornwall, for example, is so sensational and so obstinate that even a committed reformer like environmental journalist John Barr was obliged in his *Derelict Landscapes* (1969) to admit the 'lunatic attraction' of its 'savage dereliction'. And this landscape has found its own voice and its own poet, in Jack Clemo, who wrote of clay-pits, quarried mud, excavators standing at pitheads, 'the sleek belly of sprawling clay mounds': in 'The Two Beds' he compared his landscape to D. H. Lawrence's, who was 'the child of the black pit' and the underground:

> . . . You never saw
> The clay as I have seen it, high
> On the bare hills, the little breasts
> So white in the sun, all the veins running white
> Down to the broad womb with its scars.

He prefers the white cones and 'slow wash of lunar light', finding salvation in his own terrain. In 'Sufficiency' he writes:

> Yes, I might well grow tired
> Of slighting flowers all day long,
> Of making my song
> Of the mud in the kiln, of the wired
> Poles on the clay-dump; but where
> Should I find my personal pulse of prayer
> If I turned from the broken, scarred
> And unkempt land, the hard
> Contours of dogma, colourless hills?
> Is there a flower that thrills
> Like frayed rope? Is there grass
> That cools like gravel, and are there streams
> Which murmur as clay-silt does that Christ redeems?
> I have not heard of any . . .

The reclamation of industrial wasteland, so well addressed by John Barr, is a perennially interesting topic. Barr suspected that 'the obstinate, complex and sensational concentration of heaps and holes' of the Cornish china-clay tips and pits might prove beyond redemption; the local county planners at the time seemed resigned to living with them. They had not foreseen the ambitious Eden Project that sprang up in

Clemo's heartland at the beginning of the twenty-first century, which echoes the forms of the dereliction it replaced. For it too is lunar. Being on a tourist route to the West Country aided the success of this great gardening gamble, and it has proved far more popular than its modest Yorkshire cousin, the Earth Centre at Conisbrough, which struggled in vain to attract visitors. The Earth Centre was a gallant attempt to redeem the coal mines and their slag, but it was relentlessly slagged off by journalists from down south. The landscape of the Don Valley (greatly admired by Walter Scott) had been ruined by mining and by the subsequent collapse of mining. So had the local communities and the economy. Nobody wants to go on holiday to South Yorkshire. It is derelict once more.

The dramatic landscapes of mine, mountain and quarry are also celebrated in fantasy form in J. R. R. Tolkien's epics; his many descriptions of wasted and ravaged lands are clearly drawn in part from his personal memories of trench warfare on the Somme in the First World War, but they also remind one irresistibly of scenes such as the slate quarries at Blaenau Ffestiniog (home, as we have seen, to John Cowper Powys) and the burning mountains of slag in the Neath valley described a century earlier by George Borrow. From childhood on, Tolkien was entranced by the Welsh language; even the names of Welsh railway stations on passing coaltrucks – Nantyglo, Blaen-Rhondda, Penrhiwceiber – seemed charged with magic and beauty, and his later studies of Early and Middle English literature reinforced his feeling for the landscapes that this language evoked. His woods of birch and alder, his Misty Mountains and Iron Mountains with their narrow passes, lonely meres, memorial cairns, and frowning walls of sheer rock cut by ancient road-builders, are very Welsh. The dwarves, 'stone-hard, stubborn, fast in friendship and in enmity', are the hard-working underground engineers and craftsmen of Middle-earth, called 'Naugrim, the Stunted People, and Gonnhirrim, Masters of Stone'. They are the good spirits, as it were, of the Industrial Revolution, and have 'marvellous skill with metals and with stone; but in that ancient time iron and copper they loved to work, rather than silver or gold' (*The Silmarillion*, Chapter 10). The orcs and goblins, under the leadership of the wicked Sauron or Melkor, are the bad spirits, responsible for the hideous wasted plains of Gorgoroth, pocked with great craters, for the smoking chasms, and reeking furnaces of Mount Doom. The climax of *The Lord of the Rings* takes place in a ravaged nightmare of an industrial landscape:

> He was come to the heart of the realm of Sauron and the forges of his ancient might, greatest in Middle-earth; all other powers were here subdued. Fearfully he took a few uncertain steps in the dark, and then all at once there came a flash of red that leaped upward, and smote the high black roof. Then Sam saw that he was in a long cave or tunnel that bored into the Mountain's smoking cone. But only a short way ahead its floor and the walls on either side were cloven with a great fissure, out of which the red glare came, now leaping up, now dying down into darkness; and all the while far below there was a rumour and trouble as of great engines throbbing and labouring . . .

The style is heroic, the imagery grandiose; on one level Tolkien is writing about the struggle of Good and Evil, but on another level he is describing the destruction of the landscape. He was an ardent conservationist, deeply distressed by the spread of suburbs, roads, and litter through the West Midlands he had loved from boyhood, and his account of the destruction of the plain of Ard-Galen in Chapter 18 of *The Silmarillion* is in part a response to his growing fear for the countryside:

> Then suddenly Morgoth sent forth great rivers of flame that ran down swifter than Balrogs from Thangorodrim, and poured all over the plain; and the Mountains of Iron belched forth fires of many poisonous hues, and the fume of them stank upon the air, and was deadly. Thus Ard-Galen perished, and fire devoured its grasses; and it became a burning and desolate waste, full of a choking dust, barren and lifeless. Thereafter its name was changed, and it was called Anfauglith, the Gasping Dust.

Such passages – and there are many in Tolkien's works – recall the paintings of John Martin, whose portrayals of Babylon, Sodom, Nineveh and Pandemonium have, equally, a double imagery; his Biblical scenes of destruction and violence and massive engineering feats relate clearly enough, to the modern eye, to his interest in the building of the railways, to the explosions and blazing furnaces of the Industrial Revolution. Industry is the ultimate Evil, the herald of the Great Apocalypse, like Milton's Satan heroic but dreadful, sublime but destructive: Tolkien personifies its dark spirit in his rebellious Melkor, whose sin, significantly, was to seek the Imperishable Flame.

It would be hard to imagine a writer more different from Tolkien in most ways than George Orwell, yet they share a similar sense of horror at the irrevocable ruin of the countryside, and the power of the machine. *Coming up for Air*, first published in 1939, is one of the most powerful novels ever written about the threat to what we now call the environment. Tolkien, apparently, used to cry out whenever he saw a new road cutting across the corner of a field, 'There goes the last of England's arable!', and Orwell's not unhobbit-like hero, George Bowling, was heartbroken when he returned to the lost paradise of his childhood village in Oxfordshire, Lower Binfield, and found it had disappeared:

> I don't mean that it had been demolished. It had merely been swallowed ... All I could see was an enormous river of brand-new houses which flowed along the valley in both directions ... Queer! You can't imagine how queer! All the way down the hill I was seeing ghosts, chiefly the ghosts of hedges and trees and cows. It was as if I was looking at two worlds at once ...

Orwell, of course, takes no refuge in myth, and in *The Road to Wigan Pier*, with its powerful evocation of the appalling living conditions in the North of England in the 1930s, he makes an immense effort to understand the reality and its causes, an effort which Tolkien, with his almost total lack of interest in politics and modern life, would never have contemplated. He does his best to look steadily at the unfamiliar world he discovers, and tries to avoid the temptation to ignore its human misery and represent it as sublime. He writes:

A slag-heap is at best a hideous thing, because it is so planless and functionless. It is just something dumped on the earth, like the emptying of a giant's dustbin. On the outskirts of the mining towns there are frightful landscapes where your horizon is ringed completely round by jagged grey mountains, and underfoot is mud and ashes and overhead the steel cables where tubs of dirt travel slowly across miles of country. Often the slag-heaps are on fire . . . Even when a slag-heap sinks, as it does ultimately, only an evil brown grass grows on it, and it retains its hummocky surface. One in the slums of Wigan, used as a playground, looks like a choppy sea suddenly frozen: 'the flock mattress', it is called locally.

It is difficult not to quote Orwell at length, so well does he capture the essence of such scenery. Here he is, journeying through it:

The train bore me away, through the monstrous scenery of slag-heaps, chimneys, piled scrap-iron, foul canals, paths of cindery mud criss-crossed by the prints of clogs. This was March, but the weather had been horribly cold and everywhere there were mounds of blackened snow. As we moved slowly through the outskirts of the town we passed row after row of little grey slum houses running at right angles to the embankment. At the back of one of the houses a young woman was kneeling on the stones, poking a stick up the leaden waste-pipe which ran from the sink inside and which I suppose was blocked. I had time to see everything about her – her sacking apron, her clumsy clogs, her arms reddened by the cold. She looked up as the train passed, and I was almost near enough to catch her eye. She had a round pale face, the usual exhausted face of the slum girl who is twenty-five and looks forty, thanks to miscarriages and drudgery; and it wore, for the second in which I saw it, the most desolate, hopeless expression I have ever seen. It struck me then that we are mistaken when we say that 'It isn't the same for them as it would be for us', and that people bred in the slums can imagine nothing but the slums. For what I saw in her face was not the ignorant suffering of an animal. She knew well enough what was happening to her – understood as well as I did how dreadful a destiny it was to be kneeling there in the bitter cold, on the slimy stones of a slum backyard, poking a stick up a foul drain-pipe.

But quite soon the train drew away into open country, and that seemed strange, almost unnatural, as though the open country had been a kind of park; for in the industrial areas one always feels that the smoke and filth must go on for ever and that no part of the earth's surface can escape them. In a crowded, dirty little country like ours one takes defilement almost for granted. Slag-heaps and chimneys seem a more normal, probable landscape than grass and trees, and even in the depths of the country when you drive your fork into the ground you half expect to lever up a broken bottle or a rusty can. But out here the snow was untrodden and lay so deep that only the tops of the stone boundary-walls were showing, winding so over the hills like black paths. I remembered that D. H. Lawrence, writing of this same landscape or another nearby, said that the snow-covered hills rippled away into the distance 'like muscle'. It was not the simile that would have occurred to me. To my eye the snow and the black walls were more like a white dress with black piping running across it.

Yet even Orwell is tempted by the 'sublimity' argument. He admits that

even in the worst industrial towns one sees a great deal that is not ugly in the narrow aesthetic sense. A belching chimney or a stinking slum is repulsive chiefly because it implies warped lives and ailing children. Look at it from a purely aesthetic standpoint and it may have a certain macabre appeal. I find that anything outrageously strange ends by fascinating me even when I abominate it . . .

He argues, as Lawrence did, that the industrial towns of the North

are ugly because they happen to have been built at a time when modern methods of steel-construction and smoke-abatement were unknown, and when everyone was too busy making money to think about anything else. They go on being ugly largely because the Northerners have got used to that kind of thing and do not notice it.

So far, so good; this is straightforward enough. But he then continues to argue that maybe the new glittering white factories with green lawns and beds of tulips that one sees when travelling out of London, though undeniably less ugly, are somehow hypocritical, commenting, 'Perhaps it is not even desirable, industrialism being what it is, that it should learn to disguise itself as something else. As Mr Aldous Huxley has truly remarked, a dark Satanic mill should be like a dark Satanic mill and not like the temple of mysterious and splendid gods.' Here is a deep, perhaps inevitable confusion, and if Orwell is confused, no wonder others find themselves confused also, and are so to this day.

The love-hate relationship persists, though it is constantly finding new objects. Suburban sprawl became a theme for poets and novelists, and was seen by some as a greater menace than the original industrial chaos. John Betjeman and Philip Larkin both write of strange unpoetic pockets of English life, of city parks and railway stations and roads with privet hedges, and both manifest a degree of affection mingled with a degree of fear. Betjeman veers from the outright condemnation of Slough:

Come, friendly bombs, and fall on Slough
It isn't fit for humans now,
There isn't grass to graze a cow
Swarm over, Death!

to a warm appreciation of neglected Victorian churches and stations, of the quaint charms of the Metropolitan Line and the outskirts of London:

Gaily into Ruislip Gardens
Runs the red electric train,
With a thousand Ta's and Pardon's

Daintily alights Elaine;
Hurries down the concrete station
With a frown of concentration,
Out into the outskirt's edges
Where a few surviving hedges
Keep alive our lost Elysium – rural Middlesex again.

Betjeman is the poet of unsung lives and places; Highbury Quadrant, Aberdeen Park, Harrow-on-the-Hill, Bootle, Leamington Spa, Broomhill, Sheffield, Felixstowe, Margate, Filey, and the liquorice fields of Pontefract mingle in his verse with the more conventional beauties of Matlock Bath, Harrogate and Tregardock, Cornwall. Place names appear with incantatory effect: poems like 'The Metropolitan Railway: Baker Street Station Buffet' lament an age caught in its passing, that nobody else thought to miss:

Early Electric! With what radiant hope
    Men formed this many-branched electrolier,
Twisted the flex around the iron rope
    And let the dazzling vacuum globes hang clear,
And then with hearts the rich contrivance fill'd
Of copper, beaten by the Bromsgrove Guild.

Early Electric! Sit you down and see,
    'Mid this fine woodwork and a smell of dinner,
A stained-glass windmill and a pot of tea,
    And sepia views of leafy lanes in Pinner, –
Then visualize, far down the shining lines,
Your parents' homestead set in murmuring pines.

Smoothly from Harrow, passing Preston Road,
    They saw the last green fields and misty sky,
At Neasden watched a workmen's train unload,
    And, with the morning villas sliding by,
They felt so sure on their electric trip
That Youth and Progress were in partnership . . .

This is anti-scenery for the anti-hero. Kingsley Amis also catches it precisely in his poem about the meeting of two middle-aged lovers, Evans and Mrs Rhys, in 'Aberdarcy: the Main Square':

> The journal of some bunch of architects
> Named this the worst town centre they could find;
> But how disparage what too well reflects
> Permanent tendencies of heart and mind?
>
> All love demands a witness: something 'there'
> Which it yet makes a part of itself. These two
> Might find Carlton House Terrace, St Mark's Square,
> A bit on the grand side. What about you?

Philip Larkin, an admirer of Betjeman, evokes similar urban and suburban scenes, such as 'Friday Night at the Royal Station Hotel', where

> ... A porter reads
> An unsold evening paper. Hours pass
> And all the salesmen have gone back to Leeds,
> Leaving full ashtrays in the Conference Room

and the large store selling cheap clothes – 'Lemon, sapphire, moss-green, rose/Bri-Nylon Baby-Dolls and Shorties'. The synthetic paradise of what Betjeman mockingly calls 'Huxley Hall', with its electric glare and 'lightsome poplars' outside, both attracts and repels. Larkin envies the sexual freedom of the young, but is bleakly aware of the transience of all things, and sums it up in frightening little poems like 'Afternoons', which recall Bennett's despair at the sight of the wastage of provincial life:

> Summer is fading:
> The leaves fall in ones and twos
> From trees bordering
> The new recreation ground.

In the hollows of afternoons
Young mothers assemble
At swing and sandpit
Setting free their children.

Behind them, at intervals,
Stand husbands in skilled trades,
An estateful of washing
And the albums, lettered
Our Wedding, lying
Near the television . . .

At times the despair is tinged with a grim pleasure, as in 'Here', his marvellous evocation of the city where he lived, Hull, a city which few visit because it is not on the way to anywhere:

Here domes and statues, spires and cranes cluster
Beside grain-scattered streets, barge-crowded water,
And residents from raw estates, brought down
The dead straight miles by stealing flat-faced trolleys,
Push through plate-glass swing doors to their desires –
Cheap suits, red kitchen-ware, sharp shoes, iced lollies,
Electric mixers, toasters, washers, driers –

A cut-price crowd, urban yet simple, dwelling
Where only salesmen and relations come
Within a terminate and fishy-smelling
Pastoral of ships up streets, the slave museum,
Tattoo-shops, consulates, grim head-scarfed wives;
And out beyond its mortgaged half-built edges
Fast-shadowed wheat-fields, running high as hedges,
Isolate villages, where removed lives
Loneliness clarifies. Here silence stands
Like heat. Here leaves unnoticed thicken,
Hidden weeds flower, neglected waters quicken . . .

The city and the country, each in its way desolate. The old England, with its 'lost lanes of Queen Anne's lace' is going; in 'Going, going' he says of old England, 'I thought it would last my time', but concludes that it won't:

> ... before I snuff it, the whole
> Boiling will be bricked in
> Except for the tourist parts –
> First slum of Europe ...

This is a new, post-war sense of desolation, a new landscape horror. The poem was in fact commissioned by the Department of the Environment, a sign that somewhere, somehow, somebody was trying, but Larkin's mood of hopelessness is far removed from the brave spirit which designed Welwyn Garden City, and which tried to battle on with New Towns after the war.

New Towns were surrounded by a typically English mockery and defeatism from the beginning, but they had their champions, and in his extremely interesting account of one in *Late Call* Angus Wilson tries to balance the good and the bad – the enthusiasm and the failures. He resists the temptation to portray a heartless, ugly artificial community; his pioneers have a true if at times ridiculous sense of purpose. Nevertheless, through the eyes of his elderly heroine Sylvia, Carshall is a perplexing place, its architecture deeply unfamiliar: the fountain in the new Shopping Centre, with its metal arms dropping their loads of water, 'was clever but you couldn't say that it played', and the lilac and pink mural with its emerald background 'didn't have the clean lines that you looked for in modern things, and yet it didn't make any sense either'. She approves of the library, 'so well set out and clean, and so light with all the big glass windows', and is intrigued enough by the modern church to venture inside it:

> despite the odd metal steeple more like a piece of children's Meccano and the funny slots in the side of the building, it was rather plain inside – spacious and light enough, but more like a

lecture hall with unpolished wooden chairs and little tie-on cushion seats covered in jade green American cloth. Apart from the long thin silver crucifix that stood on the altar steps, you'd hardly know it for a church – not that it was at all like a chapel; it was just a big room with everything very simple and quiet, especially the thin slotted glass windows through which the sun poured with a lovely sky-blue light.

Sylvia and her creator try hard to see virtues, to accept the new world, but there is an underlying indictment. Sylvia, a country child, tries to find the true countryside of the region,

Yet, once sought, the endless 'Midlands', that lay open before her in such terrible enticement from her bedroom window, proved hard to find. The New Town, though it merged into the country, was yet cut off from it by a system of lanes and roads that turned back on themselves and eventually returned to Town Centre, as inevitably, by contrast, the paths in a maze lead away from its core. Often and again she would follow the lanes that, leaving behind the last primary school's bold colours and even the white pavilions of the last sports ground, passed on between fields of tender young wheat and stretched ahead, it seemed, to an endless rolling patchwork of fields – when suddenly there would appear a familiar green sign, white-lettered: 'Footpath to Melling' or 'Footpath to Carshall' or 'Footpath to Darner's Green' . . . After four or five days of such frustrated assaults upon the countryside, she came one afternoon upon a signpost that read merely 'Footpath', and after a sceptical quarter of an hour, she realized that she was at last moving away from the town along a path that was no more than a narrow grassy strip between two fields. She had sought it so long that she half expected some miraculous change in her feelings to come about from the discovery, to walk into some enchanted land of good or evil, but all that came from that first two hours' walk along the fields was a laddered stocking and very tired feet, for the surface was stony and bumpily uneven from molehills and deserted rabbit warrens.

The sense of loss here is not unlike John Clare's, confronted with enclosures: the countryside is distorted, the familiar made unfamiliar and frightening, the genius of the place destroyed.

In the 1960s, there was a movement to celebrate city life, a movement which recognized that cities are a natural expression of humanity, not a soulless denial of it. After all, as Jane Jacobs pointed out in *The Life and Death of American Cities*, most people live in cities because they like them, and because human beings are naturally gregarious. The Beatles, singing of Penny Lane beneath a blue suburban sky, made Liverpool the stuff of poetry, and Adrian Henri, far from recoiling with horror when he finds a litter of sweet wrappings, seems positively to welcome the evidence of human company. His Daughter of Albion, Liverpool, sits dangling her landing-stage in the water, and her daughters are colourful, cheerful, far from defeated by the urban scene:

> The daughters of Albion
> > arriving by underground at Central Station
> > eating hot ecclescakes at the Pierhead
> > writing 'Billy Blake is fab' on a wall in Mathew St
>
> > taking off their navyblue schooldrawers and
> > putting on nylon panties ready for the night
>
> The daughters of Albion
> > see the moonlight beating down on them in Bebington
> > throw away their chewinggum ready for the goodnight kiss
> sleep in the dinnertime sunlight with old men
> > looking up their skirts in St Johns Gardens
> comb their darkblonde hair in suburban bedrooms
> powder their delicate little nipples / wondering if tonight
> > will be the night
> their bodies pressed into dresses or sweaters
> lavender at The Cavern or pink at The Sink
>
> The daughters of Albion
> > wondering how to explain why they didn't go home

Christ enters cheerfully into Henri's Liverpool, in a poem which pays homage to James Ensor's *Entry of Christ into Brussels*:

City morning, dandelionseeds blowing from wasteground,
smell of overgrown privethedges, children's voices
in the distance, sounds from the river,
round the corner into Myrtle St Saturdaymorning shoppers
headscarves, shoppingbaskets, dogs.

then
    down the hill

THE SOUND OF TRUMPETS
cheering and shouting in the distance
children running
icecream vans
flags breaking out over buildings
black and red   green and yellow
Union Jacks   Red Ensigns
LONG LIVE SOCIALISM
stretched against the blue sky
over St George's hall

Henri's city is a good-hearted, swarming, jostling jumble, with Chinese Duck, bottles of brown ale, take-away curry, pie and chips, Beatles records, double-decker buses, butcher's shops, electric clocks, nylon panties, cream-painted bedsteads, PVC shopping baskets and cats waiting for their Kit-e-Kat all thrown together in an ideal (and idealized) cosmopolitan harmony – the kind of city that ought to be possible, but which people have to assemble for themselves, from unpromising materials – a collage city, for those who can love what is there, rather than yearn for what is gone.

    Few other writers achieve or indeed aim at Henri's positive response. Sillitoe's Nottingham has its moments of gaiety – the pub, the Goose Fair – but they are moments of escape, and Arthur Seaton, hero of *Saturday*

Night and Sunday Morning, in Chapter 5 responds in characteristically anarchic fashion to one of the beauties of his city:

> From the hump of the railway bridge he turned around and saw the squat front-end of the castle still sneering at him. I hate that castle, he said to himself, more than I've ever hated owt in my life before, and I'd like to plant a thousand tons of bone-dry TNT in the tunnel called Mortimer's Hole and send it to Kingdom Cum, so's nob'dy 'ud ever see it again.

Sillitoe describes his family story in a semi-autobiographical work called *Raw Material*. His family were urban working class, but with living memories of country roots, and although as a small boy he played on 'a nearby tip away from any houses, on which only waste sand and factory soot was laid, an area between the narrow River Lean and a few acres of swamp bordering the railway line, closed off from the lane by a stockade of high boards', most of his characters preserve a longing for the country: they enjoy bicycling and angling, and his long-distance runner finds himself admiring the dew on the hedges and the cow-parsley almost against his will.

Despite the vogue for provincial novels in the 1950s and '60s, and despite the success of the Liverpool scene, there are surprisingly few warm and affectionate portraits of provincial city life in the literature of this period. Douglas Dunn, writing like Philip Larkin of Hull in his first volume of poems, *Terry Street*, finds an ambiguous beauty in the back streets, but the life he portrays is harsh, the environment bleak and hard to love:

> First sunshine for three weeks, and the children come out
> From their tents of chairs and old sheets,
> Living room traffic jams, and battlefields of redcoat soldiers,
> To expand, run with unsteady legs in and out of shades.
>
> Up terraces of slums, young gum-chewing mothers sit
> Outside on their thrones of light. Their radios,

Inside or placed on window ledges, grow hot
With sun and electricity. Shielding their eyes from sun

They talk above music, knitting or pushing prams
Over gentle, stone inches. Under the clawed chairs

Cats sleep in furry shade ...

James Kirkup in his autobiography of his early years, *The Only Child*
(1957), produces an unusually vivid and warm picture of life in working-
class Sunderland, but in his poetry he flees to the far-flung and the
exotic. Michel Butor's account of Manchester in *Passing Time* is stun-
ningly dismal, a fitting successor to Engels and Gaskell: he is French, but
the damp spirit of England seems to have penetrated his style and his
narrator's soul. Manchester, in his own words, 'swathed his soul like a wet
shroud', and he produces a desolate account of an exile's vision and
refuges – news cinemas, dark pubs, neon-lit 'Amusements' with electric
billiard tables, solitary meals in the Oriental Bamboo, visits to museums
and cathedrals, trampled bus tickets. Iris Murdoch, who writes with
equal and all-embracing joy of townscapes, seascapes and countryside, is
a city lover, and confidently allows her narrator in *The Sea, The Sea* to
compare his vision of the heavens, 'that vast slowly changing infinitely
deep dome of luminously golden stars, stars behind stars behind stars',
to the changing lights in the Odeon cinema he used to visit as a child. But
such flashes are rare, rarer in literature than in life, I imagine – the
romantic tradition dies hard.

London has always been easier to love than the towns and cities of the
provinces, and poets and novelists continue to evoke it with varying degrees
of enthusiasm. C. P. Snow's Whitehall, Anthony Powell's Fitzrovia, Doris
Lessing's Bloomsbury and Earl's Court – they are all fictional creations as
well as real places. Less well-known districts have also found their writers:
B. S. Johnson in *Albert Angelo* (1964) presents a detailed, almost street-by-
street evocation of life round the Angel, Islington. His narrator is an
architect manqué, who comments knowledgeably on the pseudo-Gothic
excrescences of St Pancras Station, the Georgian terraces and squares of

old Islington, the pubs with comic tile murals, the awful smell coming from a café round the back of Sadler's Wells, the plaque to Lenin in Percy Circus, the dreary school in which he works as a supply teacher, the cheery Greek Cypriot café up the Liverpool Road where he spends his time off. Like Adrian Henri, he is unshocked by city garbage – the 'bicycle wheels, bottomless enamel buckets, tins, rotting cardboard' that litter the grass in the railinged area of Percy Circus are all part of the city itself.

But perhaps the most haunting descriptions of fringe London and depressed urban life are those of Nell Dunn, in *Up the Junction* and *Poor Cow*, both published in the 1960s. The first describes South London, a region of LCC flats, rag shops, markets, fish-and-chip shops, half-destroyed cinemas, cow-cake factories, old-fashioned laundries, pub brawls. The narrator works in a two-room sweet factory, wrapping cheap sweets. *Poor Cow* moves back and forth from Ruislip and Fulham to the outpost of Catford, where a plant like a giant pineapple, with the fruit buried, grew in the desolate garden. 'Someone had tried to light a bonfire to burn some of the rubbish but it had only burnt the top layer and gone out; beneath was a black and sodden heap of rags and paper and old soup tins, and a child's rubber ring, discarded perhaps when he learnt to swim.' Hopeless streets, hopeless rooms with cheap linoleum and the smell of poverty, dustbins piled high with rubbish – a hopeless city, hopeless lives. Yet a tender light of poetry illumines the waste land, courage and life burn steadily with a pale flame: the landscape is redeemed by love. Here are its children, set free by a teachers' strike, passing through the white-tiled alley with its millions of scrawled messages, through the playground and past the towering new flats:

On they go past the torn buildings and mud swamps, scattered with bricks and floating newspapers. 'I reckon the Queen's a show-off', says Harry. Down through the tangle of grass on the churchyard graves to the beach and to the mud stretching out to the water.

'You know what newly-weds do? Have a bit of a kiss and a cuddle. I know the facts of life, I do. What would they want to watch telly for?'

Johnny throws a stick at a swan. . . .

'Me mum don't care what time I come in of a night. She's always watching telly.'

'Well, yer mum ain't a newly-wed, is she?'

The barges glide past with small men riding on their backs. Trains rattle over the bridge from Fulham . . . Great gusts of black smoke blow sideways out of the four chimneys of Fulham gasworks across a streaky sky. . . .

Suddenly the sky splits and the black rain bounces off the river. The children scramble up the wall and run for shelter past a tin suitcase and an old piano, round a crooked tree.

'Come on, 'Arry. Mum'll kill yer if yer get wet' – Moraine catches five-year-old Harry by the hand and runs, skinny legs in her velvet dress, skipping over the puddles.

THE GOLDEN AGE

Heaven lies about us in our infancy, wrote Wordsworth, and his words are true in more ways than one. In the first place, many children destined to spend their adult lives working in the city are brought up in the country or sent there either for holidays or schooling, in obedience to the faith of Wordsworth and Rousseau. The country gives a better start in life, it protects the growing spirit from contamination, and nature is the best teacher, or so the Romantic theory goes, and many still believe it. Secondly, adults writing their fictional or factual memoirs tend to look back on childhood as a golden age, and its heavenly aspects are inevitably reinforced if childhood was indeed spent in the country; the landscapes of infancy acquire a particular radiance which the passing of time brightens rather than dims. And thirdly, those children who live in towns can travel to the country in works of the imagination: children's books are strikingly rich in evocations of idyllic landscape, and many know the Lake District only through Beatrix Potter and Arthur Ransome, the Thames Valley through *The Wind in the Willows*, the rivers of Devon through *Tarka the Otter*. How many of us have ever seen an otter in the wild?

For all these reasons, we tend to associate a certain kind of remembered landscape with childhood, and it is no accident that some of the best-sellers of our day are accounts of country childhood. We seem through them to glimpse a world that is rare, precious, vanishing. A classic of this genre is Laurie Lee's *Cider with Rosie*, first published in 1959, in which the author describes his village in the Cotswolds and a way of life that had been undisturbed for centuries. He describes the steep-sided valley, the village school, the wild cottage garden full of flowers and currants and cabbages, the owl hooting in the yew trees, the dank yellow wood with its damp, dark, hidden ruin of a cottage, the long grass of summer, the frozen ponds and icy roads of winter. It was all larger and brighter and more intense than an adult's world; indeed, on the first page Lee recalls his three-year-old vision as he arrived in the village in the carrier's cart and was set down: 'The June grass, amongst which I stood, was taller than I was, and I wept. I had never been so close to grass before. It towered above me and all around me, each blade tattooed with tiger-skins of sunlight. It was knife-edged, dark and a wicked green, thick as a forest . . .'

Laurie Lee continued to live in the valley of his youth, but he wrote that he returned constantly in dreams to the house he lived in with his mother and seven brothers and sisters: it was seventeenth-century Cotswold, built of stone, 'had hand-carved windows, golden surfaces, moss-flaked tiles, and walls so thick they kept a damp chill inside them whatever the season or weather.' It smelled, he says, of pepper and mushrooms. Although the book is about change, as are all such records, his village has changed less than many, and is still recognizable from his descriptions:

> The village to which our family had come was a scattering of some twenty to thirty houses down the south-east slope of a valley. The valley was narrow, steep and almost entirely cut off; it was also a funnel for winds, a channel for the floods, and a jungley, bird-crammed, insect-hopping sun-trap whenever there happened to be any sun. It was not high and open like the Windrush country, but had secret origins, having been gouged from the Escarpment by the melting ice-caps some time before we got there. The old flood-terraces still showed on the slopes, along which the cows walked sideways. Like an island, it was possessed of curious survivals – rare orchids and Roman snails; and there are chemical qualities in the limestone springs which gave the women pre-Raphaelite goitres. The sides of the valley were rich in pasture and the crests heavily covered in beech woods.
>
> Living down there was like living in a bean-pod; one could see nothing but the bed one lay in . . . Most of the cottages were built of Cotswold stone and were roofed by split-stone tiles. The tiles grew a kind of golden moss which sparkled like crystallized honey. Behind the cottages were long steep gardens full of cabbages, fruit-bushes, roses, rabbit-hutches, earth-closets, bicycles and pigeon-lofts . . .

A special valley, almost a secret valley, hard to get out of: nowadays coaches roll back down its steep sides, trying to clamber up like spiders out of a bath. Yet it is one of those places that strike a stranger with a sense of familiarity. Is this due to Laurie Lee, or to the valley itself, with its sense of safety and timelessness? Wombs, bean-pods, mothers, valleys, cider with Rosie in the deep grass – Laurie Lee's idyll is, like Paradise, at once secure and wonderful.

Flora Thompson's account of her cottage childhood on the borders of Oxfordshire and Northamptonshire, *Lark Rise to Candleford* (1939–43), evokes a similar lost world, though hers, both in time and in place, is more thoroughly lost. Her hamlet stood in the 'stiff, clayey soil' of the wheat-fields, 'bare, brown and windswept for eight months out of twelve', and she chronicles the lives of labourers – their working lives, their evenings in the public house, their meals, their gardens, their children, their supersti-tions, their visitors, their excursions, their songs, their rituals – May Day, pig-killing, harvest, church-going. As in Laurie Lee's world, the men worked on the land, and the girls went 'into service'. Without sentimental-ity, she recalls the poverty and the unimaginative and callous brutality of much of nineteenth-century rural life, when men had no feeling for the suffering of animals, when vicious practical jokes were thought amusing, when children were terrified by stories of ghosts and murders; far from believing in a golden age, she suggests that country people are growing more sensitive and considerate, more thoughtful if less religious – the spread of education, railways, newspapers was in her view, as in Harriet Martineau's, on the whole beneficent. Yet despite this optimistic realism, and despite her protagonist's eagerness to explore the larger world outside, her memories are inevitably charged with a sense of loss and change – wild flowers were brighter and more plentiful in the past, games were simpler and cheaper but more satisfying. The countryside has changed – aero-dromes have replaced fields, cottages have disappeared. Old Sally's cottage, described in Chapter 5, is no longer to be found, but in Flora Thompson's childhood was the most comfortable in the hamlet:

> Old Sally's was a long, low, thatched cottage with diamond-paned windows winking under the eaves and a rustic porch smothered in

honeysuckle. Excepting the inn, it was the largest house in the hamlet, and of the two downstairs rooms one was used as a kind of kitchen storeroom, with pots and pans and a big red crockery water vessel at one end, and potatoes in sacks and peas and beans spread out to dry at the other. The apple crop was stored on racks suspended beneath the ceiling and bunches of herbs dangled below. In one corner stood the big brewing copper in which Sally still brewed with good malt and hops once a quarter. The scent of the last brewing hung over the place till the next and mingled with apple and onion and dried thyme and sage smells, with a dash of soapsuds thrown in, to compound the aroma which remained in the children's memories for life and caused a whiff of any two of the component parts in any part of the world to be recognized with an appreciative sniff and a mental ejaculation of 'Old Sally's!'

The inner room – 'the house', as it was called – was a perfect snuggery, with walls two feet thick and outside shutters to close at night and a padding of rag rugs, red curtains and feather cushions within. There was a good oak, gate-legged table, a dresser with pewter and willow-pattern plates, and a grandfather's clock that not only told the time, but the day of the week as well . . .

The garden was a large one, tailing off at the bottom into a little field where Dick grew his corn crop. Nearer the cottage were fruit trees, then the yew hedge, close and solid as a wall, which sheltered the beehives and enclosed the flower garden. Sally had such flowers, and so many of them, and nearly all of them sweet-scented! Wall-flowers and tulips, lavender and sweet William, and pinks and old-world roses with enchanting names – Seven Sisters, Maiden's Blush, moss rose, monthly rose, cabbage rose, blood rose, and, most thrilling of all to the children, a big bush of the York and Lancaster rose, in the blooms of which the rival roses mingled in a pied white and red. It seemed as though all the roses in Lark Rise had gathered together in that one garden. Most of the gardens had only one poor starveling bush or none; but, then, nobody else had so much of anything as Sally.

Sally's memories stretched back to days when country people had been better off – to Cobbett's Merry England, when Sally as a little girl would mind the geese. Now, 'only the limey whiteness of the soil in a corner of a ploughed field is left to show that a cottage once stood there': Flora Thompson's description is her only memorial.

Today, most children learn of the country through books or films: it was through books that Flora Thompson learned of the town. On one occasion, when she is visiting the neighbouring small town of Candleford, with its shops and town square, its railway station and its gasometer, she catches sight of 'a narrow lane of poor houses with ragged washing slung on lines between windows and children sitting on doorsteps. "Is that a slum, Mother?" asked Laura, for she recognized some of the features described in the Sunday-school stories.' She is delighted with her discovery, though her mother hushes her in embarrassment. A similar connection is made by Herbert Read in his account of his life as a farmer's son in Ryedale, Yorkshire. In *The Innocent Eye* (1940) he writes that he was captivated as a child by a Religious Tract Society publication called 'Little Meg's Children', with its 'strange country of dingy streets and attics . . . of lack of bread and clothes, of evil and misery – it was as fairy-like as any story that I had heard . . .'

Herbert Read's own childhood reads like a fairy tale to a town child. His father's farm was near Helmsley, with the moors to the north and the wolds to the south; like Laurie Lee's, his world was secure and secluded. In *The Contrary Experience* (1963) he writes, 'I seemed to live . . . in a basin, wide and shallow like the milkpans in the dairy; but the even bed of it was checkered with pastures and cornfields . . .' He describes the duckpond, the pump, the well, the blacksmith's shop, the cows and carthorses, the Cow Pasture 'pock-marked with erupted rabbit warrens, countless mole-hills, and dark fairy-rings in the grass'; he writes of the church, grey stone with a slated roof, standing against a dark wood of firs: 'The inhuman stillness of the situation aided our friendliness; our Church was still where the monks who first built it twelve centuries ago had wanted it to be, in a wild valley, near a running beck, gray like a wild hawk nesting in a shelter of dark trees.' More changed by time were the neighbouring ruins of Rievaulx, which, he says, played an important part in the growth of his imagination, though they were on the farthest western limits of his boyhood wanderings. In a later account he comments, 'its precise geometry seems like some crystalline symbol of the natural beauty around it . . .'

Such scenery takes a lasting hold of those reared in it, and like Laurie Lee, Read returned to live in the landscape of his youth; in 1949 he went back to Stonegrave House in the village of Stonegrave, two and a half miles from his father's farm. The village is small but neat, nestling in the shelter of a steep hillside; the house – 'Sterne would have called it a "philosophical cottage", but it is about twice the size of Shandy Hall' – is 'built of honey-coloured stone and roofed with the warm crimson pantiles characteristic of all the old houses in Ryedale'. Herbert Read writes with feeling of the stone buildings of the region, and of the old quarries which provided the stone:

> The modern quarry with its machinery is often an ugly scar on the hillside, but the old quarries were soon covered with undergrowth; bramble and hazel and sometimes conifers find sufficient substance for roothold. Most of the wild life that survives has found a refuge in these oases of the deserts made by the tractor . . .

Like so many writers, he finds a special meaning in his own countryside, insisting that 'love of landscape must feed on intimacy as well as on magnitude . . .' For this reason, he loves the moors – 'Mountains I have no love for; they are accidents of nature, masses thrown up in volcanic agony. But moors and fells are moulded by gentle forces, by rain water and wind, and are human in their contours and proportions, inducing affection rather than awe.'

Herbert Read's son, novelist Piers Paul Read, was also drawn back to this same landscape, and lived for a time in Old Byland Hall, a house which bears a strong family resemblance to Stonegrave: he was moved in part, he says, by a desire to recreate his own childhood for his children, a childhood where each tree and each gate were known and numbered. The Read country of Ryedale appears again and again, almost of its own accord, in novel after novel, representing purity, simplicity, the lost innocence of infancy: Herbert Read concludes *The Innocent Eye* with the words, 'Memory is a flower which only opens fully in the kingdom of Heaven, where the eye is eternally innocent.'

There are so many excellent and moving accounts of country childhood that it is invidious to mention only a few. There is one more, however, that I cannot omit – Alison Uttley's *The Country Child* (1931), which made a deep and in many ways rather alarming impression on me when I was young. She became famous as a writer of children's stories of a cosy and undisturbing nature – Little Grey Rabbit and Sam Pig are her best-loved characters – but she also writes with an uncannily clear memory of a child's fears and superstitions, of its dread of a Dark Wood, an unkind child at school, a creaking tree, an idle adult threat. She was a farmer's daughter, brought up on a small farm in Derbyshire, Castle Top Farm at Cromford. Either her memory is sharper or her childhood was less protected and less indulged than either Laurie Lee's or Herbert Read's. Life on the farm was hard work, and humiliations always lay in store: the description of the strange old-fashioned dress she has to wear for her first day at school – warm, thick as horsecloth, ugly, with horrible large cream bone buttons with steel centres, made from an old dress found in the oak chest, belonging to a girl of a bygone age – revives nightmares of childish suffering and discomfort and dread of looking odd. 'What a figure of fun', the village children say, and the little girl who had hardly met any other children until that day is filled with horror. Susan Garland (like Flora Thompson, Alison Uttley chooses to write through a semi-fictitious third person) is an imaginative child, her mind full of 'fairies, goblins and grown-up religious talk which she had overheard in the kitchens at home'. She dreads hell-fire and punishment; to her life seems profoundly insecure, for 'at nine years old death might come at any moment'. For her as for Flora Thompson, pig-sticking day is a misery, for the pigs are her friends: she is afraid that the fearful sides of bacon will come to life again, like Lazarus, 'and run squealing back to ask why they had been slain'. Like many children, particularly lonely ones, she instinctively endows inanimate objects with life and mysterious powers, and each venture through the Dark Wood is an ordeal:

> It was no use for her to tell herself there were no giants, or that bears had disappeared in England centuries ago, or that trees could not

walk. She knew that quite well, but the terror remained, a subconscious fear which quickly rose to consciousness when she pressed back the catch of the gate at the entrance to the wood . . . In the middle of Dark Wood the climbing path rose up a steep incline, too steep for Susan to hurry, with black shadows on either side. Then it skirted a field, a small, queer, haunted-looking field of ragwort and bracken, long given to the wild wood, which pressed in on every side. A high, rudely-made wall surrounded it, through the chinks of which she was sure that eyes were watching. To pass this field was the culmination of agony . . .

The next ordeal is a rugged oak tree, behind which something is waiting for her – 'Once, two years ago, when she was seven, a pair of eyes had looked at her from behind the tree, and once a dead white cow had lain there, swollen and stiff, brought to be buried in the wood.' The nut tree, in comparison, is low, friendly and human, and the beeches rise clear of the undergrowth and let in the light: Susan breathes freely again, as she approaches the gate and sees the farm on the hilltop in the distance. Once more she has escaped.

The farm itself is ancient, a storehouse of history, built of the rock on which it stood, on the site of an old Saxon camp: 'Each window framed a distinct and lovely landscape, with fields, hedges, wood, valley, hills and distant peaks complete.' The parlours are decorated with old gilded papers, and great chests hold 'wedding dresses, in fading silks, falling to pieces, fichus in nets and hard lace, fringes and flounces, babies' long clothes, funeral cards, and packets of letters in strange crabbed writing . . .' The pig-cotes are older even than the house itself – 'Their thick stone walls were smothered in roses and honeysuckle, which covered the back in a wild tangle, unpruned and rioting. The sloping roof, with its large flat stones, was embossed with giant house-leek, great cushions of the juicy rosettes, with starry red flowers, planted in ancient days for inflammations . . .' No wonder that such a place held its ghosts, or that beauty was mingled with terror.

In her children's stories, the terror is well controlled; Little Grey Rabbit inhabits a safe little world of cowslip wine and crab-apple jelly, and the threat of the Dark Wood is always defeated. The same is true of Kenneth Grahame's *The Wind in the Willows* and Beatrix Potter's tales – although, in both, there is menace just around the corner, and many children find the adventures of Mr Tod, the rats in *The Tale of Samuel Whiskers* (1908) and the weasels in the Wild Wood unpleasantly frightening. Unlike Alison Uttley, Beatrix Potter was a town child, brought up in Bolton Gardens in London, where she was lonely and unhappy; her excursions to Scotland and the Lake District were a welcome change, and in 1905, when she was forty, she bought herself a farm in the Lake District, Hill Top Farm at Sawrey, and spent the rest of her life as farmer and farmer's wife in the district. 'It sometimes happens', she wrote when she was seventy, 'that the town child is more alive to the fresh beauty of the country than a child who is country born. My brother and I were born in London . . . but our descent, our interest and our joy were in the north country' (*The Tale of Beatrix Potter*).

Hill Top Farm, set in 'very pretty hilly country, but not wild like Keswick or Ullswater', provided the scenery for most of her best-known illustrations and stories; the farm and the farmyard, the wicket gate, the village with its village shop, the cottage gardens, the Tower Bank Arms appear in *Mrs Tiggy-Winkle*, *Tom Kitten*, *Pigling Bland*, *Jemima Puddleduck*, *Ginger and Pickles*, *The Pie and the Patty Pan*, and many others. Owl Island, in *Squirrel Nutkin*, is in Derwentwater, though this story was written before she moved north permanently. Generations of children all over the world, some of whom have never seen an English field or tree, have formed intense and acute impressions of the English countryside through her work; her observations of plant and animal life are exact and scientific, but they are more than that, and her stories open a window into an imaginative world which does not fade with childhood. She herself rejected impatiently any high assessments or profound interpretations of them, but the fact remains that readers respond to them with a peculiar intensity, as though they held some clue to a terrestrial paradise. C. S. Lewis, in his autobiography *Surprised by Joy* (1955), records that a reading of *Squirrel Nutkin* gave him one of his first spiritual and literary experiences, a sense of longing and beauty which was for him a true intimation of immortality.

The Wind in the Willows (published in 1908) affects many in the same way. Kenneth Grahame was born in Edinburgh, but was sent to Cookham Dean to his grandmother's house when he was still a small boy, on his mother's death; there he acquired his love of the Thames and riverside life, though he was to spend much of his adult life living in London and working at the Bank of England – in fact he began his story of Rat and Mole and Toad while still living at Durham Villas, Kensington. His passion for river life, for boats and ducks and moorhens and water rats and otters, is infectious, and indeed has infected so many that the reaches of the Thames he describes are now perpetually awash with craft of every kind, though there are still quiet corners and kingfishers to be found there. Most of the story, particularly the Toad episodes, is cheerful and extrovert enough, the adventures and disasters offset by plenty of descriptions of cosy interiors and large meals, but there is an undercurrent of longing and melancholy: in Chapter 7, 'The Piper at the Gates of Dawn', Mole and Rat have a vision of Pan, the spirit of the countryside, who transforms the landscape with mystical significance:

> On either side of them, as they glided onwards, the rich meadow-grass seemed that morning of a freshness and a greenness unsurpassable. Never had they noticed roses so vivid, the willow-herb so riotous, the meadowsweet so odorous and pervading. Then the murmur of the approaching weir began to hold the air, and they felt a consciousness that they were nearing the end, whatever it might be, that surely awaited their expedition.
>
> A wide half-circle of foam and glinting lights and shining shoulders of green water, the great weir closed the backwater from bank to bank, troubled all the quiet surface with twirling eddies and floating foam-streaks, and deadened all other sounds with its solemn and soothing rumble. In midmost of the stream, embraced in the weir's shimmering armspread, a small island lay anchored, fringed close with willow and silver birch and alder. Reserved, shy, but full of significance, it hid whatever it might hold behind a veil, keeping it till the hour should come, and, with the hour, those who were called and chosen.

Slowly, but with no doubt or hesitation whatever, and in something of a solemn expectancy, the two animals passed through the broken, tumultuous water and moored their boat at the flowery margin of the island. In silence they landed, and pushed through the blossom and scented herbage and undergrowth that led up to the level ground, till they stood on a little lawn of a marvellous green, set round with Nature's own orchard-trees – crab-apple, wild cherry, and sloe.

'This is the place of my song-dream, the place the music played to me,' whispered the Rat, as if in a trance. 'Here, in this holy place, here if anywhere, surely we shall find Him!'

Pantheism, pseudo-religion, mysticism, a search for the lost Golden Age of innocent childhood – however this passage is interpreted, it represents a powerful strain in English literature of this period, and it is in some way connected with the English countryside and the landscapes of childhood. Similar passages can be found in E. M. Forster's stories, where he also uses the image of Pan; in a more mature form, the same longing draws Margaret and Helen Schlegel to Howards End, that symbol of unchanging English life. Rudyard Kipling invokes the same powers in *Puck of Pook's Hill* (1906), with its vivid evocation of the Sussex countryside, though his magical spirit is not Pan but the indigenous Puck, spirit of the earth, and his magic tokens are leaves from those ancient indigenous trees, the oak, the thorn and the ash. Like Rat and Mole, Una and Dan are doomed to forget the visions that come to them during their moments of illumination; the songs fade, the presences vanish. The lament is for lost insight, as the shades of the prison house begin to close around the growing boy – but it is also for lost England, and these writers, at the beginning of the twentieth century, are consciously and unconsciously lamenting not only the death of their own innocence, but also the imminent death of a landscape.

Landscape poetry and regional novels both flourished at this period in remarkable profusion. An upsurge of patriotism, partly inspired by the First World War, made England and her rural virtues seem the more precious as they were threatened, and writers diverse as Kipling, Hilaire Belloc, Rupert Brooke, A. E. Housman, Vita Sackville-West, Edward

Thomas, Walter de la Mare, John Drinkwater, Mary Webb and Sheila Kaye-Smith contributed to a literature which later generations were to dismiss as imperialist or escapist, nostalgic or wearily imitative. Some of their work is precisely that: a glance through any anthology of Georgian poetry offers sufficient evidence of third-rate, unfelt pastoral fantasy, a feeble invocation of neo-classical nymphs and other whimsical deities. But the roots of the emotions which these writers struggle to express go deep, and cannot be dismissed so easily. The fact that many of these admirers of rural life were themselves city born and tied for much of their lives to dull jobs is in itself significant. One should perhaps see them as expressing a sense of alienation, a desire for an impossible reunion. Some of course expressed it better than others; Edward Thomas, for instance, is a fine poet whose reputation had suffered from the poetic company he kept. It is interesting to note how many of them came from similar social origins, and followed similar careers – de la Mare worked for years as book-keeper for an oil company, Drinkwater for years in insurance, Housman at the Patent Office before he became known as a classical scholar, Lascelles Abercrombie was a quantity surveyor in Birkenhead, Kenneth Grahame worked at the Bank of England. They were the sons of clerks and solicitors and stockbrokers, not of farmers: Drinkwater, born in Leytonstone, in 'Who Were Before Me' fantasizes about his own past in these terms:

> Long time in some forgotten churchyard earth of Warwickshire
> My fathers in their generations lie beyond desire,
> And nothing breaks the rest, I know, of John Drinkwater now
> Who left in sixteen seventy his roan team at plough.
> And James, son of John, is there, a mighty ploughman too,
> Skilled he was at thatching and the barleycorn brew . . .

The dream of a return to the simple life lies behind much of this kind of writing – a dream that some of them put into practice.

There lies behind it also the inspiration of one man in particular – Richard Jefferies, author of *Wood Magic* (1881) and *Bevis* (1882), and of many novels and sketches of natural history, set in his native Wiltshire, and now largely forgotten. Jefferies belonged to an earlier generation; he was born at Coate, near Swindon, in 1848, and it was easy enough for later writers to look back upon him as the true yeoman farmer, descended from generations of farmers, the living embodiment of rural England. The reality is, as Raymond Williams has pointed out, slightly different: Coate Farm had been in the family only since 1800, when Jefferies' great-grand-father purchased it, and Richard's father sold up in 1878 and moved to Bath to become an odd job gardener. Richard himself was never a farmer – he was a struggling journalist. Even his childhood was not the idyll one might guess from *Bevis*: much of it was spent with an aunt in Sydenham. Yet the image of rural England and of the Golden Age of boyhood which he presents in his work is overwhelmingly powerful; he inspired Edward Thomas, Henry Williamson, Arthur Ransome, and many others.

At first sight, *Bevis* looks much more robust and extrovert than *The Wind in the Willows* and *Puck of Pook's Hill*; it is the prototype of a certain type of imaginative open-air adventure story, and there is nothing fey or whimsical about Bevis's exploits. His problems are practical, and Pan in this book is a spaniel, not a spirit. The moorhens and swans and herons of Coate Reservoir are observed and described with a beautiful precision, but nevertheless the moorhens end up roasted with mush-rooms. Bevis is knowledgeable about plants, but he is more interested in their edible and useful properties than in their aesthetic ones. Huge five-pound tench, lurking in muddy holes at the edge of the lake, are made to be caught, and rabbits to be shot. Bevis and Mark 'thrash, thwack, bang, thump, poke, prod and kick' their donkey in a frenzy of rage, though on another page Bevis rescues a fly from drowning. Communion with nature is well concealed – but it is there, nevertheless, and Bevis from time to time falls into trance-like states, and becomes, as Mark says, 'like a tree'.

Jefferies' autobiographical work, *The Story of my Heart* (1883) is as powerfully charged with nature mysticism and pantheism as any work in the language. He describes how he used as a boy to seek out various 'thinking places', where nature would speak to him as if with voices. One particular favourite was Liddington Hill, with its ancient fort:

> Moving up the sweet, short turf, at every step my heart seemed to
> obtain a wider horizon of feeling . . . I felt myself, myself. There was

an intrenchment on the summit, and going down into the fosse I walked round it slowly to recover breath. On the south-western side there was a spot where the outer bank had partially slipped, leaving a gap. There the view was over a broad plain, beautiful with wheat, and enclosed by a perfect amphitheatre of green hills. Through these hills there was one narrow groove, or pass, southwards, where the white clouds seemed to close in on the horizon. Woods hid the scattered hamlets and farmhouses, so that I was quite alone.

I was utterly alone with the sun and the earth. Lying down on the grass, I spoke in my soul to the earth, the sun, the air, and the distant sea far beyond sight . . .

The downs and hills of Wiltshire – Wanborough Downs, Whitehorse Hill, Tan Hill, Badbury Ring – provided him with the visions that Herefordshire brought to Traherne, the Lakes and Snowdon and the Wye Valley to Wordsworth. When he moved to the South Downs in later life, in extreme ill health, he felt the landscape familiar and inspiring; from them, he could even see the sea, which he had seen only in imagination from Liddington Hill.

It is significant, however, that it is his best-known children's book that has lasted best, for there is something essentially childlike in his vision, which is not to be found in Wordsworth and Traherne. Like Alison Uttley, he endows inanimate objects with strange powers: in *Wood Magic* the squirrel tells Bevis about the trees, commenting,

Elms, indeed, are very treacherous, and I recommend you to have nothing to do with them, dear . . . Why, I have known a tree, when it could not drop a bough, fall down altogether when there was not a breath of wind, nor any lightning, just to kill a cow or a sheep, out of sheer bad temper . . .

In children, this anthropomorphizing tendency is common enough: W. H. Hudson in a chapter of his autobiography *Far Away and Long Ago* (1918) called 'A Boy's Animism' speculates that 'the sense of an apprehension of an intelligence like our own but more powerful in all visible things' is natural, and particularly marked in children brought up close to nature, in relative loneliness. He relates an anecdote of an elderly man who every night would visit the trees in his park and lay his hands on them and speak to them, and bid them goodnight, convinced that 'they had intelligent souls and knew and encouraged his devotion'. Tree-worship, Hudson suggests, was common enough amongst primitive peoples, and traces of it linger still. In literature, it has been relegated to poetry or fantasy – the Tree People, or Ents, in Tolkien being one of the most recent manifestations.

Arthur Ransome's children's books are directly descended from *Bevis*; we find the same imaginative games, the same enthusiasm for sailing, outdoor life, practical fantasy. The landscapes of the Lake District and the estuaries of Suffolk are as vividly evoked as Coate Farm and Coate Reservoir. Yet Ransome rarely describes: the scenery is evoked through the action. One might guess, however, from the peculiar and lasting impression that his books make on the reader, that his attitude to the countryside was not as simple and extrovert as his fast-moving stories make it appear, and his autobiography, published posthumously in 1976, confirms this suspicion. Like Beatrix Potter, Ransome was a town child, and spent his childhood in a Leeds grimier then than it is now; for him, holidays in the Lake District were Paradise, and Nibthwaite and Coniston Water the gateway to it. On each yearly return to the farm where the family stayed, he writes in his autobiography, 'I had to dip my hand in the water, as a greeting to the beloved lake, or as a proof to myself that I had indeed come home . . .' and he continued this salutation into adult life, indeed into old age. There is surely in this little act some clue to his ability to communicate with the child's imagination; most of us put away such childish things, but Ransome, like the old man who said goodnight to the trees, did not, and the loved landscapes of Coniston and Pin Mill live on in his books, charged with the powerful longing of a small boy exiled amidst the dirty suburban laurels, looking upon a rented farm as 'home'.

This longing for the natural world is the most powerful charge in the poetry of Edward Thomas, a friend of Ransome's, and a devoted admirer (and excellent biographer) of Richard Jefferies. Born in Lambeth, he spent most of his boyhood in London, with holidays in Wales and with his aunt and grandmother at Swindon. Rural life and country pursuits enchanted him from the first, and he was haunted by these lines of Jefferies, from *The Amateur Poacher*: 'Let us get out of these indoor narrow modern days, whose twelve hours somehow have become shortened, into the sunlight and the pure wind. A something that the ancients thought divine can be found and felt there still.' He did his best to follow Jefferies' advice, living in considerable hardship in the country in Kent, and earning his living by an enormous output of hack literary work, much of it of the highest quality – and finding time to write poetry, most of which was published after his death in Flanders in 1917. In his work can be found most of the stock themes and subjects of the period – nymphs and the Golden Age, a patriotic version of British history, praise for unchanging rural ways, fear of change, deep nostalgia, Merry England. Grahame's Pan and Kipling's Puck appear personified as the legendary Lob, an old man met in Wiltshire, for whom the poet searches after many years in vain, receiving this answer:

> The man you saw, – Lob-lie-by-the fire, Jack Cade,
> Jack Smith, Jack Moon, poor Jack of every trade,
> Young Jack, or old Jack, or Jack What-d'ye-call,
> Jack-in the-hedge, or Robin-run-by-the-wall,
> Robin Hood, Ragged Robin, lazy Bob,
> One of the lords of No Man's Land, good Lob, –
> Although he was seen dying at Waterloo,
> Hastings, Agincourt, and Sedgemoor too, –
> Lives yet. He never will admit he is dead
> Till millers cease to grind men's bones for bread . . .

Many of the poems associate patriotism, the war, imminent death and the English landscape in a way that hindsight makes peculiarly poignant; there is no place here to speak of facile emotion or a conventional death wish, but even if there were, the quality of the poetry refutes it. There are poems of Thomas's that seem to glimpse into the heart of England, to make, as R. S. Thomas has said, 'the glimpsed good place permanent'. One of his most famous poems, 'Adlestrop', catches the age and the place in four short stanzas:

Yes. I remember Adlestrop –
The name, because one afternoon
Of heat the express-train drew up there
Unwontedly. It was late June.

The steam hissed. Someone cleared his throat.
No one left and no one came
On the bare platform. What I saw
Was Adlestrop – only the name.

And willows, willow-herb, and grass,
And meadowsweet, and haycocks dry,
No whit less still and lonely fair
Than the high cloudlets in the sky.

And for a minute a blackbird sang
Close by, and round him, mistier,
Farther and farther, all the birds
Of Oxfordshire and Gloucestershire.

This is England, seen so briefly, so accidentally, so lastingly, from a passing train: who has not seen it so, and do we not all at times wonder if this is the only way to see it? There is no stopping: the train moves on.

Thomas, though born a Londoner, knew the country intimately, and most of his landscapes are precise, despite their emotional colouring; blackberries and harebells, fallow deer and snail shells, the tall chalky slope of a hill with grass and yews, the manor farm with its steep roof and tiles duskily glowing, the green elm, the ploughman with his team – all are seen in sharp focus. In contrast, A. E. Housman's poems, which contain many of the same ingredients and something of the same sense of yearning, tend to be generalized – the place-names ring out like the bells on Bredon, Ludlow and Shrewsbury, Wyre and Clee, Wenlock Edge and the Wrekin – but there is little detailed description, for Housman has not a naturalist's eye. He conveys a powerful sense of place, but it is an unattainable place, a distant shining land from which the poet is forever and inexplicably exiled.

The lonely civil servant in London, the lonely professor in Cambridge, longs in vain for lost communion with a lost country which he dreams that he once possessed,

> Where over elmy plains the highway
> Would mount the hills and shine,
> And full of shade the pillared forest
> Would murmur and be mine . . .

His Shropshire is a mythical county, infinitely remote; it is remarkably free, in view of Housman's classical interests, of classical denizens, but his rose-lipped maidens and hale yeomen, his ploughmen and carpenters, his lightfoot lads and doomed soldiers, are figments of desire, creatures from a private unconfessed world of fantasy and passion – a fantasy in which the lonely adult could consort, as he had done in his dream boyhood, with the spirits of the countryside. 'The Merry Guide' in one of his less successful poems is a remarkably insubstantial figure:

> Once in the wind of morning
> I ranged the thymy wold;
> The world-wide air was azure
> And all the brooks ran gold.
>
> There through the dews beside me
> Behold a youth that trod,
> With feathered cap on forehead,
> And poised a golden rod . . .

This pastoral youth does not become much more solid when lamented under the homelier names of Dick or Ned, though the poetry tends to be much more affecting: these are imaginary shadows of an imaginary green-wood, like Lawrence's gamekeeper, or, more relevantly, E. M. Forster's gamekeeper in *Maurice*.

Housman is not the first to use landscape as a metaphor for sex, and the fusion of real remembered place and intense lonely inner longing is something that many of us recognize, though we may not be quite clear what we are recognizing. Housman's lyrics stay in the mind when more faithful descriptions are forgotten: what could be more vague, more evocative, more painful and more deadly than these eight lines?

> Into my heart an air that kills
> From yon far country blows:
> What are those blue remembered hills,
> What spires, what farms are those?
>
> That is the land of lost content,
> I see it shining plain,
> The happy highways where I went
> And cannot come again.

At once unmistakably Shropshire, and unmistakably everywhere: an inner landscape of universal loss.

The 'land of lost content' could well describe the way in which those writers who lived through and survived the First World War saw the pre-war years of their youth. The war shattered the lives and imaginations of a generation of writers; England would never again be the same country. Some were killed: others, like Henry Williamson, were wounded mentally by their experiences and fled the reality of automobiles and unemployment, to hide themselves in a profound rustic seclusion, where animals seemed more real than men. Some were imprisoned by the memory of a golden past, by a belief that before the war everything had been simpler, sunnier, less subject to change and decay. Siegfried Sassoon, whose war poetry had been exceptionally bleak and honest, turned his back on the horror of recent memories, and wrote of Merry England in *Memoirs of a Fox-Hunting Man*, of an idyllic childhood in Kent in *The Old Century*. Others refused to look back at all, and flung themselves into a frantic urban dance, welcoming the death of the old order.

But the memories of pre-war childhood, pre-war holidays surface again and again in literature, providing an imagery of their own. The archetypal childhood holiday in fiction is Proust's at Cabourg, alas beyond our scope, but the English language provides its own masterpieces in the genre: Virginia Woolf's family holidays at St Ives, Cornwall, in the 1880s and '90s re-appear with a fierce intensity of memory and re-interpretation in *Jacob's Room* and *To the Lighthouse*; and L. P. Hartley, whose autobiographical sources are more shrouded in discretion, produced two classics of pre-war childhood in *The Shrimp and the Anemone* and *The Go-Between*.

The title of *The Shrimp and the Anemone* (1944) is almost self-explanatory. Memories of the seaside have for many of us an overpowering psychic significance; the apparently simple pleasures of beaches and rock pools expand in the mind, sibling loves and rivalries re-enact themselves endlessly against a background of cliff and sea, dim glimpses of mystic illuminations linger with the growing mind. Osbert Sitwell, at Scarborough when he was five, recalls standing on the edge of the cliff at sunset, and feeling 'at one with my surroundings, part of the same boundless immensity of sea and sky and, even, of the detailed precision of the landscape, part of the general creation . . .' (*Left Hand, Right Hand*, 1945). A precocious experience, at five, but not an uncommon one. Eustace and Hilda, in Hartley's novel (published when he was nearly fifty, and dedicated, by odd coincidence, to Osbert Sitwell), are not in fact technically on holiday, for their family lives by the sea, at a resort called Anchorstone on the Lincolnshire coast, but much of the novel is concerned with describing holiday games and their importance – digging pools, building castles, writing on the sand, riding on the sands, paper chases, excursions into the neighbouring downs. The resort itself, with its red sandstone cliffs, its zigzagging flights of often-counted steps, its Try-Your-Grip machine, its promenade and its weather-beaten tamarisks, is evoked with startling clarity; Hartley has an uncannily clear memory for the passionate, superstitious seriousness of children's play. Eustace, like the small Osbert Sitwell, is a sensitive child whose sympathies are easily aroused, and his response to the church at Frontisham in Norfolk, which the family visits on an outing, is intense; he knows the description in the guidebook off by heart, a passage which praises in particular the west window's 'beauty, vigour and originality', and concludes 'confronted with this masterpiece, criticism is silent'. Eustace stares at the window, and the seven slender tapers of stone; he imagines himself floating upwards to the gable where the tapers interlock, flinging themselves 'against the restraining arch in an ecstasy – or should we say an agony? – of petrifaction'. It is quite clear that his experience is aroused as much by the superlative accolades of the guidebook as by the architecture itself; this is a beautiful example of the way in which a literary description, even in a guidebook, can illumine and reinforce the visual impression made by a building or a landscape.

The Go-Between (1953) is another matter: not all holidays are idylls, and the one here described proved a nightmare, with psychological consequences as damaging as those produced by the war itself. Hartley's narrator looks back from middle age at the hot summer of 1900, when he was twelve, which he spent visiting the country house of a not particularly close school friend in Norfolk. The intense misery of a small boy out of his social depth, physically and mentally uncomfortable, desperately trying to make sense of the devious adult games around him, and losing his innocence in the process, is conveyed with frightening powers of recall for childhood suffering, and so too is the landscape in which these sufferings were endured, a landscape inseparable from the boy's state of soul. The size of the house, described in a directory of Norfolk, is itself overwhelming: 'Brandham Hall', young Leo had faithfully copied into his diary, 'is an imposing early Georgian mansion pleasantly situated on a plot of rising ground and standing in a park of some five hundred acres. Of an architectural style too bare and unadorned for present tastes, it makes an impressive if over-plain effect when seen from the SW.' Leo was less interested in the view from the SW than in the vegetable garden, the nearby farm, the coach house, the river with its rushes and sluices and bog cotton, though he very much liked the hall's double staircase, which he likened to 'a tilted horseshoe, a magnet, a cataract'. Hartley recalls a way of life that must have seemed everlasting to its participants – a world of rigid hierarchy, village cricket matches, Sunday mornings at the village church with each man in his proper pew, manly chats in the smoking room, bathing parties in the river. 'The past', says the narrator in his memorable first sentence, 'is a foreign country: they do things differently there'; and Hartley has recaptured the smells and sounds, the lawns and flowerbeds, the crimson canvas hammock and rhododendron shrubberies, the parched lily ponds of another world, another age.

Virginia Woolf, for reasons that she well knew and did not mind admitting, also found herself compelled to re-enter that foreign country; she needed to come to terms with the past, with the loss of her parents, with the loss of her brother. The annual seaside holidays in Cornwall had been great events for her, and when they were discontinued on her mother's death in 1895, when Virginia was thirteen, they began to acquire an even greater significance. *Jacob's Room*, written in 1921, was in some ways a preparation for the more searching and painful task of *To the Lighthouse*; the landscapes and seascapes are here overtly Cornish, with white Cornish cottages built on the cliff edge, their gardens full of gorse, with views of the Scilly Isles and Gurnard's Head, with Virginia's own memories of fishing boats and rocks and dried limpets and yellow brown seaweed and crying gulls. By the time she wrote the second novel, published in 1927, the process of transmuting memory into art had changed, and she chose to shift the scene from St Ives to the Hebrides, though Talland House where the Stephen family stayed is still recognizable, and, as one correspondent informed her, she had got the flora and fauna of the Hebrides all wrong, by transplanting them wholesale from Cornwall.

Botanical accuracy was not Virginia Woolf's purpose, however; she was describing a place in time rather than a location in space. She is describing the past, where the dead live, for one of the magical powers of art is the power of resurrection. As Mr and Mrs Ramsay, Leslie and Julia Stephen live again. The house with its tennis lawn and pampas grass and red-hot pokers waits patiently on the other side of dereliction, though Woolf, in the middle section 'Time Passes', brings about that dereliction herself: the bay with its sand dunes and rockpools and smooth rubber-like sea anemones is still there. Observed or unobserved, described or undescribed, Godrevy Lighthouse, enigmatic and ageless, subject neither to illness nor to war, sends out its incomprehensible appeal, a link between the living and the dead, the present and the past. The small picturesque town was already, before the turn of the century, popular with Sunday painters:

> But here, the houses falling away on both sides, they came out on the quay, and the whole bay spread before them and Mrs Ramsay could not help exclaiming, 'Oh, how beautiful!' For the great plateful of

blue water was before her; the hoary Lighthouse, distant, austere, in the midst; and on the right, as far as the eye could see, fading and falling, in soft low pleats, the green sand dunes with the wild flowing grasses on them, which always seemed to be running away into some moon country, uninhabited of men . . .

The past lives on, in art and memory, but it is not static; it shifts and changes as the present throws its shadows backwards. The landscape also changes, but far more slowly; it is a living link between what we were and what we have become. This is one of the reasons why we feel such profound and apparently disproportionate anguish when a loved landscape is altered out of recognition; we lose not only a place, but a part of ourselves, a continuity between the shifting phases of our life. Virginia Woolf knew that she would rediscover her lost parents in Cornwall, and she was right: for her readers, she is there too.

For most of the inhabitants of Britain, the Golden Age can never have seemed as remote as now. The vast majority of the population now lives in towns and cities; villages are dying at an alarming rate. Few can choose to live and work in the country, but this is one of the rare occasions in which the writer is unusually fortunate. There are no major obstacles, apart from temperament and the need of subsidiary sources of income, to prevent a writer from living wherever he chooses, and there are still many who choose to create their own idyll, their own version of the Garden of Eden. The successful can even have it both ways, living, as it were, in reverse – retreating to the country to work, visiting the city for society and pleasure. What could be more convenient?

The most ill-assorted of writers have made this return journey, from town to country, and written of their discoveries. Dylan Thomas is a striking example of a man who wanted both, and got them: born in a semi-detached in an ugly suburb of ugly, exciting Swansea, he became the rural poet of Fern Hill and Llaregyb, as well as the wild man of the pubs of Fitzrovia. *Under Milk Wood*, inspired by his final years at Laugharne, is a modern rural idyll, deliberately quaint and deliberately charming; the rural lust and laughter ring a little false at times, and Thomas's feelings about Laugharne itself were highly ambivalent. The house he acquired was given to him by Margaret Taylor, and his letter to her in spring 1949 on the prospect of moving there has something of the same ring as Lawrence's letter about Garsington to his patroness, Ottoline Morrell (see pp. 145–56) – writers, after all, pay their debts to their patrons in words, even now:

> O to sit there, lost, found, alone in the universe, at home, at last, the people all with their arms open! and then, but only through my tears, the hundreds of years of the colossal broken castle, owls asleep in the centuries, the same rooks talking as in Arthur's time which always goes on there as, unborn, you climb the stones to see river, sea, cormorants nesting like thin headstones, the cocklewoman webfoot, & the undead, round Pendine Head, streaming like trippers up into seaside sky, making a noise like St Giles Fair, silent as all the electric chairs and bells of my nerves as I think, here, of the best town, the best house, the only castle, the mapped, measured, inhabited, drained, garaged, townhalled, pubbed and churched, shopped, gulled, and estuaried one state of happiness!

Is not this all a little good to be true? Earlier, on 20 April 1936, he had written to Vernon Watkins: 'I'm not a country man; I stand for, if anything, the aspidistra, the provincial drive, the morning café, the evening pub; I'd like to believe in the wide open spaces as the wrapping around walls, the windy boredom between house and house, hotel and cinema, bookshop and tube-station...' Later, on 23 June 1949, just after moving into the Boat House, he broadcast these words:

> And now that I am back in Wales, am I the same person, sadly staring over the flat, sad, estuary sands, watching the herons walk like women poets, hearing the gab of gulls, alone and lost in a soft kangaroo pocket of the sad, salt West, who once, so very little time ago, trundled under the blaring lights, to the tune of cabhorns, his beautiful barrow of raspberries...

The voice of the exiled poet trembles a little with nostalgia for the Metropolis: poets are never satisfied. Less poetically, he wrote on 13 October 1949 to John Davenport:

It is bad in a small community where everything is known, temporary insolvency goes the glad rounds as swift as a miscarriage. I owe a quarter's rent on my mother's house, Llewelyn's school fees (for last term), much to each tradesman. Yesterday I broke a tooth on a minto. There are rats in the lavatory, tittering while you shit, and the official rat man comes every day to give them titbits before the kill . . . I have the hot and cold rose-flush comings and goings after elderberry wine last night in a hamhooked kitchen with impossibly rich, and thunderingly mean, ferret-faced farmers, who dislike me so much they treat me like a brother . . .

An ambiguous position, indeed. Coleridge too, one recalls, suffered from rats and mice, but was so committed to nature that he refused to kill them.

Angus Wilson was another writer caught between love of the city and love of the countryside, love of home and love of abroad: his life, divided between the three, attempted to make the best of all worlds. His childhood, years of which were spent in South Africa, was remarkably itinerant, as his adult life became; his interest in the 'wild garden' and the moral implications of the town–country dichotomy in English literature are analysed with much wit and feeling in his autobiographical work, *The Wild Garden* (1963). His search for roots in England, his 'extreme visual attachment to the English countryside', and the practical writer's need for solitude were amongst the impulses that led him to his cottage in Suffolk, near Bury St Edmunds: he writes of it,

It happened to be in a part of England untouched by any memories for me; it happened to be that undulating, yet hardly hilly country which I most love; it happened to be not too near the seaside . . . It also happened to be on the edge of a wood with a much neglected garden. Even if I were not to stay, I must do something, if not to drive the nettles back, at least not to allow them further invasion . . . It was a role for which neither my London manners nor my innate clumsiness fitted me. Yet I have gone on with it, civilizing the house, eventually turning a clearing in the wild into a carefully artificial wild garden. The symbols underlying my novels have been realized in practice, or more or less realized . . .

His attitude is very different from the distant yearning of Housman and Drinkwater, the total commitment of an Edward Thomas. He questions his motives, and the values associated with country living, pointing out that espousal of the 'country' cause in England all too easily associates itself with class arrogance and snobbery; the country gentry set themselves up against the intellectual, against artistic Bohemia. How can a writer reconcile himself to his county neighbours? This was the dilemma faced by D. H. Lawrence and Dylan Thomas, and Wilson explores it with a characteristic honesty. The conflicts and contradictions cannot be fully resolved; they are too deeply embedded in English social history for one man to reconcile them. But the wild garden, with its union of the wild and the artificial, is some kind of symbol of reconciliation, however ambiguous. It is surely significant that the most urbane and well travelled and sophisticated of our novelists should have chosen to create one, even though, as he himself points out, the only time he has described it directly in fiction (in *The Old Men at the Zoo*, 1961) he makes this garden the scene of death and defeat and destruction.

The poet's attitude to life in the country is perhaps at first sight less complex. Virginia Woolf, Dylan Thomas, Angus Wilson all needed town life, dinner parties or pubs, people: they are a source of inspiration. Ted Hughes and Sylvia Plath, two of the great poets of the twentieth century, chose the country. Hughes, unlike Plath, was country born; a carpenter's son, his early childhood was spent in the Calder valley, though the family moved when he was a boy to Mexborough, visually one of the least attractive of South Yorkshire's industrial towns. But it was not to Yorkshire that he and his American-born wife chose to move in 1961; it was to the conventionally picturesque and poetic county of Devon. Their choice, like Wilson's, was apparently arbitrary – a new part of the world, a new start. The house offered perhaps too obvious attractions; antiquity, snob appeal, beautiful surroundings. Sylvia Plath's mother, in a letter to her son Warren, describes it thus:

It is the ancient (yes!) house of Sir and Lady Arundel, who were there to show them about . . . The main house has nine rooms, a wine cellar,

and a small attic. The great lawn . . . in front, leading from a wall nine
feet high, is kept cut by a neighbor . . . All one can see from the road is
the *thatched* (honest!) roof . . . There are three acres of land – all walled
in – an apple orchard, cherry trees, blackberry and raspberry bushes,
a place that once was used for a tennis court, where they think of
making a yard for Frieda. The land backs onto a church; the village
is close by. Lady Arundel will recommend her charwoman . . .

One sees what Angus Wilson means when he speaks of the dangers of
espousing 'the country cause'. A thatched vicarage near Okehampton
might seem in some ways an unreal home for poets from origins as remote
as Massachusetts and Mexborough, but it provided Sylvia Plath with some
of the most powerful natural imagery of her late poems; the idyll/night-
mare quality of country life as she evokes it is pronounced. In *Letter in
November* she writes:

I am flushed and warm.
I think I may be enormous,
I am so stupidly happy,
My Wellingtons
Squelching and squelching through the beautiful red.

This is my property.
Two times a day
I pace it, sniffing
The barbarous holly with its viridian
Scallops, pure iron,

And the wall of old corpses.
I love them.
The apples are golden,
Imagine it –

My seventy trees
Holding their gold-ruddy balls

In a thick grey death-soup,
Their million leaves metal and breathless.

O love, O celibate.
Nobody but me
Walks the waist-high wet.
The irreplaceable
Golds bleed and deepen, the mouths of Thermopylae.

Even the beauty is ambiguous, menacing. Sylvia Plath clearly found country life and country pursuits novel and interesting; she writes enthusiastically to her mother of walks with her children, of Evensong in the chapel and foxhunts ('oddly moving, in spite of our sympathy for foxes'), of blackberry picking and log fires. She went riding, took up bee-keeping, gardened – in short, played the part properly. Yet behind the cosy caricature of country life that she presents to her mother lies the reality of the moon and the yew tree, and the bee meeting which she describes in such cheerful terms in her letter ('Today, guess what, we became *bee-keepers*! We went to the local meeting last week . . .') is transformed in her poetry into a sinister sacrificial ritual, as here in 'The Bee Meeting':

Which is the rector now, is it that man in black –
Which is the midwife, is that her blue coat?
Everybody is nodding a square black head, they are knights
    in visors,
Breastplates of cheesecloth knotted under the armpits.
Their smiles and their voices are changing. I am led
    through a beanfield.
Strips of tinfoil winking like people,
Feather dusters fanning their hands in a sea of bean
    flowers,
Creamy bean flowers with black eyes and leaves like bored
    hearts.
Is it blood clots the tendrils are dragging up that string?
No, no, it is scarlet flowers that will one day be edible.

Now they are giving me a fashionable white straw Italian hat
And a black veil that moulds my face, they are making me
   one of them.
They are leading me to the shorn grove, the circle of hives.
Is it the hawthorn that smells so sick?
The barren body of hawthorn, etherizing its children . . .
I cannot run, I am rooted, and the gorse hurts me
With its yellow purses, its spiky armoury . . .

It is hardly surprising that this attempt at country living ended badly, with bleak letters saying, 'I am getting a divorce. It is the only thing . . . I want to have a flat in London, where the cultural life is what I am starved for . . . Everything is breaking . . . even my beloved bees set upon me today when I numbly knocked aside their sugar feeder, and I am all over stings.'

Death at Primrose Hill for Sylvia Plath in 1963, death in America in 1953 for Dylan Thomas. The countryside heals and saves, but some it cannot save. In *The Bell Jar*, Sylvia Plath's narrator declares that she wants to live in the town *and* in the country, and this desire, however nonchalantly expressed, reflects a real and deep conflict. The conflict today is deeper, perhaps, than it has ever been – yet poets are still drawn to write of land-scape, of Britain, of the unchanged and changing places. Any anthology of modern poetry includes examples of a tradition unbroken from the days of Marvell and Vaughan, of Dyer and Gray, of Cowper and Wordsworth. We have inherited Donald Davie's East Anglia, Kathleen Raine's Northumberland, Ted Hughes's Yorkshire, Geoffrey Hill on Offa's Dyke, Jon Silkin's North-East, Charles Tomlinson in the villages of the Midlands as well as in Stoke-on-Trent, and Frances and Michael Horovitz in Gloucestershire. A host of others lovingly and carefully recreate in words the contours of the countries of the heart, and the topographical poem lives on in Alice Oswald's *Dart* and Kathleen Jamie's 'Cramond Island'.

AFTERWORD

This book first appeared in 1979, and this edition provides an opportunity to update some of the information in it, and one or two of the opinions expressed. But it remains of its time, reflecting the new interest in reading the landscape that had been generated by the pioneering work of W. G. Hoskins and his successors. The subject remains popular, and has diversified. It continues to interest me, the specialist, and the general reader.

Cynics might argue that our professed love of our landscape increases as our care of it diminishes. We are full of protestations of respect for what we used to call Nature and now call the Environment. Costume drama thrives, partly because of the opportunity it gives for filming country houses with their lakes and gardens, picturesque villages like those portrayed in *Cranford* and *Lark Rise to Candleford*, wild Brontë moorland, and views of Hardy's Wessex. A virtual Britain has been created on film, and sightseers visit the sites of the films of the book, which are not always the same as those described by the author of the book. Tarka the Otter now has a well-marked and signposted tourist trail named after him (although a so-called 'otter sanctuary' I visited in Devon a few years ago did not provide an uplifting experience; it was more like a shabby zoo). On the other hand, in 2008 otters were reported to have returned to St Cuthbert's Farne Islands. Nobody had actually seen one, but their tracks had been noted. There are gains as well as losses.

Gardening too has had some boom decades. A vast number of gardening books has been published in recent years, some practical and some scholarly. Television gardening and programmes about historic gardens have been popular. This is not wholly a form of escapism, as the urban garden has begun to receive as much attention as the cottage garden and the country house estate, and we are urged to make the best use of our small plots and roof tops. Programmes like the BBC's *Gardeners' World* have contributed to a new style of gardening, which may be reflected in the urban landscapes of contemporary poetry and fiction, though I have not yet collected any very striking examples.

There has also been a continuing antiquarian interest in the history of the use of land, and some ambitious restoration projects (again, sometimes aided by the medium of television) have been successful. Our interrogation of the meaning of the pastoral has been pursued by art historians, literary critics and sociologists. Biographies such as Jonathan Bate's life of John Clare have furthered the discussion. John Barrell's *The Dark Side of the Landscape: The Rural Poor in English Painting 1730–1840*, although primarily concerned with the visual arts, also provides a challenging view of poetry and the pastoral. Colin Ward, the champion of the forgotten and the unfashionable, has continued to explore small landscapes that are neither picturesque nor, in the conventional sense, popular. Waves of architectural fashion have transformed city scapes, as brutalism has given way to other styles and schools. Prince Charles's organic village at Poundbury in Dorset and the nationwide spread of the distinctive outlines of the twenty-first-century supermarket have offered us new and controversial models.

The industrial sublime still has its champions, but the decline of manufacturing has transformed dreams of power and energy into a wasteland of landfill and dereliction. As I write opencast mining seems to be enjoying renewed popularity in government quarters, but Battersea Power Station still stands derelict, attracting more photographers and painters than poets. The battle for heritage continues: some schemes of reclamation have been successful, others abortive.

The artist Edward Burne-Jones declared towards the end of the nineteenth century that 'The more telegraph poles I see, the more angels I shall paint'. Twentieth-century painters and writers accustomed themselves to telegraph poles and technology, but they also continued to describe the pastoral world and the angelic world. The twenty-first century is still young, and its imagery is still in the making, but the British landscape, in its many aspects, will remain a central theme for literature.

Margaret Drabble
April 2009

ACKNOWLEDGMENTS

I would like to thank my students at Morley College who over the years have made so many helpful suggestions. Also my mother, Marie Drabble, and my sister, Dr Helen Langdon, for their useful advice. Acknowledgments are also due to the following for permission to quote from material in their possession: John Betjeman and John Murray (Publishers) Ltd for extracts from 'Middlesex' and 'The Metropolitan Railway' (pp. 235–6); A. M. Dent Ltd, Vernon Watkins and the Trustees of the Copyright of the late Dylan Thomas for the extracts on pp. 270–71; Faber and Faber Ltd, for permission to reprint from *Terry Street* by Douglas Dunn (pp. 243–44), and, with Harcourt Brace Jovanovich, Inc., from T. S. Eliot's *Murder in the Cathedral* (p. 40) and 'Little Gidding' (pp. 29–30) from the *Four Quartets* (copyright 1943 by T. S. Eliot; copyright 1971 by Esme Valerie Eliot), *The Whitsun Weddings* by Philip Larkin (pp. 237–39), and *The Country Child* by Alison Uttley (pp. 253–54); Field, Fisher & Martineau for an extract from *Alfred Tennyson* by C. B. L. Tennyson (p. 184); Victor Gollancz Ltd for 'Stone' from *From the Wilderness* by Alasdair Maclean (pp. 103–4); Granada Publishing Ltd for 'The Hill Farmer' with extracts from four other poems by R. S. Thomas (pp. 101–3), and from *Up the Junction* by Nell Dunn (pp. 245–46); the Author's Literary Estate and the Hogarth Press Ltd, with Harcourt Brace Jovanovich, Inc., for an extract from *Orlando* by Virginia Woolf (pp. 143–44); Molly Holden and Chatto & Windus Ltd for 'The Green Man' (p. 18); Ted Hughes (copyright) for two poems from *Ariel*, published by Faber and Faber (UK) and Harper and Row, Inc. (US), by Sylvia Plath (pp. 273–75); Laurie Lee and the Hogarth Press Ltd for an extract from *Cider with Rosie* by Laurie Lee (p. 248); Methuen & Co Ltd for 'Sufficiency' from *The Map of Clay* by Jack Clemo (p. 229); the Orwell Estate on behalf of George Orwell, Martin Secker and Warburg Ltd, and Mrs Sonia Brownell Orwell, with Harcourt Brace Jovanovich, Inc., for an extract from *The Road to Wigan Pier* (pp.233–35); Oxford University Press for an extract from *Lark Rise to Candleford* by Flora Thompson (pp. 249–50); Laurence Pollinger Ltd and the Estate of the late Mrs Frieda Lawrence Ravagli for extracts from D. H. Lawrence's 'Nottingham and the Mining Country' (p. 223), and, with Viking-Penguin, Inc., from *The Rainbow* (copyright 1915 by D. H. Lawrence, 1943 by Frieda Lawrence. All rights reserved) and from *Sons and Lovers* (copyright 1913 by Thomas Seltzer, Inc. All rights reserved) on pp. 38–39, 225–26; Deborah Rogers Ltd for extracts from poems by Adrian Henri (pp. 241–42); Martin Secker and Warburg Ltd, with Horizon Press, Inc., for an extract from *The Contrary Experience* by Herbert Read (pp. 251–52) and, with Viking-Penguin, Inc. (copyright 1964 Angus Wilson), *Late Call* by Angus Wilson (pp. 239–40)

Margaret Drabble
1979

BIBLIOGRAPHY

S. Baring-Gould, *The Vicar of Morwenstow*, London, 1876

John Barr, *Derelict Britain*, Harmondsworth, 1969

John Barrell, *The Dark Side of the Landscape: The Rural Poor in English Painting 1730–1840*, Cambridge, 1980

— and John Bull, *The Idea of Landscape and the Sense of Place, 1730–1840*, Cambridge, 1972

Bede, *A History of the English Church and People*, Harmondsworth, 1968

John Berger, *Ways of Seeing*, Harmondsworth, 1972

Ronald Blythe, *Akenfield*, London, 1969

Humphrey Carpenter, *J. R. R. Tolkien: A Biography*, London, 1977

John Clare, *Selected Poems and Prose*, chosen and edited by Geoffrey Robinson and Geoffrey Summerfield, London, 1967

Kenneth Clark, *Landscape into Art*, London, 1949

Jack Clemo, *Penguin Modern Poets, No. 6*, Harmondsworth, 1964

F. H. Crossley, *The English Abbey*, London, 1935

Kevin Crossley-Holland, trans., *Beowulf*, London, 1968

— *The Battle of Maldon and other Old English Poems*, London and New York, 1965

Daniel Defoe, *Tour through the Whole Island of Great Britain*, London, 1724–27

Douglas Dunn, *Terry Street*, London, 1969

Dorothy Eagle and Hilary Carnell, *The Oxford Literary Guide to the British Isles*, Oxford, 1977

Celia Fiennes, *My Great Journey to Newcastle and to Cornwall, 1698*, London, 1888

Margaret Gelling, *Signposts to the Past: Place Names and the History of England*, London, 1978

Douglas Grant, *James Thomson*, London, 1951

Geoffrey Grigson, *Britain Observed*, London, 1975

Valerie Grosvenor Myer, *Jane Austen in her Age*, London, 1979

D. J. Hall, *English Medieval Pilgrimage*, London, 1965

Molly Holden, *The Country Over*, London, 1975

W. G. Hoskins, *The Making of the English Landscape*, London, 1955

Christopher Hussey, *The Picturesque*, London, 1927, 1967

K. H. Jackson, ed., *A Celtic Miscellany: Translations from the Celtic Literatures*, London, 1951

Henry James, *English Hours*, London, 1905

Richard Jefferies, *The Story of my Heart*, London, 1883

Barbara Jones, *Follies and Grottoes*, London, 1974

Frances Ann Kemble, *Record of a Girlhood*, London/Beccles, 1878

Desmond King-Hele, *Doctor of Revolution: The Life and Genius of Erasmus Darwin*, London, 1977

Francis D. Klingender, *Art and the Industrial Revolution*, London, 1947

Margaret Lane, *The Tale of Beatrix Potter*, London/New York, 1946

Lucien Leclaire, *General Analytical Bibliography of the Regional Novelists of the British Isles 1800–1950*, Clermont-Ferrand, 1954

J. G. Lockhart, *Life of Burns*, London, 1828

Rose Macaulay, *Pleasure of Ruins*, London, 1953

Alasdair Maclean, *From the Wilderness*, London, 1973

Edward Malins, *English Landscaping and Literature 1660–1840*, Oxford, 1966

E. W. Manwaring, *Italian Landscape in Eighteenth Century England*, London, 1925

Harry T. Moore, *The Intelligent Heart: The Story of D.H. Lawrence*, London, 1955

Ottoline Morrell, *Ottoline at Garsington*, ed. R. Gathorne-Hardy, London, 1963

James Nasmyth, *An Autobiography*, ed. Samuel Smiles, London and Edinburgh, 1883

Norman Nicholson, *The Lake District: An Anthology*, London, 1977

Carola Oman, *The Wizard of the North*, London, 1973

Michael Paffard, *The Unattended Moment*, London, 1976

Charles Peake, *Poetry of the Landscape and the Night*, London, 1967

Thomas Pennant, *Tours in Wales*, London, 1810

Nikolaus Pevsner, *The Leaves of Southwell*, Harmondsworth/New York, 1945

Sylvia Plath, *Letters Home*, ed. Aurelia Plath, London/New York, 1975

Hugh Prince, *Parks in England*, London, 1961

Canon H. D. Rawnsley, *Literary Associations of the English Lakes*, Glasgow, 1894

Arthur Ransome, *Autobiography*, ed. Rupert Hart-Davis, London, 1976

Herbert Read, *The Contrary Experience*, London, 1963

Reginald of Durham, *De Cuthberti Virtutibus*, Durham, 1835

Vita Sackville-West, *Knole and the Sackvilles*, London, 1922

Alan Sillitoe, *Mountains and Caverns*, London, 1975

Osbert Sitwell, *Left Hand, Right Hand*, London, 1945

C. B. L. Tennyson, *Alfred Tennyson*, London, 1949

R. Unwin, *The Rural Muse*, London, 1954

Virgil, *Eclogues*, trans. C. Day Lewis, London, 1963

Raymond Williams, *The Country and the City*, London, 1973

Peter Willis, *Charles Bridgeman and the English Landscape Garden*, London, 1977

Angus Wilson, *The Wild Garden*, London, 1963

D. M. Wilson, *The Anglo-Saxons*, Harmondsworth, 1971

INDEX